Praise for
The Employee Advantage

"Through an engrossing blend of stories and statistics, this book provides thoughtful guidance on how to transform your organization into an employee-centric success. Stephan Meier is one of the world's greatest applied behavioral economists, and readers are sure to return to this wisdom-packed book time and again."
>   —Katy Milkman, bestselling author of *How to Change*

"Move over, customer centricity. This book highlights that no company can afford to put employees second. With robust evidence and rich cases, Meier explains why leaders who fail to care about people do so at their own peril."
>   —Adam Grant, #1 *New York Times*–bestselling author of *Think Again*

"Meier has provided insightful thinking and compelling evidence for the win-win value of putting employees first in business rather than behind customers and shareholders. Even more importantly, he's offered a roadmap for doing so effectively and efficiently. Serious leaders of all kinds should read this book and internalize its lessons."
>   —Robert Cialdini, *New York Times*–bestselling author of *Influence*

"An engaging look at the complex relationships that connect pay, respect, culture, autonomy, purpose, and more to employee experience and company value. *The Employee Advantage* shows that employee experience remains a worthy bellwether for company success."
>   —Amy C. Edmondson, Novartis Professor of Leadership, Harvard
>   Business School, and author of *The Right Kind of Wrong*

"Meier presents a compelling, evidence-based way of transforming the workplace into an environment where employees feel valued, uplifted, and empowered. This comprehensive guide shows that when companies prioritize their employees, they create a ripple effect of positive outcomes that extend to customers and shareholders alike."

—Sheena Iyengar, S.T. Lee Professor of Business, Columbia Business School, and author of *The Art of Choosing*

"From one of the biggest researchers in behavioral economics and motivation, this book will keep your organization on top of its game through the ever-shifting landscape of work."

—Erin Meyer, author of *The Culture Map*

"This brilliant book is a clarion call for leaders to embrace an employee-centric mindset as a strategic imperative. With insights drawn from behavioral science, Meier makes it crystal clear: the future belongs to companies that go all-in on their employees."

—Hubert Joly, former CEO, Best Buy; senior lecturer, Harvard Business School; and author of *The Heart of Business*

"Meier seamlessly and intentionally tackles a conversation at the heart of every organization. His terrific work rooted in real-world examples emphasizes an employee-centric mindset, encouraging leaders across levels to do the same."

—James P. Gorman, executive chairman, Morgan Stanley

The Employee Advantage

How Putting
Workers First
Helps Business
Thrive

Stephan Meier

PUBLICAFFAIRS
New York

PublicAffairs
Hachette Book Group
1290 Avenue of the Americas, New York, NY 10104
www.publicaffairsbooks.com
@Public_Affairs

Printed in Canada

First Edition: October 2024

Published by PublicAffairs, an imprint of Hachette Book Group, Inc. The PublicAffairs name and logo is a registered trademark of the Hachette Book Group.

The Hachette Speakers Bureau provides a wide range of authors for speaking events. To find out more, go to hachettespeakersbureau.com or email HachetteSpeakers@hbgusa.com.

PublicAffairs books may be purchased in bulk for business, educational, or promotional use. For more information, please contact your local bookseller or the Hachette Book Group Special Markets Department at special.markets@hbgusa.com.

The publisher is not responsible for websites (or their content) that are not owned by the publisher.

Library of Congress Cataloging-in-Publication Data
Names: Meier, Stephan, 1972– author.
Title: The employee advantage : how putting workers first helps business thrive / Stephan Meier.
Description: New York : PublicAffairs, 2024. | Includes bibliographical references and index.
Identifiers: LCCN 2024000844 | ISBN 9781541703889 (hardcover) | ISBN 9781541703902 (ebook)
Subjects: LCSH: Employee retention. | Employee motivation. | Management—Employee participation. | Personnel management. | Business planning.
Classification: LCC HF5549.5.R58 M56 2024 | DDC 658.3/1 4— dc23/eng/20240129
LC record available at https://lccn.loc.gov/2024000844

ISBNs: 9781541703889 (hardcover); 9781541703902 (ebook)

MRQ

Printing 1, 2024

To Susan

because working together works!

Contents

Introduction

O
N JULY 8, 2000, J. K. Rowling published the fourth book in her Harry Potter series, *Harry Potter and the Goblet of Fire*. Like previous installments, it was poised to be a publishing phenomenon, as millions of fans eagerly waited to dive back into the adventures of Harry and his friends as soon as it was released. Scholastic and Bloomsbury, Rowling's US and UK publishers, were so bullish on the book's prospects they ordered a combined five-million-copy initial print run and made the unusual decision to publish the book on a Saturday—so that kids could read it over the weekend.

Scholastic and Bloomsbury were not the only companies making big bets on the book. Jeff Bezos, the founder and CEO of Amazon, then a six-year-old struggling online book retailer, also gambled on Pottermania. Bezos decided to discount the book by 40 percent and offer express delivery for the price of regular delivery. He knew how important it was to get the book in readers' hands on publication day. This decision, however, would cost Amazon hundreds of dollars per order, for a book that was costing consumers under twenty dollars. As you might imagine, not everybody was thrilled about it. Wall Street analysts, already annoyed with the fact that the company had not turned a profit for years, felt that Bezos's *Goblet of Fire* action was just another example of wasting money to make customers happy. Even the executive in charge of Amazon's book business, Lyn Blake, had her doubts: "I was thinking, holy shit, this is a lot of money." But Bezos was convinced that delighting the customer in such a way would build invaluable customer loyalty. He refused the notion that the relationship with customers was a zero-sum game where

1

if customers win, shareholders lose. In the summer leading up to the release of *Goblet of Fire*, Bezos said, "That either-or mentality, that if you are doing something good for customers it must be bad for shareholders, is very amateurish."

From the very beginning, Bezos was convinced that putting customers first was the way to build a successful e-commerce company. His obsession with customers was apparent from his first letter to the Amazon shareholders in 1997, in which he wrote: "We will continue to focus relentlessly on our customers...[rather] than short-term profitability considerations or short-term Wall Street reactions." He realized that, with the rise of the internet, the time for customer-centricity had come. Digital technologies were creating customers that were better informed about alternatives than ever before, and as a result, customers were becoming more demanding. Switching to a competitor was just a click away, and customers wanted not only great prices but a great customer experience. The digital revolution also allowed companies to collect massive amounts of data about customers in order to, among other things, tailor a sales experience to their individual needs.

Amazon would go on to become one of the most customer-centric organizations in the world. Bezos, one of the richest people on the planet, read customer emails himself until the day he retired from his role as CEO of Amazon. If he saw a customer complaint, he would forward the email to his executives. Those famous forwarded emails had a single character in the text: a question mark. No salutation. No other comments. Certainly no "thank you for dealing with this." Just a "?" The executive whose team was responsible for fixing the problem understood what the email meant: deal with this problem immediately. That team would then drop everything and work day and night on the problem to fix the customer's complaint. This customer obsession, the result of Amazon's philosophy that it must constantly learn from its customers and evolve with their needs, has led to a reputation for unparalleled customer service. In 2016, Bezos wrote in his shareholder letter: "There are many advantages to a customer-centric approach, but here's the big one:

Customers are always beautifully, wonderfully dissatisfied, even when they report being happy and business is great. Even when they don't yet know it, customers want something better, and your desire to delight customers will drive you to invent on their behalf."

So Bezos was right on his bet on *Goblet of Fire*. Lyn Blake had to admit later: "We were able to assess all the good press and heard all these stories from people who were meeting their delivery men at their front doors. And we got these testimonials back from drivers. It was the best day of their lives." Delighting the customer created a lot of loyalty. And Amazon got great press during the time of the *Harry Potter and the Goblet of Fire* release. Customer-centricity was and still is at the core of this unparalleled success story—and has inspired many other companies to follow.

The news about Amazon since then has been less positive. While Amazon is still clearly obsessed with pleasing its customers, the company seems to have ignored another important stakeholder: its employees. In 2015, a now famous *New York Times* investigation into Amazon revealed another side of the company: a grueling work culture that "experiment[s] in how far it can push white-collar workers, redrawing the boundaries of what is acceptable." Turnover at Amazon is famously higher compared to other tech companies. And a Business Insider analysis from 2021 showed that Amazon was also losing employees it really wanted to keep. The average rate of "regretted" attrition, an internal metric that indicates the proportion of employees Amazon didn't want to lose, almost doubled to 12.1 percent in 2021 compared to previous years. And while the work culture for its white-collar workers is problematic, the situation is even worse for blue-collar workers, the thousands of people fulfilling and distributing all those Amazon orders. Another *New York Times* article in 2021 looked at the situation inside Amazon's warehouses. The stories and descriptions from more than two hundred interviews reveal why Amazon has a staggering 150 percent turnover rate (almost double the industry standard): it has created a culture in which employees are under enormous pressure, constantly monitored by technology to be productive and worried about being laid off for taking a bathroom break that could be seen as unnecessary by an algorithm. An outcry by a worker on an internal feedback board said: "It is very important that area managers understand that associates are more than just numbers. We are human beings. We are not tools used to make their daily/weekly goals and rates."

The discrepancy between how Amazon cares about customers and how it treats its employees is striking. If you study Bezos's shareholder letters, you can see the starkly different emphasis placed on each stakeholder: he talked about customers five times more than his employees.

Amazon may be one of the most prominent offenders, but it certainly isn't alone in focusing on customers above all else. In 2021, after reading about Amazon's work culture, I became obsessed with how other companies handled this issue. My colleague at Columbia Business School, Nandil Bhatia, and I analyzed earnings calls of around eight hundred publicly traded companies and showed that, on average, these companies talked nearly ten times more often about their customers than their workforce. And when these executives did talk about employees, they used cold, impersonal terms like *cost* and *risk*. Customers, meanwhile, were discussed using words like *growth* and *opportunity*. Our results are similar to those found in multiple related studies, showing an undeniable trend. Many managers claim that their "people" are their most important assets, but this simply isn't true. What we do know for certain is that it's customers *and* employees that make a company successful. So why are so many companies ignoring this fact?

As the James P. Gorman Professor of Business Strategy at Columbia Business School, each year I teach hundreds of students about business strategy and how companies can create a plan to achieve a sustainable competitive advantage and be profitable. Customers and employees are at least equally important if a company wants to grow and be profitable. In some ways, employees are even more important—especially when it comes to implementing a business strategy. Yet the textbooks do not reflect this. Even they include about three times more mentions of customers than employees! And from 2000 to 2022 the *Harvard Business Review* had 40 percent more articles about customers than about the workforce, people, or culture. Given that imbalance, it is maybe not so surprising that boards have more members with marketing experience than human resource experience. If I'm being honest, I also have spent more time throughout the whole of my career discussing customers than employees in my strategy classes. Only in the past few years have I shifted to reflect the importance of focusing on employees—in my strategy course and in my new elective and executive education course, "Future of Work." As the chair of the management division, I saw firsthand that even at my own institution (which I love) we are not putting enough emphasis on the experience and motivation of our staff. There is plenty of emphasis on "customers" (aka students) and on faculty, but not on the people who clean our classrooms, the staff responsible for admissions and student affairs, or the dedicated administrators in divisions and centers ensuring everything runs smoothly.

My own change in thinking reflects a broader societal shift—the realization that the issue of how companies are treating employees can no longer be ignored. Not surprisingly, given the lack of focus on the workforce, employees are dissatisfied and disengaged. More than 67 percent of US employees, and more than 86 percent of employees worldwide, report being unengaged in their jobs over the past fifteen years—according to Gallup. This has been a problem for quite some time, but the COVID pandemic made things worse: people are reassessing what they want, resigning, striking, or calling for unionization in droves (Amazon, Starbucks, screenwriters and actors, and autoworkers are the most recent prominent examples of workers being dissatisfied and getting organized). Many organizations' efforts to diversify their workforce are stalling, and they are struggling to create a workplace environment where underrepresented minorities (URM) can thrive. In surveys about return-to-office policies, a larger share of URM say that they want to stay at home—presumably because their current workplaces are not welcoming or supportive of them.

There are four distinct forces that have been pushing businesses toward customer-centricity for years. Now, those same forces are reshaping the way organizations must approach managing their employees.

We know businesses are operating in an environment of rapid technological change, and organizations must be **agile and adaptable** to keep pace with these changes to satisfy customers' needs. But keep in mind, it is actually the employees who are coming up with the innovations, and it is they who implement those changes. They are the ones who are asked to be agile, which requires a new way of being managed. Not a top-down and command-and-control way of leadership but empowering employees—providing autonomy and a safe space to be creative.

Second, the proliferation of information has made it easier than ever before for customers to compare products, services, and brands. This has led to an increased demand for **transparency and accountability** from businesses. Brands that are transparent about their promises and willing to engage with customers in an open and honest way are more likely to build trust and loyalty. But transparency and accountability are now required when it comes to the workplace and corporate culture. Glassdoor.com is for employees what Tripadvisor.com is for customers.

Third, the availability of data about customers has driven the shift toward customer-centricity. Advances in big data and analytics have made it possible for businesses to **collect and analyze vast amounts of data** about their customers in order to identify customer needs and preferences and to personalize interactions and experiences. Obviously, there are also vast amounts of data about employees, allowing organizations to move away from a one-size-fits-all to a personalized employee experience.

Finally, the expectations of customers have changed and accelerated the shift toward customer-centricity. Customers **expect more from companies** they do business with. They expect personalized experiences, fast and efficient service, and a high level of responsiveness. They also expect brands to come with a purpose and to act in ways that align with their values. Employees also expect more from their work in terms of meaning and experience. The organizations and teams who understand those trends and embrace an employee-centric mind-set will flourish.

Some business leaders are starting to realize that we need to change. When I spoke with Indra Nooyi, the former CEO of PepsiCo and a board member of Amazon, in the summer of 2020, she recommended that I tell all my students to read *Deaths of Despair and the Future of Capitalism*, a book by prominent Princeton health economist Anne Case and Angus Deaton, a Nobel Prize laureate in economics. The book paints a bleak picture of the current labor market for low-skilled workers, showing how the stress of being working class in America is making workers sick and even, in some cases, causing them to die. But Nooyi's concern for the well-being of struggling American workers is shared by too few of her peers. If we are to turn those grim statistics around, more leaders must realize that they are missing the mark in creating an engaging and motivating employee experience and that doing so would help not only their employees but their organization as a whole. A key point for anyone looking at their bottom line (so basically everyone): there is a way forward in which the employee experience can improve, and it does not need to come at the expense of profits. In fact, being employee-centric can, when done right, *increase the size of the pie.*

Throughout this book, I profile business leaders (top executives and emerging leaders) from large organizations like Best Buy, Costco, and DHL Express, but also from smaller organizations like the grocery chain H-E-B or the Whitney Museum of American Art, who also understand that being employee-centric helps their business. Even Jeff Bezos in his last letter to the shareholders as a CEO in 2020 wrote: "We have always wanted to be Earth's Most Customer-Centric Company. We won't change that. It's what got us here. But I am committing us to an addition. We are going to be Earth's Best Employer." If Amazon can pull that off, it will likely continue its run of unparalleled success. But that change in company culture won't be easy, and it will require much more than a paragraph in a letter to shareholders: it will require major mind-set shifts, as well as an entire suite of short-term and long-term strategies applied at every level of the organization.

Being truly employee-centric will require full commitment and dedication from everybody in the organization. The same is also true for being customer-centric. Just mentioning that employees should come first or having a lofty mission statement is not enough. Amazon ultimately added a leadership principle about "striving to be Earth's Best Employer" to its fourteen core principles: "Leaders work every day to create a safer, more productive, higher performing, more diverse, and more just work environment. They lead with empathy, have fun at work, and make it easy for others to have fun. Leaders ask themselves: Are my fellow employees growing? Are they empowered? Are they ready for what's next? Leaders have a vision for and commitment to their employees' personal success, whether that be at Amazon or elsewhere." Although this is a good start, it is not enough if the mind-set shift is not internalized and Amazon doesn't become as obsessed about employees as it is about customers. This is where *The Employee Advantage* comes in. It provides a comprehensive road map that any organization, large or small, can implement to reap the profitable benefits that come from putting its employees first. It requires combining insights from business strategy and behavioral science to fundamentally shift how you think about your business and grasp the core motivations of your employees. Too often when we talk about organizations and competitive advantage, we forget that humans are at the center of everything organizations do. To humanize work is to truly understand the behavioral science of motivation and leverage technology to amplify these motivators.

My hope is that *The Employee Advantage* will provide valuable lessons not only to CEOs, but also to leaders at every level in both large and small organizations—and indeed to anyone who wants to be a force for employee-centric change. It would, of course, be wonderful if Jeff Bezos could use this book to help Amazon become the Earth's best employer. But the real dream is to populate the Earth with better employers. Together, we can create a future of work that is truly engaging and employee-centric.

PART I

Employees Are the New Customers

CHAPTER 1

The End of the Status Quo

THERE ARE DECADES where nothing happens, and there are weeks where decades happen." Vladimir Lenin's famous quote may have been about the slow—and then sudden—onset of the Bolshevik revolution, but his words could just as easily be used to describe the cultural changes brought about by the COVID-19 pandemic that spread around the globe in early 2020. That health crisis had a dramatic impact on many aspects of our lives and accelerated trends that had already appeared. In the world of business, the pandemic accelerated a movement toward greater customer-centricity that had already been going on for decades. Digitalization, personalization, and convenience all got an extra boost by the efforts of companies to serve their homebound consumers better. People got used to online shopping, remote doctors' appointments, contactless delivery, and curbside pickup. Telemedicine appointments, to give just one example, increased tenfold during the pandemic. Those accelerated digitization efforts increased customers' expectations and the need for customer-centricity in order to focus on delivering amazing customer experiences.

This was all great for customers. But the story for the employees of these fast-changing businesses was very different. As the COVID pandemic restrictions began to be slowly lifted and (work) life started to return to seminormal, a new term began to go viral on the social media platform TikTok: quiet quitting. The term and the phenomenon hit a nerve especially among Gen Z workers and was taken by many as a sign that bosses had gone too far in pushing workers, especially amid the dangers and the demanding workplace conditions imposed by COVID.

But while some were quietly quitting and just phoning it in on the job, others were resigning completely or starting to fight for better working conditions through unionization. The pandemic led to historic levels of actual quitting, too, which became known as the Great Resignation. For months, there were reports of people leaving their jobs to spend more time with their family or on their hobbies, often with no other source of income lined up. Stories about young workers quitting their jobs in order to move to a less expensive area became a common feature on news sites. But the trend of resignations might actually be more of a great reassessment, in which workers were fundamentally reevaluating the importance of work in their lives. It was not just a temporary phenomenon caused by the pandemic. This was a culture-wide reassessment of work-life balance—a permanent shift in what employees expect about their work.

And then there are the workers who instead of quitting (quiet or not) became active in efforts to unionize their workplaces. Other workers already unionized, such as UPS workers, screenwriters, and autoworkers, pushed for better working conditions (all in 2023). Since its heyday around 1950, union membership has declined precipitously in the United States. In the last thirty-five years, the percentage of workers with union membership has dropped from around 20 percent of employees in 1985 to around 10 percent in 2021, according to data from the US Bureau of Labor Statistics. But while union memberships are declining, unionization efforts have gained in prominence at various famous retailers. Amazon's fulfillment workers and Starbucks's baristas are the most prominent examples of this movement to create unions in the United States. At Starbucks, for instance, three hundred stores had unions in 2022, up from zero a year prior. While this is less than 5 percent of all Starbucks stores in the United States, unionization is gaining momentum and has caught the attention of Starbucks executives—especially Howard Schultz, the founder and ex-CEO who came back as interim CEO in 2022 to deal with the labor movements.

The baristas are unhappy with a number of issues at Starbucks, from tipping options to training for baristas (well, the lack of both). While

Starbucks continues to focus on customers and sell more and more coffee, the baristas feel they got left on the sidelines. An order of Edward, a customer in a Los Angeles Starbucks store, that went viral illustrates the customer-centricity at Starbucks that drives the baristas crazy. Edward customized his Venti Caramel Crunch Frappe with thirteen ingredients including, among other things, five bananas, caramel, a few different syrups, and extra whipped cream. He did nothing wrong and just took advantage of the option of making incredibly complicated and personalized drinks. Josie, the barista who prepared the drink, got frustrated, posted the order on Instagram, and only half-jokingly added: "This is why I wanna quit my job." The post went viral, and many baristas shared Josie's frustration. The joke had hit a nerve among baristas that the company had gone too far in satisfying customers' (sometimes very complicated) needs without caring about the implications for baristas. And it feels very personal for them. In a story on NPR, a barista expressed their view about the company: "They don't seem to really care about us at all." Howard Schultz, in particular, "has lost faith of so many of us that really believed in him."

The COVID pandemic put a spotlight on the deep dissatisfaction of some employees about existing workplace policies. And some executives seem concerned—or at least pretend to be—if public statements by executives such as Amazon's Bezos or Starbucks's Schultz are to be believed. But their begrudging acknowledgment of their employees' anger and unhappiness was a response to the emergency of the pandemic and the acute crisis it created for businesses. All will be well once the world returns to normal, they seemed to say. But of course, the problems the companies face run much deeper and were a long time in the making. If they and other CEOs believe the dissatisfaction of workers will fade now that the pandemic has receded, they are deeply mistaken.

Before Quiet Quitting, There Was Microsoft Solitaire

Of course, issues of misguided workplace policies, mismanagement, and terrible bosses and the resulting dissatisfaction of workers are nothing new. Workers have been phoning it in for a long time. One of the prime historical symbols of this disengagement was Microsoft Solitaire. This collection of solo card games started to be preinstalled on Microsoft Office in 1990 and became one of the most played video games of all time— many of those hours played in the office. In a wry acknowledgment of the role the game was likely to play in many people's working lives, the developer of Microsoft Solitaire allegedly programmed a "boss key" into the prototype, which would open up a fake Excel sheet so that employees could pretend they were working. This command never made it into the official version, which is a pity for the employee who got fired by New York City mayor Michael Bloomberg in 2006 for playing the game at work and the many others who got into trouble with their bosses for being distracted by the game while working. Perhaps Homer Simpson said it best when he advised quiet quitting back in 1995: "If you don't like your job, you don't strike. You go in every day and do it really half-assed. That's the American way."

In fact, worker disengagement goes back even further than that. The Gallup corporation has been tracking engagement levels of millions of workers for decades. The results of those surveys are more than alarming: in the United States, only about *a third* of the employees are engaged at work. While this number fluctuates a little, it has remained relatively stable for the last twenty years.

If you think the engagement level in the United States is alarming, the numbers for the rest of the world are even worse. Across the world, only around 20 percent of employees are engaged at work. We should be worried about the other 80 percent—the employees who are psychologically detached from work or quiet quitters. In a sample of forty-seven countries, about 25 percent of workers find their jobs socially useless or are not sure about the impact they are having.

There are direr consequences than just feeling bored or unfulfilled in your work. Low-skilled men in particular tend to have meaningless jobs—a trend that has increased over the last twenty-five years. Two prominent Princeton economists, Ann Case and Nobel laureate Angus

Deaton, go one step further and argue that the lack of meaningful work for low-skilled workers is one of the triggers for a spiral that leads to drug overdoses, suicides, and alcohol-related liver failure. These "deaths of despair" are believed to be the culmination of worsening prospects in the labor market and family life. According to Case and Deaton: "Jobs are not just the source of money; they are the basis for the rituals, customs, and routines of working-class life. Destroy work and, in the end, working-class life cannot survive. It is the loss of meaning, of dignity, of pride, and of self-respect that comes with the loss of marriage and of community that brings on despair."

Amid this consistently worrying level of disengagement and unhappiness among the workforce over at least the past thirty years, another movement has unfolded in business. Over the past two decades, there has been an obsession with customer-centricity, driven by trends that provide insights into the importance and methods of prioritizing another stakeholder: employees.

The Customers Get a Seat at the Table

Before customer-centricity, there was product-centricity. Companies would create the best products that they could possibly design—adding as many bells and whistles as they could. They would push the technological frontier and make the products better and fancier because—well, because they could. Back then, the prevailing idea was that more features equated to better quality and that product designers know best what is cool. A company would then use its sales and marketing machinery to sell those products to the consumer. In doing so the company would tout the many new and advanced features of the product. The product and its technical features would come first, and what the customer actually wanted or needed came second. This all started to change with customer-centricity about a decade ago.

Compare this with Amazon, where, in recent years, the customer literally got a seat at the boardroom table. Jeff Bezos would allegedly bring an empty chair to meetings. The chair, he would announce, was reserved for the customer, "the most important person in the room." Obviously, every company knows customers and clients are important. But the empty chair symbolized a real departure from product-centricity toward an obsession about customers. Their needs and experience became front and center, and everything at the company was aligned around them.

The development of the Kindle e-reader at Amazon illustrates how customer-centricity is altering the way companies innovate. Bezos was inspired by Apple's iPod, which had changed the way people listened to music, and he wanted his company—which had no experience whatsoever in designing hardware—to come up with a device that would revolutionize the way people read books. He gathered a small team to run this division, and from the very beginning it was all about how to improve the experience of the customer. Colin Bryar and Bill Carr, two Amazon executives who were involved in the development of Kindle, remembered that Bezos would reject many ideas as "copycat thinking, emphasizing again and again that it had to offer a truly unique value proposition for the customer."

The development of the Kindle was not driven by the product or the capabilities (or lack thereof) of Amazon to develop an e-reader. It was driven by what customers needed so they could have a seamless experience in ordering, searching for, buying, and reading e-books. "When we worked backwards from the customers' needs with digital books," Bryar and Carr remembered, "it became apparent that we needed to invent a device ourselves, even though it might take years, and even though we had no experience in hardware." Kindle was born and did indeed revolutionize e-reading and the book industry. As Bezos said: "If you're competitor focused, you have to wait until there is a competitor doing something. Being customer-focused allows you to be more pioneering."

Amazon is not the only customer-centric organization, of course, and there are many more that aspire to be. But companies that want to emulate Amazon had to do more than just have an empty chair in meetings. They needed everything and everyone in the company to be focused on putting customers first.

There are four trends that explain why, for at least a decade, companies have tried to be customer-centric. And they are integral to understanding how to make the transition from a customer-centric to employee-centric organization.

First, *rapid technological change* sparked the need for constant innovation to better serve customers and to outcompete the host of new start-ups that came onto the scene. Consider wealth management: this $100 trillion industry has been disrupted by technology, such as artificial intelligence (AI), and new, global competitors, from financial technology (fintech) start-ups to big tech companies. Traditionally, wealth management was straightforward: financial advisers would help their wealthy clients make the right decisions regarding their investments and sell them different products to invest in. In return for this expertise, clients paid a fee and companies made massive amounts of profits. UBS Wealth Management alone, the Swiss company and largest wealth management firm in the world, makes about $4 billion in profits (before taxes) each year.

But technology is disrupting the industry. Algorithms can provide more tailored advice and at large scale. Robo-advising, in which financial advice is not given by a human but by an AI-driven virtual financial adviser, alone is expected to grow to a $24 billion market by 2028, and new competitors are entering the market in droves. A new generation of customers want to be more in control of their investments and are much more comfortable with using digital tools themselves rather than talking to an adviser on the phone or in a lunch meeting. Large companies such as UBS or Morgan Stanley, the largest US wealth manager, need to be prepared for the disruption and know how to compete with smaller and more agile competitors. This requires a renewed focus on customer experience and the changing expectations of clients. Morgan Stanley, for example, has invested heavily in AI-supported systems that complement their financial advisers. According to Jeff McMillan, managing director and chief analytics and data officer for Morgan Stanley Wealth Management, investments in technology will improve customer experience. "The future will see a world in which every company utilizes AI to deliver customized experiences to each client based on his or her unique needs or preferences, with the intent of providing value to clients in ways they never anticipated."

Second, the sheer *amount of information* about brands and the *speed* at which news spreads is also changing the way organizations engage with their customers. Not only is the competition just a click away, but customers are also using the vast amount of information on the internet to compare products and services. But it is not only information provided by the companies that is influencing customers; the customers themselves are generating content on comparison and review sites. Jeff Bezos commented that "if you make customers unhappy in the physical world, they might each tell six friends. If you make customers unhappy on the Internet, they can each tell 6,000." Information is also flowing about services and products in the physical world. For example, Tripadvisor, a site that collects reviews about airlines, lodgings, and restaurants, absolutely changed the travel industry. Customers post one billion reviews every year on Tripadvisor alone. And those reviews can make or break the future of a hotel, a bar, or any destination activity as nine out of ten customers read reviews before they make a purchase. For example, when tourists in Rome have easier access to Tripadvisor while exploring the city (after mobile roaming charges were abolished by the EU in 2017), closure of low-rated restaurants is doubling and revenue of high-rated restaurants is increasing by 3 to 10 percent. This research shows that Tripadvisor affects restaurants significantly—and ends tourist traps. Peter Ducker, chief executive of the Institute of Hospitality, is very clear about the broader impact: "The online world has changed pretty much every industry, but hospitality beyond recognition."

And third, information goes both ways. The availability of almost limitless *data about customers* has allowed organizations to better customize (pun intended) products and services to individuals. Stitch Fix is a fashion retailer founded in 2011 that generated $2 billion in revenue in 2022 and has around 3.5 million clients in the US and UK. They use data from many sources (surveys, social media profiles, engagement on their site, and direct consumer feedback) to understand the needs of their customers and personalize their experience and product offerings. The offerings and recommendations from businesses that use this model—other examples include Netflix and Amazon—get better the more the companies know about their customers. And who knows more about individuals and can provide the most tailored recommendations than social media companies? This has led to the birth of social commerce in which social media platforms are not only used for individualized marketing but also build out their e-commerce offering. The hashtag #tiktokmademebuyit is already generating billions of views on TikTok and sets up the platform's new shopping feature as one of the leaders in the social commerce space. Part of the success of such platforms is that customers absolutely love the personalized experience. According to Accenture, a consultancy company, about 80 percent of customers were willing to share their data for a personalized experience.

Fourth, and ultimately, all those trends have affected the *expectations of customers* profoundly. Consumers of today experience a different level of customer service than in the past—and as a result have higher expectations. Growing up, I used to fight with my sister all the time about what to watch on our only TV in the house. There is no fighting about this in our house today. In fact, my wife and our three kids can watch five different shows on five different devices, each tailored to our tastes, whenever and wherever we want to watch them. We now expect that type of personalized customer service from all companies. According to Salesforce research in 2022 and based on its survey of around seventeen thousand consumers around the world, 88 percent say that the consumer experience is more important than a company's product or service—up from 80 percent in 2020. In addition, the values of companies also need to match. Sixty-six percent of customers have stopped buying from a company whose values didn't align with theirs—up from 62 percent in 2020.

To differentiate themselves in a hypercompetitive environment, companies need to provide a top-notch customer experience. These four trends shift the power to the customer: *rapid technological change* requires constant innovation to better serve customers and to outcompete new rivals; *information and transparency* about brands make it easier than ever to distinguish between good and bad customer experiences; more *data about customers* allows the best companies to offer an even more personalized experience; and these three trends consequently lead to the fourth trend of *changing customer expectations*. So it's not surprising that many companies strive to be customer-centric and align everything they do around the customer experience and that the truly customer-centric organizations will come out on top.

But the same trends that hit the consumer market are also affecting the labor market—and only the employee-centric organizations will flourish in this environment. In fact, the four trends that have led to customer-centricity have their equivalents in the labor market. Regarding changing expectations: employees and customers are the same humans, after all. Those employees (as customers) have higher expectations and care about values and experience. In terms of information and transparency: employees also have more information about companies and their culture. Additionally, they are accustomed to a highly personalized approach due to the abundance of data as customers, and they become frustrated with a one-size-fits-all approach in the workplace. Regarding the necessity for companies to continually innovate to remain competitive, employees actually play a pivotal role in creating innovative and agile organizations. Let's start exploring the impact of those four trends by first looking at changing expectations of employees.

Employees Expect More from Work, No Matter Their Age

People (if they are consumers) expect more from brands today than they did in the past, and they are making their purchase decisions based on more than just product or service attributes. The experience they have interacting with organizations and the values of the brands are critically important. Those same consumers are also employees. And people (if they are employees) are also demanding more from their employer and their work. As consumers, they are used to a very personalized experience with lots of choices—which affects their expectations as employees. Experiences that people have—especially when young and during their formative years—affect their job preferences for life. One of my studies shows, for example, that growing up in times and regions with bad macroeconomic conditions affects people's job preferences for the rest of their lives. These individuals place more importance on income. People who grow up in better times, however, care more about meaning at work beyond income, and they will place greater value on their experiences at work.

The debate about shifting attitudes toward work is often reduced to discussions about newer generations and their work attitudes. A good example is an article in *Fortune* magazine, titled "Managing Gen Z Is Like Working with People from a 'Different Country,'" which implied that younger generations have very different (and strange) values when it comes to work. Generation Z is the term for people born roughly between 1997 and 2012. They are digital natives and came of age after the Great Recession in 2008 and so know nothing before our current era of extreme personalization and consumer choice. While millennials (born between 1981 and 1996) also grew up with the internet and computers (and also have a particular reputation when it comes to work), Gen Z do not know a world without smartphones and laptops and the expectation of one-day delivery. Those experiences allegedly affect what they expect from their work: more choice, a healthy work-life balance, and meaning at work—not just a paycheck. But at the same time they are said to value loyalty less and switch jobs more easily for a better paycheck. Entire books are written about how to manage new generations of workers such as millennials or Gen Z, and HR teams have developed specific strategies to recruit, motivate, and retain younger generations. While members of those younger generations are the most vocal on social media and therefore get a lot of attention, the focus on shifting work attitudes of only the newer generation is missing the point that attitudes are changing across the board.

Obviously, attitudes toward work differ by age. The young are always different from their elders. So to accurately reflect attitudes between generations, we would need to compare their experiences at the same age, that is, a twenty-year-old Gen Z employee with a twenty-year-old baby boomer. Indeed, when we compare what people from different generations value about their job at a specific age, we see a lot of similarities. For example, when comparing how much people care about income compared to meaning or impact, we see that, across generations, it is the older workers who care more about meaning and impact. This is not that surprising as people who are just starting their career and their adult life are more concerned with financial stability and income than workers who have already been in the workforce for a while and have built a financial cushion. The latter group is more likely to be reflecting on what they want to get out of work and life. Focusing too much on younger generations ignores the slightly older workers who care more about other aspects of employment than just money. Given that we live longer and healthier lives, which means that employees are productive into more advanced age, companies need to pay attention to older workers as well as the younger generations.

Most importantly, everyone's expectations are changing. Only considering how younger generations, such as Gen Z or millennials, view work ignores how changes in the labor and consumer market are affecting everybody. Expectations about work are changing across the board. In surveys that ask workers about the importance of different aspects of a job (such as income, job security, working independently, doing something helpful for society, etc.), there is a clear trend that workers find more attributes important. That means, all workers today want high income *and* making an impact *and* having flexibility *and and and.* They then also want to work in a company that shares their values. More than half of responders in a survey by Qualtrics would not consider working for a company that doesn't share their values. This indicates a difficult dilemma for leaders who are more and more forced to publicly take a stance on social and political issues. Although some employees may require so-called CEO activism, others who do not agree with the position may be turned off. Consider if you're overly focused on the younger generations and are overlooking the broader workforce's aspirations. Leaders need to recognize that every employee, not just the more vocal Gen Z or millennials, expects more from work and wants to work for companies that share their values.

Just as it is getting easier for consumers to compare brands, it is also getting easier for employees to compare organizations and figure out which potential employer shares their values. Travis Kalanick learned the hard way that information about work culture is spreading faster than ever.

Increased Corporate Transparency

Travis Kalanick was the founder and CEO of Uber from its launch in 2010 until 2017. The ride-sharing company reached a billion-dollar valuation (which is the threshold for being called a unicorn) in just three years, and in 2022, it was valued at around $50 billion. Kalanick personally made about $2.5 billion from Uber's initial public offering (IPO) in 2019. While the company is still struggling to make a profit, Kalanick's idea and his company have completely disrupted the taxi industry and revolutionized transportation. In spite of the staggering influence of the company under his leadership, it only took one viral video starring Kalanick to bring about his fall at Uber and his resignation as CEO. And it has everything to do with Uber's treatment of employees and workers.

The famous video shows Kalanick arguing with an Uber driver at the end of a trip that he took with friends. The dashboard camera recorded the interaction that went viral. The driver complained to Kalanick about falling prices and that he is in bankruptcy because of Uber. That is when Kalanick got personal. "Some people don't like to take responsibility for their own shit," he replied. "They blame everything in their life on somebody else. Good luck!" Then he slammed the door. The video was emblematic of the company's poor treatment of workers and toxic corporate culture. Only a couple of months before, a blog post by a former employee that alleged sexual harassment culture at Uber went viral, leading to internal investigations that confirmed widespread harassment and discrimination. In the wake of the investigation, Uber fired a number of employees, including senior executives. Since the advent of social media, such scandals can spread like wildfire and can have a major influence on the behavior of consumers. In the case of Uber, #deleteUber started trending again (originally a consumer protest when allegations arose that Uber tried to capitalize on President Trump's immigration ban), and many customers began choosing different travel options. But a widely shared anti-employee episode like this also affects the hiring of talent and workers because—guess what?—the same consumers that are uneasy about the treatment of workers are also potential employees.

Sites like Expedia.com for price comparison, Tripadvisor.com for reviews, and Wirecutter for consumer experience and product quality have allowed consumers to easily compare products and services, which has intensified competition among companies.

Rich Barton, the founder of Expedia and Zillow, websites that brought transparency to the travel and housing markets, respectively, applied the same idea to the workplace by cofounding the webpage Glassdoor.com in 2008. Glassdoor has a powerful review feature that serves as a Tripadvisor for corporate culture. He said: "We were empowering people with information and tools that they didn't have before." Glassdoor, now valued at over a billion dollars, has reviews for over one million companies, and more than fifty million reviews are written about those companies by current or former employees. Glassdoor is only one of the many sites (like Indeed, Vault, Kununu, or Fairygodboss) that allows employees to compare their current or future workplace with other options. The increased transparency is getting noticed by executives. Beth Comstock, a former vice chair of General Electric, said it's changed the way business leaders think. "There'd been a march for more transparency that had come along with the digitization of business. But suddenly it became very personal. People were, like, 'Wait a minute, they're going to be rating *me*?'" Leaders are right to be taking notice as around half of job seekers are looking at review sites before applying for a job.

Comparison and review sites like Glassdoor.com definitely decrease wage discrepancy. Potential employees now go into wage negotiations after first checking review sites to know the acceptable range of wages. The hope is that such transparency is also reducing wage inequality. But reviews also have an important impact on another aspect of work that can be difficult to see: corporate culture. Research shows that after getting reviewed on Glassdoor.com, companies improve their workplace practices, measured by corporate social responsibility scores on employee relations and diversity. The increased transparency is putting a public spotlight on shortcomings in a company's culture and can be a substantial threat to a company's reputation and their employee brand. The scandals at Uber and other companies regarding toxic cultures and sexual harassment show the power of this transparency. Bad behavior that went on for years is being revealed, going viral, and leading to change. Jennifer Berdahl, who studies workplace sexual harassment at the University of British Columbia, said: "This is just putting on the Internet what's been going on forever—women whispering about bad experiences they've had within companies." The transparency requires leaders to finally tackle problems within their organizations head-on and to figure out how to improve employees' experiences. Current and potential employees will know (and share) whether their bosses succeeded and will reward those who are employee-centric. Reflect on whether you give equal emphasis to your employee brand as you do to your consumer branding. In light of the heightened corporate transparency, both hold equal significance.

In addition to the changing expectations of employees and customers and more transparency about brands and workplaces, more data is also available about employees.

More Data Means More Personalization

Vast amounts of data about customers and their preferences allowed for consumer-centricity and hyperpersonalization. Gone are the days in which customer segmentation was mainly based on sociodemographics such as young versus old, rich versus poor, or male versus female. Today, products and services can be targeted and personalized based on personality traits, preferences, or attitudes beyond simple sociodemographic variables. And people have gotten used to it. At many workplaces, however, employers are still either doing a one-size-fits-all approach or simple segmentation based on demographics. Any approach, for example, that is based on the idea that the younger generation wants X and older workers want Y is too simple and will be ineffective. There are clearly meaningful differences among employees of the same age, as well as of different ages, in what they want, need, and aspire to be. Gathering more data will allow us to capture those differences and personalize the employee experience, which will motivate employees to be more engaged and productive at work.

The amount of data about employees is rapidly increasing and enables companies to go beyond the observable attributes of employees and capture personality traits or people's relationships within an organization. In addition to data from widely adopted human capital management solutions that link human resource data with performance indicators, data also comes from "the *digital exhaust* of a company"—that is, the vast amount of data generated, for example, through email accounts, text exchanges, chats on Slack, Zoom meetings, and file transfers. This data captures who is communicating with whom and when in an organization and allows companies to analyze not just who people are in an organization but also *who people know*. It can show who is influential and well connected and who is isolated, as well as which teams lack the diversity needed to be productive and innovative. A study mentioned in the *Harvard Business Review* involved a software company that mapped the connections of their engineers. The analysis showed that the company was divided into multiple cliques, that is, smaller groups in which members mainly talked only to one another. But good ideas are often created by combining different and novel information, and so just talking to the same people is not a recipe for generating ideas. A smaller number of engineers connected and communicated with the various smaller networks or cliques. Those were the individuals who came up with the best ideas. Management was then able to target those engineers and make it easier for them to do what they do. As a result, the company saw an increase in both the quantity and quality of their ideas. This kind of tailored approach is only possible because of these new types of data.

The vast amount of data enables organizations to personalize recruitment—how the new hire is integrated, trained, and, in general, communicated with. While some of the data already exists in organizations, other types of data need to be collected in order to personalize. The same way customer-centric organizations react to feedback from customers, employee-centric organizations need to use analytics from employee feedback to personalize employee experiences. Most organizations have a long way to go. Take deciding about and planning for the future of the workplace. While it should be obvious that decisions should be data driven, a report by Slack about the future of work indicates that 66 percent of executives are designing their postpandemic workforce policy without any or only minimal input from employees. The companies that personalize the employee experience will have an edge in attracting the best and keeping them motivated and engaged. Reflect on whether you are equally dedicated to crafting a tailored employee experience as you are to shaping a personalized customer experience. The sheer amount of new data will be key. As with consumer data, it's crucial to consider the quality and privacy concerns surrounding the data. Leaders should have a clear strategy concerning potential employee data—staying true to being employee-centric. That means that organizations need to be transparent about the use of the data and only apply it to enhance the work experience and not misuse the data to control their employees. As we will see later in this book, this will require a shift in how employers view their employees.

Last but not least, the rapid pace at which companies must innovate and adapt impacts customer-centricity and at the same time necessitates a shift toward employee-centricity.

The Key to Becoming a Successful Agile Organization: Employees

In recent years, being innovative is not enough—you must now innovate at speed. For example, digitalization and developments in artificial intelligence and data analytics require constant changes to companies' business models. New entrants—either international firms or smaller and much nimbler start-ups—require quick competitive reactions. Rapidly changing consumer preferences for different purchasing channels (such as self-service on a computer or mobile phone or an online chat) or product and service attributes are making historic competitive advantages obsolete. The unprecedented level of volatility, uncertainty, complexity, and ambiguity (collectively known as VUCA) in organizational environments requires organizations to keep up with the rapid pace of change. Innovation is now a given for high-performing organizations. The ones that do not figure out how to keep pace will not survive. The solution is to create agile organizations—and agility is almost by definition people-first.

Agile organizations are set up to react quickly to changes in trends in the marketplace and the environment. But to achieve that, companies need to completely change their organizational structure and processes. A hierarchical and top-down organization must give way to a flat organization in which power and authority go to employees and teams. The whole organization should be set up in cross-functional teams that are encouraged to experiment, fail, and learn. Those teams have end-to-end responsibility, which means that they are autonomous in delivering new products without having to rely on other parts of the organization. This is a substantial shift for managers. Not only do many have to transition from managers to "just" team members, but they need to relinquish the control that comes from planning and reporting, which does not fit this agile model.

ING, the global bank headquartered in the Netherlands, successfully undertook such an agile transformation starting in 2014, one year after Ralph Hamers was named its new CEO. Hamers realized that the bank needed to change in light of significant shifts in its business environment. Customers had become accustomed to fast and personalized service from tech companies such as Amazon, Apple, and Spotify and were getting more demanding as a result. Once people are used to one-day delivery, waiting multiple weeks to get approved for credit can be quite frustrating. ING's quality of customer experience and customization now had to keep up with these customer-centric tech companies. The digital companies were not only much better at offering their services online; they were also much quicker in coming up with new features and products. Many of the new fintech competitors such as PayPal, Square, or Venmo (or Amazon with its short-term loans to small and medium-size companies) also offered disintermediation, meaning it was possible for customers to interact directly without going through a bank. ING needed to adapt.

Transforming a large and established bank such as ING is not an easy task. Large organizations in general are difficult to change, and banks are known for being particularly slow to transform. ING first had to completely overhaul its organization. It got rid of layers of hierarchy and organized the whole company into squads. These squads are cross-functional teams of around nine people who have end-to-end responsibility—that is, they are able to come up with a new product without the help of anybody else in the organization. As a result, the bank got much faster and more innovative. ING went from having "five big releases a year to thousands of new releases a month." Releases can be new product launches but also smaller changes, such as new search functions in payment apps or a software update.

At the core of any successful agile transformation are people. ING's former chief operating officer, Bart Schlatmann, defines agility as the "flexibility and the ability of an organization to rapidly adapt and steer itself in a new direction. It's about minimizing handovers and bureaucracy, and empowering people." ING's agile transformation required a completely new employee-centric way of working, as all the initiatives had to come from employees. The bank was very explicit that agile innovation would only happen if it prioritized people over processes and tools. That meant a stark departure from working with strict protocols and tools to providing freedom, support, and resources to employees. ING organized "pizza sessions" in which employees were asked to give honest feedback about what was working, and what was not working at ING. As the name of the sessions suggest, ING would provide the pizza and communicate the received feedback to the board. For example, in those sessions it became clear that employees hated meetings and thought that most of the meetings were a waste of time. Schlatmann explained that as a result of input from those sessions and from reimagining work as employee-centric, ING "gave up traditional hierarchy, formal meetings, over-engineering, detailed planning and excessive 'input steering.'" After ING's transformation, Schlatmann said that "there is so much more freedom, happiness, and empowerment."

ING's people-first agile transformation was unquestionably a business success: its innovation speed increased, customers were more satisfied (as reflected in an increased net promoter score), and its financial performance improved. But the bank also became a better place to work. It moved up two ranks, from seventh in 2014 to fifth in 2017, in the Dutch equivalent of the *Fortune* 100 Best Companies to Work For list. But it's important to point out that being employee-centric was not the result of the agile transformation, but the necessary precondition for being agile.

The four trends all point in the direction that companies need to put employees first and be truly employee-centric. But to be really employee-centric and generate the benefits of it requires more than mentioning in a letter to shareholders (as Jeff Bezos did) that "we are going to be Earth's Best Employer." It requires a mind-set shift: putting employees first does not put profits second. Leaders must have internalized that, rather than creating higher costs for a company, employee-centric strategies will provide more value. Just like a customer-centric organization in which both customers and shareholders win, being employee-centric results in mutual gains for both employees and the organization itself.

Unfortunately, the either-or view that *either* employees *or* shareholders win is still very prevalent—a lesson that 3M, the company that created the Post-it note, learned the hard way.

CHAPTER 2

Not Either-Or but Win-Win

F EW COMPANIES EXEMPLIFY an innovative people culture better than 3M. We can see this in the story of how it created its now-ubiquitous product, the Post-it note. The history of Post-it notes is by now well known—but the lessons it offers on how a business can foster a people-first innovation culture are less so. It all started with a failure. In the late 1960s, Dr. Spencer Silver, a 3M scientist, was working on developing an ultrastrong adhesive for use in aircraft construction. He was unsuccessful but in the process created a weak, pressure-sensitive adhesive containing "microspheres," which retained their stickiness and could be used again and again. It was obviously useless in the production of planes, and for years Silver could not find an application for his invention. But he would not give up. He talked to his colleagues about it constantly—including Art Fry, another 3M scientist. Fry sang in his church choir and needed to mark the songs they performed for each mass. To his frustration, the paper slips he put into his hymnal would always fall out. He needed something that would stick and then unstick, as the program changed each week: the Post-it note's moment had arrived. Silver's unusual adhesive not only solved Fry's hymnal problem; it also became an invaluable tool now used in every office around the world.

Post-its are just one of the over sixty thousand different products manufactured by 3M today. That's quite a change from the early 1900s, when the Minnesota Mining and Manufacturing company (where the name 3M comes from) was a small and unprofitable organization just beginning to realize that it needed to diversify and innovate to survive. At that time its leaders decided that instead of focusing solely on mining, its engineers should start to experiment with different materials and apply their discoveries to new products. Over the decades that followed, the company produced a wide variety of technological breakthroughs, including everything from Teflon to skin creams to industrial chemicals to the first asthma inhaler and even a proprietary theatrical blood that was used in the 1978 horror film *The Dawn of the Dead.* Their resulting success through innovation made them a perennial member of the Fortune 500 list.

By 1995, 3M had created so many ingenious products it was honored by the US government with its highest award for innovation, the National Medal of Technology and Innovation. Today, a third of 3M's sales comes from products invented within the past five years. One of 3M's practices to foster innovation is to give its people 15 percent of their time during the week to work on anything they care about. This is when Silver and Fry worked on the Post-it note. The 15 percent rule at 3M was introduced in 1948—fifty years before Google announced its own version, the 20 percent rule. What both companies realize is that giving their employees freedom and autonomy encourages creative scientists and engineers to join the company. It creates a culture for serendipitous discovery.

It's also important to note that Post-it notes were not an immediate success. The company was, in fact, initially skeptical of their commercial viability. For years after they developed the product, Silver and Fry struggled to get the support they wanted from top management. But eventually they did. The culture within 3M remained open to the persistence of the two scientists as they embraced a more long-term view. Only multiple years after the invention did the product become the invaluable product we know today—all thanks to 3M's culture, which believed in its best innovators: its employees.

Unfortunately, 3M's people-first culture of innovation would not last—because of a widespread either-or mentality.

The Six Sigma Black Belt Who Killed Innovation

Today, managers and Wall Street investors are skeptical of putting people first by creating autonomy and job security. This approach is more expensive than the typical command-and-control model and requires long-term commitment. If an executive does not believe these strategies will promote innovation, then they will be seen as doing little more than increasing costs and inefficiency. This was the view of James McNerney, who became CEO of 3M in 2000. McNerney had learned his trade from Jack Welch at General Electric (GE), who, it should be said, was not really known for being an employee-first kind of manager. David Gelles, a journalist who studied the views and influence of Welch, described his profound influence in his book *The Man Who Broke Capitalism*: "The changes he [Jack Welch] unleashed at GE transformed the company founded by Thomas Edison from an admired industrial behemoth known for quality engineering and laudable business practices into a sprawling multinational conglomerate that paid little regard to its employees and was addicted to short-term profits. And we all went along for the ride."

Welch was famous for implementing the set of management tools and techniques known as Six Sigma at GE. The goal of Six Sigma is to streamline work processes to reduce error rates and improve operational efficiencies. If you have as a target an average quality or cost, you don't want the variability from that goal to be too high. According to the Six Sigma method, you want to be within six standard deviations, three above and three below the mean. (In statistics, the term *sigma* indicates the standard deviation in a distribution.) The method involves determining and planning the goal or output, documenting the process, analyzing and making adjustments, improving the process, and continuing to monitor and refine (referred to as "define, measure, analyze, improve, control"). It can also introduce a rigid adherence to statistical analysis and arbitrary milestones.

McNerney brought the ruthless scientism of Six Sigma to the people-centric culture of 3M. All employees got training in Six Sigma to get a green belt certification in the methodology. High potentials received black belt training—overseen by McNerney personally. But McNerney brought over another "trick" from Welch as well: eliminating 10 percent of the workforce when efficiency increased. The process was welcomed by Wall Street, as operating margins grew from 17 percent in 2001 to 23 percent by 2005.

Six Sigma was indeed able to bring costs down at 3M—at first. But it also limited innovation and creativity. This in turn limited growth and new product development. The original corporate culture at 3M of serendipitous discovery, tolerance for failure, and entrepreneurship and self-initiatives did not square well with Six Sigma's mantra of planning, accountability, and control. Not to mention the fear of failure Six Sigma could instill in workers. A divisional director at the time noted: "Six Sigma has this terrifying thing of not wanting errors. But if you do innovation the way we do, pure risk is something you have to be able to admit and accept." The constant reviews and monitoring of Six Sigma would have prevented the invention of the Post-it note and stifled innovation at 3M. During those years the number of innovative products developed by 3M dropped significantly, and engineers were frustrated by the process—a disaster for a company that thrived on innovation.

Eventually, 3M took a step back from full Six Sigma to allow innovation to be less planned, less focused on short-term thinking, and less controlled. In 2005, 3M's new CEO, George Buckley, kept the best of Six Sigma in production, like some uniform language and greater concern for risk management, in order to keep its cost-cutting and efficiency-improving qualities. But he also exempted many of the research processes from the strict Six Sigma protocols that had stifled innovation. When people feel empowered, trusted, and secure, innovation sparks. It might be less efficient at first, but it actually creates value. 3M found its way back to being an innovation powerhouse by giving its employees more freedom. In fact, in 2010, it was voted by Booz Allen to be the third-most innovative company in the world—just behind Google and Apple. Even today, when 3M faces declining demand in its core markets, it still appears on lists of the best and most innovative workplaces. In 2023, it was the finalist on *Fast Company*'s list of Best Workplaces for Innovators in the Sustainability category and among the twenty most innovative companies by Boston Consulting Group.

Unfortunately, it is a widespread belief that being employee-centric comes at the expense of profits, that is, *either* employees *or* shareholders benefit but not both. We can see such zero-sum thinking not only in how McNerney treated workers at 3M but also in the way analysts and the stock markets react to investments in the workforce. Costco, the US retailer known for being the most employee-centric in the industry, is frequently criticized by analysts and investors for this approach. A headline in the *Wall Street Journal* from 2004 captures the either-or attitude of some analysts and investors: "Costco's Dilemma: Be Kind to Its Workers, or Wall Street." And an analyst at Sanford C. Bernstein & Co., a brokerage firm, is even more explicit: "Whatever goes to employees comes out of the pockets of shareholders." This is zero-sum thinking again: when employees are happy, the company loses.

When in the fall of 2020, Costco announced that it spent $282 million in bonuses and safety measures for its employees, the stock dropped 1.27 percent—despite the fact that Costco in that quarter exceeded earnings and growth expectations. The concerns were partly that the investment in their workforce would be a drag on the company's profit in the long run. Jim Cramer, the engaging but controversial host of the investment show *Mad Money* on CNBC, actually got it right when he commented about this either-or thinking: "With all due respect, these concerns are moronic. [...] Costco has always paid its employees better than every other store. And it's always been a good investment."

This either-or mentality remains widespread and ingrained in many leaders' thinking and their decisions. As we've seen, when executives talk about their employees in earning calls, they tend to use words like *cost* and *risk*. This is how Jack Welch and his disciples, such as James McNerney, thought about labor. Employees were not an asset but a cost that either needed to be eliminated or tightly controlled.

If you want to reap the rewards of being employee-centric, you need to move away from this either-or thinking. People, whether they are customers or employees, are much more complicated than a variable on a spreadsheet. I've already described how businesses like Starbucks and

Amazon reaped benefits from their concerted focus on customer service. They understood the psychology of consumers and showed how, by valuing them, you can win their loyalty. These lessons can also tell us why being employee-centric works. To understand this better, let's start by thinking about how value and profits are created.

Create Value for Customers and Employees and Profit Will Follow

How and why does helping others (customers and employees) increase profits? I'll use a simple framework and visualization, based on work by Adam Brandenburger and Harborne Stuart, known as the value stick (and shown in Figure 1). This concept nicely illustrates how value and profits are generated and how customer-centricity (and then also employee-centricity) creates benefits for companies. The framework is used across the globe in business schools to teach how to craft successful value-based business strategies. The value stick shows that the same logic that makes customer-centricity profitable also applies to employee-centricity.

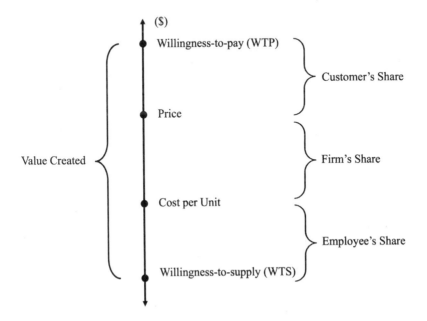

Figure 1: Value Creation and Value Capture

Let's first focus on customers (and the upper part of the value stick) and how customer-centricity works. The intuition of the framework is that successful companies are the ones that create the most value. They do so by increasing the willingness to pay (WTP) of the customer. WTP is the absolute maximum the customer would pay for a product. By making the service and product better and improving the customer experience, WTP increases.

Increasing WTP is great for customers, but how does this increase profits? In the end, profitable companies are those who increase prices and lower cost. That is where profit margins come from and how companies capture value. But for any of this to work, they first need to *create* value. In order to increase the price, companies basically negotiate with customers. In the bazaar of Marrakesh, where I teach every year, or any other market without fixed prices, you can clearly see that prices are negotiated. Stall after stall of similar shops fan out in every direction. Pricing, in these conditions, seems like a zero-sum game: if I pay one dirham less for the fake Liverpool jersey for my son, the vendor has one dirham lower margin and I have one dirham more in my pocket (and a gift to bring home). *Either* the vendor wins *or* I do, but this isn't how it works most of the time when businesses are selling differentiated products. In order to have pricing power, companies need to first create value and then they can capture some in the form of a higher margin. They need to be different from each other—something that the vendors in the Marrakesh market are not because I can always go to another vendor who has the exact same jersey. Companies will always compete with other companies, and those who create the most value for customers will win.

But how can you create value? This is where customer-centricity kicks in. Zappos.com, the online shoe retailer that is now part of Amazon, is a great example of a company that increases WTP by putting customers first. In fact, the company's number-one core value is "Deliver WOW Through Service." I experienced this firsthand on a gloomy January evening in New York City in 2014. I had just moved from a building on 64th Street and West End Avenue to a building closer to Columbia

University's campus in Morningside Heights. My previous apartment was in a huge doorman building that probably had around two hundred units (at least).

On this particular evening I was in my new, much-smaller prewar building suffering from a severe cold, wondering why the sneakers I had ordered on Zappos.com had not arrived yet. The website said that the shoes had been delivered, but the package was not in my lobby. That is when I decided to call customer service at Zappos.com—and one phone conversation converted me into a loyal Zappos.com customer. The call center employee was super nice, and we had a good chat (unlike any other call center experience I ever had). She lived in Las Vegas, where the Zappos.com headquarters was, and according to her, the weather in Las Vegas was much nicer than in New York on that January day. Upon hearing that I had a cold, she gave me tips on how to deal with it (hot tea, lots of lemon, ginger—and a shot of whiskey!). Only then did we look at what went wrong with the delivery. It turns out I did not update my address after moving, and so my Puma sneakers were lost somewhere in the building at 101 West End Avenue. Clearly, my mistake! Imagine my shock when she decided to send me another pair free of charge and upgraded me to VIP member. While I never needed to call customer service again, Zappos.com got my loyalty then, and I will never forget that moment. My WTP is higher for shoes on Zappos.com, and I have since bought more than fifty pairs of shoes from Zappos.com.

Moments like this illustrate how customer-centricity becomes win-win instead of either-or. Lowering prices is not customer-centric, but increasing WTP is. As a result, the customer is willing to pay a higher price. While this is primarily a customer-centric play, companies like Zappos.com also need to make their employees happy in order to create such a superior customer experience. The customer rep that picked up my call clearly enjoyed her job: Zappos.com gave her the autonomy to talk with me without a strict script or time limit, and she was happy to use it. As we discuss later, only happy employees will create happy customers. In terms of customer-centricity, customers win and get value, but companies are now also able to capture more value and eventually increase prices—instead of lowering them.

There are still leaders, investors, and analysts who do not buy the customer-centricity mantra. Jeff Bezos calls this either-or mentality, when it comes to customers, "very amateurish." Since Bezos started his company, we have come a long way in realizing that in order to capture value, companies need to first create value by helping customers and increasing their WTP through superb and hard-to-imitate customer experiences and by constantly innovating.

Be Obsessed with WTS

When it comes to employee-centricity, many leaders are, however, still stuck in the either-or mentality, despite the fact that the logic about value creation and value capture is the same as for customers, only it relates to their willingness to supply (WTS)—and the lower part of the value stick shown in Figure 1. WTS indicates the lowest wage for employees or cost for suppliers they would accept. Improving the work and the employee experience will decrease the WTS for a company's employees. If a job is unattractive or dangerous, WTS increases, and workers will need to be compensated more for accepting the job.

Employee-centricity and customer-centricity are both integral to adding value. And just as a business's investment in customers can be win-win, so can investment in employees. Value is created when employees are happy and their willingness to supply (WTS) their labor and effort is lowered. That is the equivalent to increasing WTP discussed before. So, compare two jobs: one has a terrible boss and one has a good boss. Most people would rather have the job with the great boss and would even accept a lower wage or work harder to work for one.

But WTS for companies is not just about lower turnover. These employees are more productive and engaged, which lowers the cost. We'll talk more later about how to lower your employees' WTS. Being employee-centric truly adds value, a strategy that notably prevented Best Buy from collapsing.

In 2012, Hubert Joly took over as CEO of Best Buy, an electronics retailer. Everybody thought that he was absolutely insane to take on this job. Best Buy was being crushed by e-commerce in general and Amazon in particular. One of the major problems was "showrooming": customers would go into a Best Buy store to see, feel, and compare products like flat-screen TVs, and then go home and order their choice on Amazon. This behavior was shrinking Best Buy's sales numbers. By the time Joly took over, sales and profits had declined, and the share price had plummeted. As a consequence, Best Buy's workforce grew extremely frustrated and disengaged. It seemed an easy prediction that online retailers would destroy Best Buy like they had Circuit City, a competing electronics retailer that folded in 2009. RadioShack, another competitor, filed for bankruptcy in 2015. Everybody expected a similar fate for Best Buy.

But Joly, an unlikely CEO choice from France, was crazy enough to leave his job running the travel company Carlson to try to save Best Buy. After he started, Joly got a lot of advice (solicited or not) on how to turn around the company, and most of it was focused on how to squeeze the employees more. Some even suggested he get rid of many of his employees. Joly remembered: "Everybody was saying, 'You better cut, cut, cut, close stores, fire a lot of people.'" Sound familiar? It was the conventional either-or logic: margins improve if employees lose. But Joly did not follow this advice. Instead, he conducted a people-centric turnaround. And in the process, he pulled off one of the most remarkable business reversals in decades.

He started the turnaround by wearing a "CEO in Training" tag and listening to the "blue shirts," the front-line workers who wear Best Buy's iconic blue shirts, at a store in St. Cloud, Minnesota, which is about sixty miles north of Best Buy's headquarters. As Joly describes in his book about the turnaround, *The Heart of Business*, he learned more in a couple of days from talking to the blue shirts than he did analyzing spreadsheets and talking to a bunch of executives. They knew what was going wrong and could express what was frustrating the workforce. For example, the company reduced employee discounts a couple of months earlier.

Reducing this perk hit the blue shirts hard as most worked at Best Buy because they were electronics geeks. The discount was exactly the right perk to attract the right employees: somebody who really cares deeply about electronics, even though the discount was a small thing. Joly got from the blue shirts many other ideas on how to make both the employee and customer experience better.

"When a business is in trouble," Joly later wrote, "listening to the individuals on the front line is the best place to quickly identify what 'crazy, goofy, or stupid' things…have been getting in the way." He then went on to improve the experience of employees by removing stupid rules, providing more autonomy, and increasing investment in the blue shirts' development and training. Joly also expanded employee benefits to include paid caregiver leave, expanded mental health benefits, paid time off for part-time employees, and backup childcare. Reducing head count was the absolute last resort. Joly did exactly the opposite of "cut, cut, cut." "When a business is in critical condition," Joly said, "its people are the key to a successful turnaround. Survival depends on them, how energized they are, and how much they care about customers and all other stakeholders." Focusing on employees creates value, leads to an engaged workforce (at Best Buy engagement was at its all-time high after the turnaround), and creates a situation in which both employees and the company win.

But being obsessed about WTS requires knowing what employees actually want and what is motivating to them. A listening tour such as the one Hubert Joly did helps get insights. The second part of this book will discuss this important point further and present the behavioral science behind employees' work motivation. It will provide the basis of creating a customer-centric team or company.

Beyond case studies, there is research analyzing large numbers of organizations across the globe to evaluate the overall benefit of being employee-centric on profits. An early set of studies by Alex Edmans of London Business School showed that companies that were listed on the

Fortune 100 Best Companies to Work For in America generated between 2.3 and 3.8 percent higher stock return per year than their peers over a twenty-seven-year period. A more recent study looked at a sample of around thirty-five hundred companies across forty-three countries. They analyze the effect of different indicators for an employee-friendly (EF) culture on company performance. Organizations with more EF culture are valued higher and perform better measured as return on asset or return on equity. Similar studies across the globe looking at best places to work lists or employee evaluations from review sites such as Glassdoor.com confirm the case studies that being employee-centric is not either-or but win-win; that is, business benefits as well.

Being obsessed with reducing WTS is the first insight from the value-based strategy. But there is another crucial element to being employee-centric: to make a workplace attractive it needs not only to be motivating for workers (i.e., lowering WTS), it also needs to be hard for competitors to imitate.

It Will Be Difficult...and That Is a Good Thing

I assume that at one point there was a hotel that figured out that customers like it when there is chocolate on their pillow before they go to bed. While this might have marginally increased the WTP, it does not add to the hotel's competitive advantage because it is easy to copy. Now every hotel provides sweets. And this is another reason why price decreases are not customer-centric in a way that creates a significant competitive advantage. Every company can lower its prices if it wants to. Unique value is created only if it is hard to pull off.

For a company to create value compared to its competition, it needs to decrease WTS in a way that is hard to imitate, similar to how companies need to differentiate to increase willingness to pay. If it is easy to copy, everybody else will do it. This is no different when it comes to attracting employees and talent. Think about organic energy bars: if those bars are attractive to employees and affect their WTS, then every company will have break rooms with organic energy bars. This perk is too easy to imitate and therefore offers no competitive (employee) advantage. While there is some low-hanging fruit in terms of employee-centricity, as we will discuss later in this book, the best changes that companies can make to improve work for their employees (and for their bottom line) are hard to implement and require dedication and strategic thinking. This is another reason why focusing just on wage and monetary benefits does not create value. In addition to leading to an either-or situation, these approaches are, like organic energy bars, easy for competitors to copy.

Best Buy's turnaround was difficult to pull off—which is why it worked and could not be copied easily. Joly remembered, "Our main challenges were: How do you create these new strategies? How to get 100,000 people to embrace them?" One theme of Best Buy's turnaround was creating purpose for its employees. As we will see later, just having a flashy mission statement is not cutting it—again, everybody can and is doing that. The changes need to show dedication and be authentic. "'Authentic' is about credibility—something aligned with what the company does, that it is able to deliver, and that is at the core of its DNA," according to Joly. But what is at the core and defines a team or company's DNA requires strategic thinking about what type of employee-centricity is aligned with its business strategy.

As I will discuss in Chapter 4, what works for one company might not work for another. This is where differentiation comes in. Before the pandemic only 22 percent of executives in a survey by the consultancy firm Deloitte said that their companies were "excellent at building a differentiated employee experience." Finding a differentiated way is similar to the process for customers: some companies focus on one segment of the population while other companies serve a different segment. Companies then figure out what affects the WTP of their respective segments. Same with employees: What do we want to achieve? What kind of employees do we want? How do we make those employees happy and engaged? Answering those questions and being dedicated to them will create unique value that will be hard for the competition to imitate.

Long Term, Not Short Term, Wins

Focusing on creating value will eventually lead to higher profits. But this is not a short-term strategy maximizing short-term margins and growth. It will require investment and dedication and being obsessed about customers and employees. And it requires a shift from an either-or thinking to a win-win mentality. Before the turnaround, Domino's Pizza was stuck in an either-or and short-term-win mentality. As executive vice president of communication Tim McIntryre explains: "We were making independent changes that in small doses seemed like good ideas. For example, people were trying to drive a little bit of cost out of sauce and so they cheapened it and they said: 'we can save some money here and nobody's going to notice.' And another team did the same thing with cheese and another team did the same thing with meat. And what happened was that there was a collection of individually good ideas that all added up to one bad idea."

Domino's turnaround moved away from the logic that to benefit the bottom line, it needed to make the pizza slightly worse for customers. The company focused on the quality of its product and the customer experience, and as a result, the business could not have been better. Domino's (which dropped *pizza* from its name after it expanded its food offerings to sandwiches and pasta, among other products) has done phenomenally well. Its stock price increased by around 4,000 percent from January 2010 to December 2022, while the S&P 500 only increased by 250 percent. In the same period, Amazon's stock price "only" increased 1,200 percent. The pizza chain outperformed the tech giant by more than three times! Domino's understood that in its industry focusing on the customer experience by digitizing its operations was win-win. The company took the number-one spot from Pizza Hut as the largest pizza chain in the world in revenue and number of restaurants. Moving away from short-term, either-or thinking seemed like a much better long-term strategy that benefits both customers and the company's bottom line.

This customer focus also influences its employee strategy. At least one-third of the two hundred employees working in Domino's headquarters in Ann Arbor, Michigan, work in technology with a lot of autonomy to be innovative. Domino's is also not outsourcing its delivery operation to gig-work apps such as Uber Eats or DoorDash. "It is all about our execution on delivery. And we do that extraordinarily well," said former CEO Patrick Doyle. While in 2023, it revised its stand on gig platforms and is available on Uber Eats and Postmates, Domino's still does the delivery with its own workforce in order to control customer satisfaction.

As with customer-centricity, you will only see the benefits of putting employees first in the medium or long term. When Hubert Joly stepped down as CEO of Best Buy in 2019, the company was alive and kicking. He was able in just seven years to improve customer satisfaction, increase employee engagement, gain market share, grow revenue, and improve margins. The Renew Blue turnaround had many aspects, many of them customer-centric, but as Joly said: "Engaged employees were the engine of Best Buy's successful turnaround and remain the number-one reason for its continued success today. Yet you cannot find them on the balance sheet. As a result, investing in people [...], like we did at Best Buy, can depress profits in the short term." Unfortunately, businesses are not in the practice of accounting for the long-term benefits of investing in employees—not yet.

Other companies that distinctly focus on and invest in their employees are also doing well in terms of profits. Costco is paying much higher wages than Walmart's Sam's Club, offers generous benefits, and provides its employees with a clear career and development path within its organization. It shows in employee reviews on Glassdoor.com: Costco receives four stars while Walmart has 3.3. Seventy-seven percent of employees would recommend Costco to a friend to work, while only 56 percent would do the same for Walmart. As discussed earlier, Costco is getting a lot of heat from analysts for being "too nice." But James Sinegal, Costco's founder and longtime CEO, counters: "On Wall Street they're in the business of making money between now and next Thursday. I don't say that with any bitterness, but we can't take that view. We want to build a company that will still be here 50 and 60 years from now." And the business results confirm Sinegal's view: Costco is doing really well. Revenue and profits are growing fast, which is reflected in its stock price. The share price increased by 690 percent from 2010 to 2022. In comparison, Walmart stock price increased only by 160 percent in the same period. So, I guess, Sinegal was right when he said: "We pay much better than Wal-Mart. That's not altruism, that's good business."

In order to craft a successful employee-centric strategy leaders need to dig deeper and see where the benefits accrue and how to differentiate. And it turns out, the perfect example of this can be found dangling above the Toyota assembly line.

CHAPTER 3

Benefits of Putting Employees First

I N 1984, TOYOTA AND GM formed a joint venture to produce cars and light trucks in a factory in Fremont, California. The new joint venture, called NUMMI (New United Motor Manufacturing, Inc.), would produce high-quality small cars under both the Toyota and the GM/Chevy brand. It was no secret that the Fremont plant before the joint venture was an absolute disaster. It had "the worst workforce in the automobile industry," according to Bruce Lee, who oversaw Fremont Union Local 1364 of the United Auto Workers. "Everything was a fight. They spent more time on grievances and on things like that than they did on producing cars. They had strikes all the time. It was just chaos constantly." And statistics backed up Mr. Lee's assessment: the plant was the worst in quality, productivity, absenteeism, and worker safety. Illegal drugs and alcohol were rampant on the premises. And the workforce was not just unmotivated but actively destructive. There were instances of employees retaliating against management by scratching finished cars or even sabotaging safety features of the automobiles. Two years before NUMMI took over, GM had had enough: it closed the plant and laid off thousands of workers.

Though the Fremont plant was the worst within GM, all the other plants at GM were bad, especially by Toyota standards. It took GM about thirty hours to assemble a car. Toyota took half the time. Assembly defects per one hundred cars were around 130 for GM and only 45 for Toyota. And the quality differences in the cars resulted in about a 20 percent price premium for a Toyota car compared to a nearly identical GM car. Toyota just produced higher-quality cars in fewer hours of work. How did the company do it? The answer was the Toyota Production System (TPS), a set of principles and processes that should—if applied correctly—lead to lean manufacturing and just-in-time production. Toyota was willing to teach GM in the NUMMI plant in Fremont how to do it and in the process figure out whether the Toyota system could work in the US context.

And the system did work out well in Fremont. In fact, it even worked with the same, still-unionized workers from the miserable Fremont plant. Two years after GM closed the Fremont plant and fired the entire workforce, Toyota hired almost all the people whom GM had laid off to work at NUMMI—the old team made up 85 percent of the new team. GM was vehemently against hiring the same crew again. Why would you hire the same unionized workers who created so much trouble in the past? But Toyota was confident it could make those same people work productively. And it did. Toyota management came into the plant, and within just a couple of months, productivity and quality improved tremendously. Within just one year, NUMMI produced the highest-quality GM cars. And not just that, employees actually started to enjoy coming to work. Absenteeism and grievance filing by the union fell dramatically. And the workers were really proud of their work on the new Chevy Novas, the GM car produced at NUMMI based on a Toyota Corolla.

But this isn't the end of the story. While things improved significantly, the lessons from the NUMMI plant would not fully transform GM manufacturing for another fifteen years. Productivity and quality of GM cars from other plants still lagged. Why? The answer lies in a small nylon rope that hangs above the assembly line: the andon cord.

To Pull or Not to Pull?

An important part of TPS is *kaizen*, a short word with a long definition. It means "continuously improving business operations through innovation and evolution." The philosophy and insight of kaizen is that everything can and should be improved constantly, and everybody in an organization—independent of their hierarchical rank—is expected to come up with innovations to improve process and quality. The andon cord symbolizes this philosophy. In Japanese, an *andon* is a lantern, traditionally made out of paper and bamboo. On the assembly line, andon cords hang down from the ceiling, and workers are expected to pull them whenever they see a problem in the quality or the process that needs fixing. Pulling the cord produces a blinking light that illuminates the section in which a problem has occurred. The supervisor and the worker's whole team then try to fix the problem right away. If not fixed within a couple of minutes, the assembly line stops. To be clear, the inability to quickly fix the problem does not lead to a discussion about whether to stop the line. It's automatic. Production literally stops, then and there, until the problem is resolved. This may seem like a recipe for chaos. Pulling the andon cord is a risky and costly undertaking. Stopping an automotive assembly line costs around $15,000 per minute. In fact, in most manufacturing lines, it is close to a capital crime to stop the assembly line. But the andon cord system allows for process and quality to be constantly improved with instantaneous problem-solving and innovation. Toyota's superior metrics on productivity and quality proved it.

After the NUMMI plant adopted the andon cord, all GM plants were equipped with cords. But there was a problem. Nobody at the other GM plants would actually pull the cord and make suggestions for improvements. Turns out that having the processes and equipment in place is not enough: if you want to spark innovation through genuine, employee-centric strategies, you need a profound mind-set shift. To get innovative suggestions on the production line, workers need to be empowered to make suggestions, be assured that their improvements are taken seriously, and trust that it will not lead to them being replaced once the process is improved. The implicit or explicit understanding between workers and the organization needs to be that workers can and should make suggestions that would potentially make the worker's job redundant—without fear of actually being laid off. At the same time, supervisors need to dramatically change from a command-and-control structure to a team-based approach where decisions are delegated down to the team level. This requires a shift for managers and supervisors away from the view that workers try to slack off whenever they can (and might pull the cord to get a break) toward trust in the unique abilities and good intentions of workers.

NUMMI had implemented an employee-centric culture. One crucial pillar of the TPS is "Respect for People." Without it, nothing works. Toyota extensively invested in training and empowering its workforce at NUMMI and its other plants. It shifted to a team-based model, in which not only shop-floor workers worked in a team, but the supervisors also actively worked alongside the workers to solve problems. Supervisors would respond to an andon cord pull with the recognition and gratitude that the worker did their part in improving the organization. And importantly, Toyota committed to a no-layoff policy. In the end, a lot of those practices depend on a culture of trust—and only actions can reinforce the foundation of trust. For example, while many NUMMI workers might have been skeptical about the no-layoff commitment, Toyota followed through with its promise: even when capacity at the end of the 1980s dropped to 65 percent, it did not lay anyone off. Such trust and empowerment lead to constant innovation and improvements. In a Toyota plant in Georgetown, Kentucky, assembly plant workers made eighty thousand improvement suggestions in one year, of which 99 percent got approved. Being employee-centric paid off.

GM at large was not able to implement this shift for decades. It hadn't developed a culture of trust. Workers at GM were convinced for the longest time that GM only wanted to implement the Toyota way to speed up production, create more pressure on employees, and cut head count. And indeed, in the midst of the recession at the beginning of the 1990s, GM CEO Robert Stempel was not able to convince his board or Wall Street that losses in those years were not a sign of mismanagement. So, he closed twenty-one plants and cut seventy-four thousand jobs. This certainly did not help with building trust and credibility. While GM did install physical features of Japanese-style lean manufacturing, it was clear that the culture had not changed. Managers and workers remained at odds, and employees on the assembly line grew scared of pulling the cord lest they get yelled at by their supervisors. In the end, a few plants took down the andon cords altogether.

The key lesson here is that it was not the andon cord itself that created innovation and improvements; it was how Toyota treated their employees. Toyota understood how humans actually work, and that led to increased engagement and innovation. It seems counterintuitive, but in order to create a lean, innovative, and hyperefficient manufacturing process, Toyota had to substantially invest in people, foster autonomy and teamwork, and build trust and job security. It helped enormously that the objective of innovation at Toyota was clear: to be as productive as possible and create the best-quality cars for its customers. Its methods were well suited for the iterative process of improving automobile manufacturing. But does a people-first approach also work for innovating from the ground up?

The Next Post-It Note?

Innovations can come in two flavors. There are more incremental changes that exploit current capabilities, such as improving assembly-line processes, adding a new feature to an existing software, or adding twists to established brands, like pineapple-flavored Haribo Gummy Bears or Milk Chocolate Honey Graham M&Ms (both new flavors in 2022). And then there are more dramatic ideas, like distribution innovations or a completely new product category. The former is less risky as these changes are merely variations on already successful themes, while the latter is riskier, starting from scratch and going into often uncharted territory, but also exciting because it leads to more transformative changes.

If organizations want to uncover those dramatic new opportunities, their employees need to be empowered, given security, and ultimately trusted. The problem with new innovations is that they often fail. To encourage employees in the face of this risk, the incentive system needs to protect them from the consequences of early failure and provide more discretion to the innovator. We can see this clearly when looking at some of the best experts on innovation: scientific researchers.

Researchers doing groundbreaking work on biomedical science have two major sources of funding opportunities in the United States. One is the National Institutes of Health (NIH). The NIH is the primary US government agency supporting biomedical and public health research. It is the largest public funder of biomedical research in the world and, according to its webpage, invests around $32 billion a year in research. Two of the NIH's more well-known discoveries include the use of fluoride to prevent tooth decay and the hepatitis B vaccine. Another source of funding comes from the Howard Hughes Medical Institute (HHMI), a nonprofit medical research organization that is very important in biomedical research support. Every year, HHMI supports medical research with more than $650 million in grants. While both institutions have the same goal—breakthrough or radical innovations in biomedical research that improve people's lives—the incentives and structure of evaluations of their funding are very different.

Funding by NIH through its Research Project, or RO1, program typically lasts only three years. Renewal after that depends on early success of the research and is relatively unforgiving to failure. Furthermore, NIH grants are tied to particular projects with clearly defined deliverables. In contrast, scientists at HHMI are rewarded for longer—typically funded for five years—and their funding is often renewed at least once, making HHMI more forgiving to early failure. In addition, HHMI selects "people, not projects," which allows scientists to reallocate funds to new ideas if the initial attempts at one line of research do not look promising. NIH is more controlling, while HHMI is putting more trust into its scientists to create long-term innovation.

So, does HHMI-style management and incentives lead to more valuable ideas? A research team from the Massachusetts Institute of Technology (MIT), UC San Diego, and UC Berkeley carefully studied the research output of NIH- and HHMI-funded scientists. The results are clear: the HHMI approach leads to more high-impact research output. The impact of scientific discovery is normally measured by the number of citations to a paper. Significant ideas will be cited more often in other papers. The researchers found that HHMI-supported scientists have a much higher proportion of articles in the top 1 percent of most-cited articles. They also produce more research that is not cited very much at all, which is exactly what we would expect when scientists work on more high-risk, but high-reward projects. The trust that HHMI puts into its scientists clearly pays off.

Such trust in employees allowed the discovery of the Post-it note at 3M and supports the company's continuous success in being innovative. The case of Six Sigma at 3M discussed in the last chapter illustrates that you can only create such an innovative environment if all practices and policies work in concert. It is insufficient to introduce only some and not others. At 3M, telling people that they should be innovative but, at the same time, signaling to them that the company does not trust them by controlling them and making them document all failures did not work. My former colleague, the late Casey Ichniowski, and his coauthors studied HR practices in many industries and consistently found that the combination of different practices is more important than individual practices. For example, providing autonomy for workers is not enough. Workers cannot make good decisions and suggest innovative improvements if they are not properly trained and informed, or if they fear that their suggestions would cost them their jobs. Companies have to go all in on being employee first and reimagine all their HR practices in concert. Just implementing some employee-centric practices and not others will not work out. But the benefits of going all in on employee-centricity on productivity and innovation can be quite substantial. Studies confirm the effect of employee-centricity on innovation: companies that are employee-centric (identified by their inclusion on the *Fortune* 100 Best Companies to Work For list) file over 86 percent more patents than companies not on the list.

The benefits of innovation from employee-centric policies are not only for companies that are in the business of finding the next Post-it note. Employees often have the best insights into how to improve production processes or product offerings. They do know when and why to pull the metaphorical andon cord. Zeynep Ton of MIT studies employee-centric strategies of retailers like Walmart and Aldi. Not exactly the places you would start looking for innovation or agility. But in any industry, employees, if treated right, come up with game-changing ideas. Mercado, the largest supermarket chain in Spain and a champion when it comes to putting employees first, relied largely on suggestions from its store employees to cut costs during the 2008 financial crisis. As a result, it was able to reduce its prices by 10 percent during the crisis (which is a big deal in an industry that has razor-thin margins). The retailer came out of the crisis stronger than before—thanks largely to its employees. So, whether finding the next Post-it note, creating an agile organization, making a car assembly line more productive, or figuring out how and what to shelve in a supermarket, putting employees first will lead to innovation and creativity. But that is only one of the benefits for businesses to put their employees first.

Let the Sunshine In!

As we've seen, making an organization or a team more attractive to work for, thus decreasing the willingness to supply, will actually lower the company's cost. This argument heavily relies on the assumption that happy employees are more motivated and productive. But are they? And is it possible to create an atmosphere that is too cozy, where team members are not being pushed enough? Certainly, some leaders would say that employees who are too relaxed and comfortable are not being pushed hard enough (this is either-or mentality again combined with a notion that work by definition needs to be hard). Jack Welch, with his "tough love" personnel management style, was definitely in this camp.

Even tech companies that have been incredibly generous with perks in the past are changing their tunes. Nadia Rawlinson, the former chief people officer at Slack, wrote in an op-ed in the *New York Times* about the general layoffs at the end of 2022 and beginning of 2023: "The layoffs are part of a new age of bossism, the notion that management has given up too much control and must wrest it back from employees. After two decades of fighting for talent, chief executives are using this period to adjust for years of management indulgence that left them with a generation of entitled workers."

Is this true? It's a trickier question than you might think because even if we observe that happy employees are more productive, we can't be sure what caused it. Maybe it's not true that if employees are happier they become more productive. Maybe it's that productive employees happen to be also happier. It's almost impossible to know. And that is why sunshine comes in handy.

The sun has two properties that are extremely useful when you want to study the effect of happiness on productivity: First, we know that sunshine makes people happy. Second, the sun has its own schedule and is obviously not affected by whether a person or a team is productive. So, a group of researchers looked at whether a worker got out in the sun in a certain week (that is, whether they got lucky enough to have a week with a lot of sunshine). This allowed them to analyze the effect of well-being or happiness (which is higher when you're exposed to sunshine) on productivity. They looked at the productivity of 1,793 telesales employees at British Telecom (BT), a multinational telecommunications company headquartered in the UK and the largest private employer in the UK that also operates in around 180 other countries. The job of BT's telesales workers is to deal with incoming (and to a smaller degree outgoing) calls from existing and potential customers and to try to convert those calls into sales. The researchers measured productivity (primarily through weekly sales) using administrative data and elicited happiness levels in weekly surveys. Importantly, they knew which of the eleven regional BT offices the employees worked in and whether each employee's office had windows or not. So, some got more sunshine (and were happier) in certain weeks and others in different weeks, and so on. The results showed that happier employees are more productive employees. If reported happiness increases by 1 point on a scale from 0 to 10, weekly sales increase by 12 percent. It is not that they worked more hours (in fact, I would probably punch out earlier on the rare sunny day in Britain), but the happier telesales workers were more productive and converted more calls into sales. Other related studies had similar results.

Increasing employee happiness—and productivity—by creating more sunshine is, unfortunately, not a practical solution for leaders (well, except for designing workspaces that allow for natural light). But knowing that happy employees are more productive employees is still extremely useful. Team leaders just have to figure out how to introduce employee-centric policies that make workers happy or more satisfied. And that is just what successful companies are doing.

In the 2010s the call centers at Quest Diagnostic were caught in a negative spiral: low motivation, high turnover, and unhappy customers. The high turnover alone was costing Quest about $50 to $70 million annually. And customers were going to the company's competitors. Quest Diagnostic, a Fortune 500 corporation, is a leading clinical laboratory company that operates in the United States, Puerto Rico, Mexico, and Brazil. But it also has partnerships with many hospitals and clinics across the globe. The call center workers (like the ones at BT) deal with incoming and outgoing calls from physicians, hospitals, and patients. In 2015, MaryAnn Camacho was hired as executive director to deal with the mess at Quest's customer service centers.

Camacho improved the job for call center employees holistically: not only did she increase their base salary and incentives that rewarded tenure, but she also created a clear career path, introduced technology that added self-serve options for customers in order to reduce the call volume, increased training and skill building, and started to explicitly celebrate great achievements with awards, team-based bonuses, and ceremonies. And the employee-centric approach worked: answer rates increased by 40 percent, live call volume reduced by 17 percent, and the fraction of calls answered within sixty seconds increased from 50 to 70 percent. Also, turnover dropped from 34 to 16 percent, and unplanned absences fell from 12.4 to 4.2 percent. An amazing turnaround by bringing the equivalent of some sunshine into the jobs.

Camacho's strategies are just some of the methods leaders can use to create metaphorical sunshine at work—and benefit from it. I get into those ideas in the second part of the book and also show the behavioral science on which good employee-centric policies are based. But we have just started with the benefits for companies of being employee-centric. More than just improving innovation and higher productivity, putting employees first will increase retention, consumer satisfaction, and diversity efforts.

And there is nothing better than a crisis to expose the strengths and weaknesses of a strategy.

Stop the Job-Hopping

Crises put a bright spotlight on problems in an organization. The pandemic, a worldwide crisis, was hard on employees and was particularly brutal for front-line workers. Unable to work from home, they instead exposed themselves to danger from the people who were at home and sick. Neglected for years, many people working in health care, delivery jobs, or vital government services were suddenly labeled essential workers and were forced to risk their lives to serve the rest. But once the pandemic was over, they had had enough. Resignations increased dramatically, and their employers soon realized that finding people to take their place was particularly hard. In nursing, for example, a shortage that was already a problem before the pandemic has grown into a full-blown crisis.

DHL Express, one of the largest parcel delivery companies in the world, employs many of those front-line workers. Its yellow trucks, planes, and employee uniforms are well-known sights in countries around the world. DHL Express, which is headquartered in Bonn, Germany, and is part of Deutsche Post, employs more than 120,000 workers. The job of those front-line workers is hard all the time, not just during a pandemic, and the surge in e-commerce increased their workload even further. Turnover is a problem for many companies in this industry but less so for DHL Express. As Sunjoy Dhaawan, vice president of human resources of DHL Express, proudly pointed out in 2022: "At DHL Express, the attrition rate in the past five years is less than 5 per cent." They are at a third of the rest of the industry, which is steady at 15 percent.

The fact that employees want to stay at DHL is not an accident but part of DHL's plan. As the CEO of DHL Express, John Pearson, explains: "Attracting people is one thing, but the best weapon in the war for talent is retention. Let's keep the people we have and let's really understand our frontline employees that are leaving and why they're leaving." DHL did not only have low turnover in general, but during the crisis, their people-first strategy paid off even more. And that philosophy comes from the very top. Frank Appel, former CEO of Deutsche Post DHL Group, has said: "People got us through the financial crisis in 2008, people got us through the Icelandic ash cloud crisis in 2010, (when not one plane flew above Europe for 30 days). And then here we are in 2020, with our people getting us through the biggest thing that has happened in 102 years, since the Spanish flu."

Since the beginning of 2009, DHL Express has invested heavily in being a people-first culture. It changed communication and transparency in the company by eliciting constant feedback from its employees. It celebrated employees' successes and made sure employees' benefit packages were up to par. Central to DHL's cultural initiatives was a thorough overhaul of its learning and development program. DHL Express poured $100 million into creating the Certified International Specialist program, an in-house training program for all staff, and the Certified International Manager Curriculum, tailored for current and upcoming leaders. Costing several hundred dollars per participant, these programs educate all employees on the company's strategy and provide specialized courses in, for example, sales and leadership. This not only boosts knowledge and confidence but also enhances engagement. Additionally, the management training hones the leadership abilities of team and division leaders. As Pearson remarked in 2022: "My predecessor said the customer is at the center of everything we do. I twisted that around and said that our people are at the center of everything we do." So at DHL Express, employees are indeed the new customers. DHL Express was the number-one best place to work on the World's Best Workplaces 2022 annual list, compiled by the Great Places To Work Institute, research partner of *Fortune*. Let that sink in. DHL was the *best* workplace of all companies in the *entire* world in 2022. In fact, 2022 was the second year in a row that it was the best place to work in the whole world—according to that list (in 2023 DHL slipped to second place). In 2017, the first time DHL was featured on the list, it was number eight. All the company's investments in employees have paid off in lower turnover and higher loyalty. Oh, and did I mention that DHL is also extremely profitable?

The same benefit of lower turnover can be seen at other companies that invest in their employees. Costco not only pays substantially more than its competitor Walmart but offers health insurance benefits and gives its workers a lot of career opportunities. Costco's turnover rate is one of the lowest in the industry: just 17 percent overall, and 6 percent after one year of employment. Meanwhile, turnover at Walmart is 44 percent a year, close to the industry average. The cost savings from lower turnover is substantial. In addition, inventory shrinkage (the industry term for shoplifting and employee theft) at Costco is much lower compared to its competition. CFO Richard Galanti told Barron in 2019 that its shrinkage is between 0.11 and 0.12 percent. That would be around 13.5 times lower than the industry average of 1.62 percent in 2019 reported by the National Retail Federation. So, in 2019, a year in which Costco made $155 billion in revenue, it also saved $2 billion in lower shrinkage, of which employee theft is the largest contributor.

If employees (even on the front line) feel respected and appreciated, they do not want to leave. Researchers at Harvard Business School conducted a large investigation on behalf of the Bill and Melinda Gates Foundation about the lives and motivation of low-wage workers in the United States. About 44 percent of American workers are employed in such low-wage, front-line jobs. They show that the shockingly high turnover numbers (in most industries about three-quarters of low-wage employees leave within five years) are not inevitable. Many workers in those jobs actually would like to stay with their employer. And when asked what would make them stay, "62 percent of surveyed workers indicate the prospect of upward mobility"—in addition to predictable and stable pay and working hours. But the report also shows that "today, most companies devote surprisingly little effort to retaining and nurturing their incumbent talent at the lower levels of their organization." But those who do work on retaining and nurturing talent and try to understand what really motivates their workers, such as DHL Express or Costco, are rewarded. Costco's cofounder and longtime CEO said: "We're trying to turn our inventory faster than our people. Obviously, it's not just wages that motivate people. How much they are respected, and whether they feel they can have a career at a company, are also important."

On every level, in every industry, and in every team, turnover can be reduced if leaders really try to understand what motivates their employees or team members and act accordingly. Many of the executives (and I hear it often from the ones I teach) want to put the blame on younger generations such as millennials. They claim that those younger employees do not value commitment or loyalty anymore. They go further and say that those "job-hoppers" change their jobs like they change their clothes. If this were true, turnover could be attributed to this new type of worker. That would still be annoying and costly for companies but convenient for leaders, who could say there's nothing they can do about their inability to retain employees. But it is not true. In fact, tenure at companies— that is, how long people stay within a company—is actually going up and not down. According to the Bureau of Labor Statistics, median tenure at companies slightly increased since the 1980s and is around four years right now. Even younger workers are not changing employers more often than young workers did twenty, thirty, or even forty years ago. Research supports that a substantial benefit of being employee-centric is keeping and attracting talent—who then also happen to be more innovative and productive.

Remember the effect of sunshine on productivity at British Telecom? Happy employees are more productive employees. But what do happy employees do, exactly, to be more productive? In the telesales case, they are better at sticking to their prescribed daily work schedule, and they work faster by taking more incoming calls. But the biggest difference between happy and unhappy workers is that the happy ones are more efficient in converting calls into sales. Their better mood helps them tap into their social and emotional skills and allows them to sell more bundles and convince customers to renew their contracts. And importantly, they are particularly good at dealing with angry and dissatisfied customers. That brings us to one of the most significant benefits of being employee-centric: happy customers!

Customers Feel It

On September 21, 2002, a familiar scene played out outside a store in Frisco, a suburb of the Dallas–Fort Worth metro area. In this northern Texas neighborhood, which is home to the National Videogame Museum and the Dallas Cowboys' training site, a large crowd of people waited hours for a store to open at 6 a.m. According to the local news, around fifteen hundred shoppers stood in line for up to twelve hours. DJs and the Wakeland High School drumline kept the waiting crowd in good spirits. What was unusual about this scene is that the crowd was not waiting for the newest Apple gadget or the next batch of MoonSwatches, the hard-to-get-ahold-of new watches from the Omega X–Swatch collaboration. There were also no Taylor Swift tickets on sale or a celebrity to spot. No limited edition anything or special deals. The people were just excited that this particular grocery chain had finally opened a store in North Texas. It was H-E-B, the Texas grocery chain that has a cultlike following, and it is kicking Amazon's and Walmart's butts. It also happens to be one of the best places to work in the United States, and that is the key to its success.

H-E-B is a privately owned grocery chain headquartered in San Antonio, Texas, that has more than four hundred stores in Texas and northeastern Mexico. The success story really started when Howard Edward Butt (now we know where the name H-E-B comes from) took over his family's grocery store in 1919 and started expanding it. The chain grew mainly in South Texas, has about sixty-four stores in Mexico, and in

2022 expanded its H-E-B stores to North Texas, that is, the Dallas–Fort Worth area with the Frisco store with the long lines. In an industry that is plagued by low margins and substantial competition, the privately owned company is doing very well. Part of its strategy is that in the United States it only has stores in the state of Texas. It's a huge state, and there's plenty of room to expand. If you didn't already know, Texans love Texas. Therefore, H-E-B has hundreds of goods that are shaped like the state. That includes Texas-shaped cast-iron pans for $20.58 or Texas-shaped corn tortilla chips for $2.97 (their bestseller). But this is hardly a competitive advantage as you can buy many Texas-shaped goods on Amazon or on Etsy.com. Rather, from the very beginning, the company understood that its employees were its "competitive advantage." Or, as the president of H-E-B, Craig Boyan, put it: "If you take care of your employees as number one, and then customers as number two, then the shareholders will be served as an outcome of taking care of employees. It makes a huge difference."

The company invests heavily in its employees, gives them stock options in the company, and supports the communities in which their workers live. H-E-B has an extensive Hunger Relief Program that supports local food banks. It also supports education in Texas by giving around $10 million each year to teachers and schools across the state. In addition to directly caring about its employees, the company also gets a lot of praise for its reactions to crises and catastrophes such as Hurricane Harvey or the COVID-19 pandemic. The company has humane and swift responses to such crises. Back in 2017, the *Texas Monthly* compared H-E-B's relief efforts after Hurricane Harvey to those of the Red Cross, the Salvation Army, and other first responders. In fact, the grocery chain employs a full-time director of emergency preparedness and has mobile kitchens, a disaster relief unit, and water tanker trucks. All those would be employed to provide fast help in affected areas. H-E-B's reaction to the coronavirus was also swift and praised. It added a hotline for employees months before other retailers followed its lead. When the power grid in Texas failed in 2021, H-E-B stepped in. Its competent response to the terrible situation caused the *Houston Chronicle* to only half-jokingly comment: "We'd all be better off if H-E-B took over the Texas power grid."

As a result, the employees love the company. On Glassdoor.com, H-E-B's CEO Charles C. Butt was in the top-ten CEO list of 2021. The list is determined by employee choices, and he got a 97 percent approval rating. As you can imagine there were no other grocery or retail chains in the top ten. Being number seven on that list, he was just behind Satya Nadella, CEO of Microsoft. And the engaged and motivated employees lead to an amazing customer experience as reflected on amazing scores on customer satisfaction indexes—and long lines of devoted fans when a new store opens. The employee-centric culture at H-E-B is responsible for incredible employee engagement and retention. People officer Tina James explains: "That is what really distinguishes us. When you treat people like their whole life matters to you, they engage heavily and are loyal and take care of their customers." The loyalty allows H-E-B not only to hold its own compared to the much larger and mighty competitors, Amazon and Walmart, but to actually beat them. In 2022, the annual Retail Preference Index by Dunnhumby, a leader in customer data science, ranked H-E-B as the best US e-commerce grocery retailer—before Amazon and Walmart. As a grocery expert commented: "H-E-B has consistently ranked at the top of consumer preference polls for its store experience. Now, it's taken the top position in a rigorous new index focused on e-commerce shopping."

When you look at the companies that create superior customer experiences, they are, almost without fail, also employee-centric and have policies in place that create engaged employees. Remember the customer service representative at Zappos.com who made me a loyal customer by being super nice? That is no coincidence and can be traced back to how Zappos.com treats its employees. Tony Hsieh, an early investor of Zappos.com and CEO for twenty-one years, from 1999 to 2020, understood that to make people comfortable buying shoes online, the customer experience and service need to be absolutely top notch. Think about it, shoes often do not fit even when you get the right size, look terrible when you actually wear them, or just do not feel comfortable on the feet. Not exactly a product that is ideal for online shopping!

In order to create its much-needed customer service, Hsieh deviated dramatically from the industry norm of how to run a call center. The so-called best practice of running an efficient call center is to provide a lot of structure and control. This means call center agents must follow tight scripts, can only spend a couple of seconds with each caller, and are restricted in what they can offer the customers. This is either-or thinking in which the company tries to squeeze out as much efficiency from the worker as possible. In such a regime, the call center agent would never have asked me about my cold or offered her suggestion for a hot drink that could help it. But at Zappos.com, there are no strict scripts and no time limits. The employee has a lot of discretion and autonomy to deal with the caller. A call center employee told a *Forbes* reporter who visited the center located in Las Vegas that she once spent two hours with a caller, and Hsieh found out about the call and approached her. She thought that she might be in trouble. But he just asked: "Did you make them happy?" After she replied, "I sure did," Hsieh said, "Great job! Keep it up." He then told the reporter that "trusting your employees to keep customers happy will eventually lead to return customers, loyal customers, and higher sales. If you've hired the right people, then trust them to do whatever they feel is the right thing to do for the customer."

Sounds so easy and intuitive. As we see later, it is not exactly that easy to pull off (which is good if you want to create a unique employee advantage). For example, the phrase "hire the right people" is a crucial part. But Hsieh, who unfortunately died way too early at the age of forty-six, was very passionate about *delivering happiness* (which is also the title of his bestselling book) to his customers *and* employees. And it clearly paid off in delivering outstanding customer service and experience—same as with other companies who follow the same mantra, such as Southwest Airlines or—a new entrant—Zoom. As Eric Yuan, founder and CEO of Zoom Video Communications, said in 2020: "If I can make our employees happy, together we can make our customers happy."

The effect of employee satisfaction and customer experience, expressed in either customer satisfaction or loyalty, can also be seen in studies across many companies and industries. The meta-analysis of 339 academic studies mentioned before shows that employee satisfaction is associated with higher productivity, higher profitability, and lower turnover (all discussed before). But the largest effect found in all those studies is on customer loyalty. Employee satisfaction is highly associated with higher customer loyalty, and the relationship is large and robust. The economic research team at Glassdoor analyzed 293 large employers in thirteen industries over a ten-year time span to analyze the connection between employee and customer satisfaction. The results support other studies that show that each 1-point improvement in the Glassdoor 5-point company rating is associated with a 1.3-point increase (out of 100) on the American Customer Satisfaction Index. By the way, H-E-B is in the top five companies with both high average Glassdoor ratings *and* high customer satisfaction ratings. And how valuable is higher customer satisfaction? Research shows that a 1 percent improvement on customer satisfaction is associated with a 4.6 percent boost in valuation of a company. The Glassdoor report further documents that while across all industries positive company ratings affect customer satisfaction, it is particularly strong in industries in which many employees have direct contact with customers, such as retail, restaurants, bars, food services, travel and tourism, financial services, and health care. In those industries, the correlation between positive company rating and customer satisfaction is more than twice as large as the average across all industries. Combining those results with the effect of employee satisfaction on stock prices, which leads to a one-star improvement on the Glassdoor company rating, would imply an 18.9 percent increase in market value in industries with direct contact between employees and customers and a 7.8 percent increase across all industries.

In addition to the direct impact on the customer experience of putting employees first, many customers also generally care about how workers are treated when making purchasing decisions, and they react negatively when employees are mistreated. Nike famously got boycotted starting in 1996 when a scandal about child labor in its supply chain got revealed. The hashtag #deleteUber, which encourages riders to delete the ride-sharing app, surges whenever new labor issues (either sexual harassment charges in Uber's headquarters or treatment of gig workers) come to light. And with social media, mistreatment of employees can go viral (and not in a good way) and negatively affect a brand.

Employee-centricity always comes back full circle to customer-centricity. As with being agile, organizations need their employees to be customer-centric. If not, they will not pull the andon cord and will also not wow the customer. And employee-centricity generates another advantage: it helps with efforts to increase diversity at organizations.

Celebrate the Diversity in Diversity

My Spotify account looks nothing like yours. Yes, there are classic rock recommendations typical for somebody born in the 1970s, but there is also a lot of African music inspired by (a) my teaching in Morocco, Ghana, and South Africa, (b) Peter Gabriel's early collaboration with Youssou N'Dour (which I love and which featured prominently at my wedding), and (c) an amazing concert I saw with my wife in Dakar, Senegal, of Élage Diouf. My stay in Barcelona with the Erasmus exchange program in Europe explains the Spanish albums that get recommended. The opera and classic tunes on my home screen are because I often listen to them while working (or writing this book). And there are a lot of suggestions for "Drei ???" episodes or equivalent. "Drei ???" are stories of three (*drei* in German) kid detectives who solve crimes and mysteries. These last recommendations reveal that despite the fact that I live in New York, I am speaking and listening to Swiss German with my son. The account reveals a lot about me, my life, and my preferences. A big part of customer-centricity is about understanding and embracing differences in identity and preferences and then personalizing the experience. Employee-centricity should do the same and as a result would help with increasing diversity. But many organizations are still miles away from understanding differences in their workforce.

Seventy-five percent of responders report in 2013 that they suppress some of their identity. Among straight white men, 50 percent hide their identity, and among blacks, 94 percent do so. This does not sound like workers who are comfortable celebrating their differences—especially for minorities. The employee experience reflects that diversity is not celebrated. The consulting company McKinsey and Lean In, the nonprofit founded by Sheryl Sandberg, the former COO of Meta (formerly Facebook), conducted in 2022 a large study on the status of women in the workplace. The report reveals a number of shocking, but unfortunately not that surprising, results: female employees with a traditionally marginalized identity are enduring negative work experiences such as microaggressions and a lack of manager support, allyship, and psychological safety. So, for example, when asked whether they "feel comfortable disagreeing with coworkers," 62 percent of men do so, 57 percent of white women, but only 45 percent of Latinas and 44 percent of Black women do. Not so surprisingly, minorities are in no rush to come back to the office and are also leaving organizations to a greater degree. Why would you want to go back to the office to experience microaggressions or a lack of psychological safety? While 18 percent of men would like to work mostly on-site, only 10 percent of women do.

Some of the differences come from different responsibilities at home that make remote work more valuable. And those differences in life outside the workplace are also very important to consider. And then the employee experience in the office does the rest in explaining why minorities do not want to come back. Thirty-six percent of women of color report experiencing "othering" microaggressions when mostly on-site, but only 23 percent do so when working remotely. A Black woman vice president said: "A lot of people have said I should be worried about not having face time, but there's another perspective, which is that people of color don't want to be in a work environment where they don't feel like they can be themselves." Quotes like this indicate that we have a long way to go to be welcoming to all. But organizations are lagging on diversity not necessarily because of lack of good intentions, but because they are not putting employees first and thinking of them as customers. Diversity is all about understanding the differences among workers and personalizing employees' experiences.

Eli Lilly, the large pharmaceutical company that makes Prozac, Cialis, and Trulicity, realized a couple of years ago what many other organizations have also seen in their data: Black employees and women were far less likely to be promoted to executive roles. Its traditional DEI initiatives had not moved the needle at all. So, it turned to a process that its customer team was using: customer journeys. Through customer journeys, Eli Lilly gains insights into how different groups of patients experience every step of being on a certain drug treatment. Tools, such as focus groups or individual interviews, and surveys help the company understand what its customers are going through and pinpoint moments in their journey that really matter and are worth improving. It is, in a sense, about understanding and then celebrating the differences in patients' experiences.

In 2015, Eli Lilly took this process and applied it to employees to map the employee journey of their underrepresented minorities. The company literally took the customer experience team and redeployed it to map the employee experience, with an initial focus on women workers. The survey produced immediate results. The resulting quantitative and qualitative data provided executives at Eli Lilly insights into those experiences and ways of addressing them. Being focused on each individual's unique experience helped Eli Lilly get closer to its diversity goal. From 2016 to 2020 the percentage of women in management increased globally from 41 to 46 percent.

And Eli Lilly was only getting started. Soon the company began to apply these techniques to other underrepresented groups. "It became a catalyst," Kelly Copes-Anderson, the global head of Diversity, Equity, and Inclusion, later said. "We're like, 'Wow, there was such a striking difference for women employees. What is [the experience] for minority group members?'" Lilly then did employee journeys for Blacks, Latinos, Asians, and LGBTQ employees. For racial and ethnic minorities and other nonmajority members in the United States, management representation increased from 16 to 22 percent between 2016 and 2020. Across all levels of its workforce, Eli Lilly saw increased representation for minorities in the United States and women globally. Feeling more included not only affected those employees but the resulting diversity also increased productivity of the whole team and organization. It has also improved Lilly's talent acquisition and retention. The CEO of Lilly, Dave Ricks, has also observed the way the company's efforts have affected the corporate culture in a broader way. "There is also an emotional side," he said in a 2020 interview, "which is about engaging your workforce. We found that as we engaged on a big lift in D&I and focused on those differences and those underrepresented groups, it unleashed positive energy." Those encouraging results at Lilly were achieved by literally using the tricks of customer-centricity inside the company.

There are many benefits to companies who "let the sunshine in" and put their people first. The employee advantage comes from innovation, productivity, turnover, customer experience, and diversity. As Costco's president and CEO, Craig Jelink, said before the US Senate Committee on the Budget in 2021: "This isn't altruism. [...] [but] makes sense for our business and constitutes a significant competitive advantage." So, why exactly are many organizations or teams not able to figure it out? Turns out that as with customer-centricity, being employee-centric is not that easy and requires not only being strategic and dedicated, on all levels of the organization, but also understanding that those ping-pong tables in the break room are not cutting it. And that is a good thing if you really want to unlock the employee advantage.

CHAPTER 4

Employees Don't Play Ping-Pong

THE HEALTH OF A BUSINESS is normally measured using revenue or profits, same-store sales, customer churn rate, or investment activities. But in 2016, the *Wall Street Journal* offered a different indicator of business health: ping-pong. Or rather, the sale of ping-pong tables to businesses. According to the article, which analyzed ping-pong table sales in the Bay Area, a significant decline in table sales in the first quarter of 2016 coincided with a significant decline in start-up funding over the same period. Coincidence? Simon Ng, the owner of Billiard Wholesale, a store in San Jose, California, that sells ping-pong, foosball, and pool tables, doesn't think so. He believes that ping-pong table sales track the health of the tech businesses. When companies are doing well, they buy tables, and when they are not (as in the first quarter of 2016), they stop ordering tables. This "ping-pong index" isn't the only unusual tracker of (tech) business health: other unusual proxies for company performance over the years have included the size of the signature of a CEO, the length of women's skirts, and the average duration of PowerPoint presentations. If the ping-pong index is true, we should be worried about ping-pong companies, given the massive layoffs among tech firms at the end of 2022 and 2023.

Whether ping-pong table sales really track tech success is unclear, but ping-pong tables have, since the first dot-com boom in the late 1990s, become a symbol of what an innovative, employee-friendly workplace should look like. Proponents of ping-pong tables claim that it brings fun to the office, breaks down hierarchies, gives people engaging breaks, and improves corporate culture. (Full disclosure, when Columbia Business

School opened its new $600 million building a couple of blocks north of the main campus in Manhattan in 2022, we also got…a ping-pong table.) As much as ping-pong tables (and free KIND bars or kombucha taps) symbolize a fun and innovative workplace, they also illustrate why it is so difficult to be truly employee-centric and why the complexity of this problem is actually a good thing for companies who really want an employee advantage.

It is understandable why so many employers have grown so fond of using ping-pong tables to raise employee morale. It is a fun and competitive game that most people can pick up easily, which makes it great for bonding. There is no doubt that the workplace design affects productivity. Playing ping-pong is also good for you, unlike other workplace perks, like free snacks, and ping-pong tables are free of the widespread suspicion that perks like free food, beer taps, or nap pods are only there to keep workers at their desks for longer—and as such might be detrimental for their well-being. Nevertheless, ping-pong tables highlight two problems for business leaders who want to truly adopt employee-friendly policies.

First, if ping-pong tables actually increased innovation and employee motivation, then the solution to that ever-thorny management problem would be easy and no one would need this book! You'd just need to spend $2,000 (if you want a fancy table) and free up a room in which to put it. Voilá! Job done. Let the innovations commence. It's the same with many other perks. If KIND bars are the kicker to motivate employees, what happens if everyone provides them? What about *monetary* employee benefits? If a signing bonus is all it takes, then everybody could offer signing bonuses. These things might be great for employees, but none are a true distinguishing factor for a business. What's worse, they may give CEOs the *idea* they are making employees happier and more productive, when in fact they are accomplishing nothing at all.

The same holds true for other ostensibly employee-focused programs, such as wellness programs. Nine out of ten organizations provide some sort of wellness benefits, and three out of five have dedicated wellness budgets. These programs subsidize gym memberships or yoga classes to incentivize a healthy lifestyle. I applaud this growing trend of companies to prioritize their employees' well-being and health, but I believe many of these programs miss their intended mark. Although they are often well intended (either to reduce health-care expenses or increase productivity), there are several issues.

First, many wellness programs rely on easily measurable metrics, like body mass index, to gauge health, but these metrics can be highly controversial as reliable indicators of overall well-being. Second, it remains questionable whether these programs genuinely contribute to improved wellness. Some studies merely analyze whether participants in these programs become fitter, but the results are often skewed because those who enroll are generally already healthier and would have improved their health regardless. Rigorous research investigating the *causal* effects of wellness programs finds little significant impact, as the incentives are often claimed by employees who would have pursued healthier lifestyles regardless, leaving others feeling discouraged. Finally, if merely offering a bonus for gym attendance could boost wellness and productivity, every company would adopt this approach.

In reality, such programs are similar to metaphorical ping-pong tables, as they are easy to imitate and fail to address broader factors impacting employee well-being. A more comprehensive approach to wellness initiatives should encompass mental stress, work-life balance, and toxic workplace culture to make a substantial and lasting impact on employee health and productivity. "As an employer," the McKinsey Health Institute said, "you can't 'yoga' your way out of these challenges." That brings me to the next problem with all of these perks: not only are they potentially easy to imitate, but they are also simply not enough. You can have a ping-pong table and still have a toxic work culture.

The video-game industry is notorious for having cool offices and terrible work cultures at the same time. Activision Blizzard, the maker of some of the most successful video-game franchises such as *Call of Duty*, *World of Warcraft*, and *Candy Crush Saga*, is one of those companies. They have accumulated a litany of abuse and harassment allegations and lawsuits over the years. In response, workers have organized walkouts and protests. Microsoft bought Activision Blizzard for $68 billion in 2022 and knew from the jump that it needed to fix the culture. Satya Nadella, Microsoft's CEO, announced in a conference call with investors shortly after the acquisition that fixing the culture was one of his top priorities. "It requires consistency, commitment, and leadership that not only talks the talk but walks the walk," said Nadella. After the merger was approved, Activision Blizzard appointed a DEI officer and began a holistic evaluation of the corporate culture problems. As a consequence, the percentage of women or nonbinary employees rose to 26 percent of the company's total workforce in 2022, an increase of 2 percent compared to the previous year.

But many different practices and policies need to change and support one another to create an employee-centric environment. In the end, all the different practices at work need to be aligned to support an employee-centric atmosphere. This is good news for organizations that really put in the work to put employees first. They can set themselves apart from the crowd and gain an employee advantage.

All In!

The pandemic created an interesting experiment to see how remote work affected various companies and teams differently. It allowed people in my line of work to address some questions, such as what type of work cultures and work practices made work from home (WFH) easier. How does WFH depend on a company's prepandemic employee-centric practices (or lack thereof)? Of course, the pandemic was a shock to many aspects of work and life. Demand collapsed for certain industries (think hospitality) or went through the roof for others (such as e-commerce). In certain occupations, remote work is either not possible at all, like manufacturing, or leads to suboptimal outcomes, as with education. (I painfully experienced this first-hand with my three children and while teaching remotely.) Researchers say that about 37 percent of jobs in the United States can be done remotely.

So, does the prepandemic treatment of employees matter for the success of remote work? Absolutely! Take two hypothetical companies in the same industry. Both were forced to operate completely remotely during the pandemic. One company always trusted its employees and gave them a lot of autonomy. It evaluated the outcome of the work, not input. The other company had more of a control-and-command approach in which bosses monitor mainly inputs, like whether employees put in the appropriate number of hours.

The latter type of company is not uncommon at all. In fact, studies show that most companies promote based on input and not output. One study compared the productivity of call center employees who were randomly selected to work from home with another group who worked in the office. According to their findings, the WFH group was more productive. Nevertheless, the employees who worked from home were *less* likely to be promoted, indicating that output is not the only metric used for promotions. In this case, "out of (office) sight" led to "out of mind" for the person who evaluated employees and decided on promotions. You can only imagine that in such a company, WFH is not as effective or popular as it could be because performance evaluations are not set up for WFH.

Italy was the first country in Europe to be hit by the COVID pandemic and to enact an order to stay and work at home. Four Italian researchers found that companies that were better managed and were more employee-centric did much better during the pandemic. This was mainly due to the changes they put into place to organize remote work more efficiently. Similar studies across the globe support the view that employee-centric management styles were extremely helpful during the most extreme WFH period of the pandemic. US companies with higher engagement levels on Glassdoor before the pandemic rebounded faster from stock market decline and exhibited positive growth rates. The shift to WFH during the pandemic shows that the success of a policy change, like permitting remote work, heavily relies on various other management approaches, for example, how much management built up a trusting work environment. All the management techniques are interlinked, and therefore if there is a change or a shift in one, the entire management and leadership system requires an overhaul.

Having different employee-centric management practices that support one another is the key to success here. My colleague and former chair of the management division at Columbia Business School, Casey Ichniowski, studied this idea and provides one of the best pieces of evidence of how important it is to implement a bundle of employee-centric practices. Ichniowski and his coauthors investigated different workplace practices in the steel industry. Their research shows that individual practices such as more training, flexible job assignments, or more team autonomy do not, on their own, affect productivity much. However, if you bundle these practices together, productivity and profits increase substantially. Companies and teams have to go all in.

How to accomplish this? Think about WFH days. Just allowing workers to work from home a couple of days a week does not necessarily make the workplace more motivating and engaging. In fact, it could make it worse if nothing else is adjusted. We saw this during the stay-at-home period in the pandemic. It needs to go hand in hand with trust, performance evaluations, systems that award output, support systems that check on employees' well-being, and training and mentoring models. The organizations and teams that deliberately change all the practices to be employee-centric and to complement one another will have a sustainable employee advantage. But everybody needs to be on board—whether you are the CEO of a large organization or an emerging leader of a small team.

All Hands on Deck

During one of my executive education teaching sessions about the future of work, I mentioned to my audience that I thought employees are the new customers. Afterward, I was approached by Kimie Page, who works for the Whitney Museum of American Art in New York City. She told me that customer-centric principles guide the way she treats her team. I found this particularly interesting because Page and her team are directly responsible for handling complaints from members of and visitors to the Whitney.

As you can imagine, Page's team does not always have pleasant interactions with visitors and members. After all, people rarely contact customer service to deliver unsolicited praise. Page and her team use a fundamental set of customer service principles in their responses. At the Whitney, they are called the "visitor and member experience principles," and their goal is to approach customer service interactions with consistency, while respecting the individual needs of each member and visitor. It is an important part of customer training, which team members re-emphasize and practice over and over again. As Page said: "We do all the training within the context of these customer experience principles to help keep customer service at the front of everyone's mind because that's who we are: the customer service team." That is customer-centricity right there.

But it started to become clear to Page that the same principles her team was using for interacting with customers could be applied to the team itself. "The principles are so ingrained in our brains that, at some point years ago, I started realizing that I was using the same techniques that I would use for customer service when I was responding to staff management situations as well." Whenever she encountered a team challenge or situation, she began reminding herself and her team members to ensure that their interactions with others on the team aligned with the thoughtful approach of their customer experience principles. As a result, turnover within her team is low. This is particularly remarkable in the museum world, which relies on part-time and seasonal staff with generally high turnover rates. The Whitney is not immune to this, and in her role, Page can't unilaterally address institutional issues. But she knows that on every level of the organization, employee-centric management practices matter.

Remember Casey Ichniowski, my colleague who studied employee-centric management? Ichniowski was very passionate about the holistic approach to create an engaging workplace, and he instilled it in our small team of academics. The chair of a division cannot change compensation or any other fringe benefits, but when Ichniowski was in this role, he implemented many different employee-centric practices that he did have control over. Perhaps the most important in our team was getting together and celebrating successes. At the beginning and end of the teaching semester, we'd organize a social gathering at a bar or restaurant. There, Ichniowski would highlight the semester's achievements and applaud everyone's individual contributions to them. It might surprise you, but these practices often matter more to employees than money—and every leader of even the smallest teams can make a difference by acknowledging successes. Casey Ichniowski's approach did in our division. Unfortunately, he died way too early and was not able to see the long-lasting impact his leadership had. But to this day we call all of our social events "Caseys" in his honor.

As I discussed in Chapter 3, the employee-centric focus of companies like Costco or H-E-B is the result of top-level decisions, and you can see the benefits throughout the organization. To be employee-centric, the executive team needs to be on board. John Pearson, CEO of DHL Express, emphasizes that people are "critical to our business. Lots of people say it, but then not everyone backs it up." As with customer-centricity, most of the work actually happens through daily interaction. As Hubert Joly of Best Buy said: "If it just stays in the executive suite that doesn't do anything. [...] So the bulk of the work is about creating the environment where people can connect." So, what is the role of the emerging leaders in an organization, those individuals whose job it is to coach and motivate their team but who cannot influence corporate policies?

One way to see the difference emerging leaders can make is by looking at how engaged and productive employees are in *different* teams in the *same* organization. Just go from one Starbucks or Dunkin' franchise to another, and you can feel the difference in vibe and culture among the employees. Productivity and performance vary among stores, and those differences come from the actions of the store manager. A study entitled

"Can a Workplace Have an Attitude Problem?" rigorously analyzed the differences among branches of a large commercial bank. Workplaces (here, bank branches) can have an attitude problem. The study found that branches with an attitude problem, in addition to having disgruntled employees, are also less profitable and even more likely to close in the future. While some employees are more positive than others, the branch and its manager still matter a lot: employee-centric managers create a positive workplace, which becomes contagious: new employees become more positive when surrounded by good managers and positive employees.

Emerging leaders in the branches make a huge difference. While they cannot affect corporate HR policy, they can have a massive impact on performance. One study analyzed the productivity of around twenty-four thousand workers who have a technology-based service job, such as call center operator or airline gate agent. How important were the around two thousand bosses who mentored and motivated them? The study showed that having a boss whose management skills rate in the top 10 percent has the same effect as adding an additional worker to a nine-member team. Good bosses will coach and motivate the whole group but also work individually with workers. Under the stewardship of a good boss, productivity increases, and the boss is also more likely to be promoted. Drilling further down into what makes a good manager shows that interpersonal skills are particularly important for emerging leaders. When interpersonal skills are better—for example, a manager consults with employees for decision-making when appropriate or most employees agree that the manager can be trusted—turnover decreases by 60 percent. What this tells us is that employees are not leaving bad jobs—they are leaving bad bosses. And remember, these good bosses are working within an organization where they have no control over corporate policies, such as increasing wages or approving new benefits. What they are doing is affecting the experience of work beyond the paycheck—which matters a lot.

To create the employee advantage, everybody in an organization—from the CEO to the emerging leader who manages a small team—needs to be on board and do their part. Your interest in reading this book indicates your desire to develop as a more employee-centric leader. Whether you hold the position of a CEO within a company or are an emerging leader overseeing a small team, this knowledge can have a profound impact. Ultimately, it's imperative that everyone within the organization is aligned and comprehends what drives their team members or colleagues to foster a motivating and engaging employee-centric workplace. Achieving an employee-centric approach requires the collective efforts of the entire team.

But before we talk about what actually motivates employees, let's get one of the elephants out of the room: Does being employee-centric mean business owners need to treat their employees like kings and queens?

Are the Employees Always Right?

Josh Silverman did not exactly receive a warm welcome from his employees when he took over as CEO of Etsy.com. The first question he got in his first all-staff meeting on the morning of May 3, 2017, at the company's headquarters in Brooklyn, New York, reflected the sentiment of many employees: "Yesterday felt impersonal, un-empathetic and decidedly un-Etsy," the employee said. "What is the new leadership planning to do to earn our trust and maintain the empathetic and human culture that is the entire reason that many of us chose to work here?" The workforce was afraid that their beloved employee-friendly atmosphere would be sacrificed for profits. Just the day before, their admired CEO, Chad Dickerson, was fired by the board, along with another 79 employees. Silverman, who was an Etsy board member and the former CEO of Evite and Skype, was tasked to shake things up. This included plans to lay off another 140 employees within just two months after taking over and cutting back on a number of employee-friendly policies that made Etsy such a special workplace. A public petition by employees read: "We believe these changes represent a move away from Etsy's mission and values, and we are feeling uncertain about what the future holds for us as Etsy employees and for Etsy's community of creative entrepreneurs."

Etsy is, indeed, a very special company and workplace. The company was founded in 2005 as an alternative to eBay or Amazon for artists and craftspeople to sell their handmade goods. The cofounder and first CEO, Robert Kalin, was a furniture maker himself and wanted to build something that supported crafters on the internet: "This is what Etsy stands for: The little guy being able to organize a better marketplace." The site was an instant success and attracted thousands of sellers in a short period of time. The next CEO was Dickerson, who took over in 2011. He increased the company's revenue fourteenfold, and then took it public in 2015. Both Kalin and Dickerson had created a unique workplace that was true to their belief that profits and people go hand in hand. At the IPO, Dickerson said: "We don't believe that people and profit are mutually exclusive. We believe that Etsy can be a model for other public companies by operating a values-driven and human-centered business while benefiting people."

The workplace was unique and took care of its employees. Etsy had one of the most generous benefit packages of any tech company. Employees were allowed forty hours of paid time a year to do volunteer work, health insurance was fully covered, and wages were around 40 percent above local living wages. The parental leave policy of six months for both parents was more generous than Facebook or Google. Its beautiful Brooklyn office was built from sustainable material, and rainwater irrigated the vertical garden. Etsy had a "breathing room," where employees could sit quietly in a device-free room and meditate; it offered yoga, pottery, printmaking, and cooking classes. The company had many other self-actualization programs, and its meal program, called Eatsy, was one of the best in the industry, with organic food sourced from socially conscious and local (often high-end) vendors. Etsy's office made ping-pong tables look like child's play. An article in *New York* magazine ridiculed the workplace as "an extremely cozy private welfare state" for employees.

The employees were extremely happy, but there was one big problem. The company was losing money and lots of it: $30 million in 2016 alone. Meanwhile, the growth of the platform's most important metric, gross merchandise sales, which measures the total value of transactions on the site, was stalling. That is when Silverman came in to turn the company around and try to save it from being sold.

Silverman laid off employees, rethought all the company's expensive perks, and shut down many of its far-flung projects. According to *Businessweek,* these included programs such as "'office hackers,' a group responsible for developing cool stuff for Etsy employees, like a paint-by-numbers mural and a system for tracking office waste." Silverman had to make many hard decisions that many employees did not like. Attrition increased, and ratings on Glassdoor.com dropped like a stone. At first glance, Silverman's leadership looks like the opposite of an employee-centric turnaround. But in truth, it illustrates a successful way of implementing a sustainable employee-centric approach. Employee-centricity (and this is no different from customer-centricity) still challenges leaders with trade-offs and requires deep strategic thinking, choosing the right employees and figuring out what really motivates them. There are three important principles for guiding the implementation of an employee-centric strategy: aligning employee-centric strategies with business strategies, choosing the right employees, and choosing the right incentives.

Align your employee-centric strategy with your business strategy. Obviously, putting your people first is not doing any good if the company is not making money. The mission of Etsy is to help the millions of crafters on the internet sell their products. But the company was not fulfilling its promise and was on the brink of being sold off. Silverman said in an interview at Harvard Business School: "It was really hard for me to find a measure in which Etsy's social impact was outsized to the positive. Well, except one. I think the employees were treated unusually well." Etsy needed to focus on its business objective and do so without falling back to an either-or mentality when it came to its people strategy. Silverman shut down projects that were too peripheral to the core mission, which was to provide an amazing marketplace for crafters. Employees are critically important in that regard, but there were too many metaphorical ping-pong tables that were not actually supporting the mission.

When we're talking about an employee-focused approach, leaders need to figure out how having happy, engaged employees will help the company reach its main goals. Chapter 3 discusses how these benefits can be anything from sparking new ideas and making customers happy to just getting more work done. These big wins then help shape how a company sets up and brings together practices that put employees at the center. For example, for Etsy, it is clear that diversity is an important principle. Eighty-one percent of Etsy's four million sellers and the vast majority of the eighty-one million buyers identify as women. Diversity efforts were always an important part of Etsy's culture, and Silverman strengthened it further. Around 50 percent of the executive team and of the board are women, more than 30 percent of its engineers identify as women or nonbinary, and more than 30 percent are people of color. Employees at Etsy work there because they strongly believe in its mission. Silverman made a significant effort to make the mission much clearer and stronger. He involved employees in the process, and they came up with "Keep Commerce Human." This purpose is combined with a clear strategic vision.

In general, employee-centricity has to be combined with such strategic clarity. Analysis of half a million employees in more than four hundred companies clearly shows that only the combination of a sense of purpose with a feeling that "management has a clear view of where the organization is going and how to get there" leads to superior performance. Employee-centricity is not a substitute for business strategy but is a powerful tool to be used in combination with it.

Choose the right employees. There is the saying that "the customer is always right." Peter Fader, a professor at the Wharton School of the University of Pennsylvania and author of a book entitled *Customer Centricity*, disagrees: "The customer isn't always right. Rather, the right customer is always right. And yes, there is a difference." A big part of customer-centricity involves finding the right customer segment and tailoring the product to its needs. The same is true for employees. Figuring out who are the right employees and what is the right mix of employees is key. In the end, this is a segmentation exercise that is the bread and butter of everybody in marketing. It requires a deliberate decision to determine what the "right" employees are for a given employee-centric strategy.

Recall the words of Tony Hsieh, founder and CEO of Zappos.com, when he said: "If you've hired the right people, then trust them to do whatever they feel is the right thing to do for the customer." In a system in which trust and providing lots of autonomy is at the core, choosing people who appreciate and are motivated by such a policy and who do not exploit it is critically important. Zappos.com goes out of its way to figure out who fits into such a culture. They pick up candidates who come from out of town at the airport with a shuttle bus and bring them to their interview. To gauge if the candidate is genuinely kind, the recruiter will check in with the shuttle driver at the day's end to see how they were treated during their interaction. "It doesn't matter how well the day of interviews went, if our shuttle driver wasn't treated well, then we won't hire that person." Research shows that choosing the right candidates is key for a successful business based on autonomy. Without proper screening, employers shouldn't give employees freedom in their roles. It's essential to hire trustworthy employees who won't misuse this freedom, whether at Zappos.com or any other company.

But the ultimate selection mechanism at Zappos.com comes after it has already hired an employee. After an extensive training period in which the new hire experiences what the job and the corporate culture are all about, Zappos.com offers to pay the new hire $2,000 if they decide to leave the company they joined just days ago. Why is Zappos.com offering monetary incentives if the employee decides to quit—*after* the company has just spent lots of money on selecting and training the new employee? Because for someone to be the right employee, not only must the organization and the team feel they are a good match from the hiring manager's perspective, but the new hire must also feel the same way. It's like dating—both sides need to be happy. Importantly, the selection, on both sides, has to go beyond the skills required for the job or just the job description. Whether the corporate culture is a good fit for the job applicant is hard to tell from the job description.

Herb Kelleher, the cofounder of Southwest Airlines, famously said: "Select for attitudes, train for skills." He was referring to his belief that it is easier to hire a happy employee, who then makes customers happy, than to train happiness. Apparently, during Southwest Airline job interviews, a potential cabin crew member is asked to tell a joke. This was the airline's way of selecting for being funny and fitting into their culture. But Kelleher's quote is more generally applicable. Companies need to determine what makes the right employee, beyond skills and degrees, for their setting and culture and then select accordingly.

Choose the right incentives. Finally, after aligning the business strategy with the employee-centric strategy and choosing the right employee, organizations and teams need to figure out **what actually motivates** those employees. And it needs to be a whole set of practices on all levels that support employees—not just free snacks and nap pods. Silverman at Etsy involved all his employees in this process of homing in on what the core purpose of Etsy was. As noted earlier, they determined that serving crafters and "keeping commerce human" was key. As such, sustainability and diversity efforts became the core of its employee-centric policy. In the end, Silverman turned the company around—without giving up its employee-centric attitudes (or maybe because of them). The stock price rebounded, analysts started to love the company again—and employees did too. In a 2019 survey, 92 percent of the staff said it's a "great place to work," while the national average is 59 percent. Furthermore, 96 percent of them felt proud to tell others that they worked at Etsy. Etsy's purpose was clear and valued by its employees. In 2022, Etsy had the largest increase in engagement levels of any companies in the *Wall Street Journal's* Management Top 250 companies. Sales on the platform and stock performance of Etsy similarly improved. But the work by Silverman was necessary to secure the benefit for employees and create social impact—and make money.

In the end, it requires hard work to figure out how to align the employee-centric strategy with the business strategy, and it all starts from the first mind-set shift: to become a flourishing employee-centric organization is to realize that treating your employees nicely and being employee-centric is not an either-or situation but actually creates a win-win situation. Just having metaphorical ping-pong tables will not cut it; significant commitment on all levels of the organization is required. Only the organizations that put employee-centricity in the center of their business strategy will be able to profit from the employee advantage. In Part II, we'll explore what drives people in their jobs and how to create a captivating and humanized work environment. Changing the work environment will require the second mind-set shift: moving away from the belief that primarily monetary benefits motivate employees.

How to Humanize Work

CHAPTER 5

More Than Money at Work

I N 2015, DAN SCHULMAN left his job as group president of enterprise growth at American Express to take over as CEO of PayPal, which had just spun off from its parent company, eBay. PayPal is in the business of facilitating payments between sellers and buyers and, through its Venmo platform, between peers. PayPal's mission focuses on providing financial services to merchants and buyers who were overlooked by the conventional banking system. When Schulman stepped in as CEO during a period of stagnant sales growth, he emphasized and expanded on this core mission. Under his leadership, PayPal's guiding principle became the democratization of financial services. As its mission statement highlights, PayPal firmly believes that "easy and affordable access to financial services should be a right for everyone, not just a privilege for a select few."

In 2019, Schulman commissioned a report on the financial well-being of his roughly twenty-six thousand employees. In line with the company's democratic mission when it came to its customers, the report was especially focused on the thousands of entry-level and hourly workers who were employees at the company. Many of them worked in customer service, where they addressed the needs of both merchants and buyers. Schulman would later admit he felt confident that he would get good news because the pay at the company was at or above market rates in all PayPal's locations across the United States and the world. "I did [the survey] because I thought I was going to get back this great information," Schulman said in a TED interview in 2020. "I was going to talk at an employee meeting about how well we pay."

But when Schulman got the results back, it was not what he expected. Instead of getting confirmation that all was great, he learned that 60 percent of the company's entry-level employees or hourly workers were struggling to make ends meet, even though they were being paid at or above market rates. For Schulman it was "simply unacceptable" that so many of his employees were struggling financially. "I think the number one responsibility that we have is the health—financial health—of our employees, because nothing could be more important to a company than to have financially secure, passionate employees working for you."

Schulman commissioned another study shortly after to calculate the net disposable income (NDI), which is the money left after living expenses, for PayPal's employees. Personal finance experts recommend that a person's NDI should be about 20 percent of their pay. This provides a buffer for unexpected expenses, such as a car repair, a visit to family members, or a medical emergency. NDI is a much better measure of financial worries than just looking at wage levels. At PayPal, more than half of its employees had an NDI of 4 to 6 percent. Not so surprisingly, those employees would fall behind on payments and be stressed about their finances. To address this issue, Schulman implemented a four-point plan, which increased the base pay where needed (about 7 percent, on average); gave all employees, not just the top executive team, stock options; reduced the health-care cost for employees by 58 percent; and offered financial literacy training. The plan increased the NDI to 16 percent, which cost PayPal tens of millions of dollars. Despite the high cost, Schulman firmly believed that "taking care of our employees, taking care of our customers, will benefit us in the long run multiplefold over the costs associated with doing that. If people are struggling to make ends meet, they are not as productive at work."

Schulman's belief is backed by research showing that financial stability improves worker performance. A study among manufacturing workers in India quantified the effects of financial worries on productivity. To do so, the researchers manipulated not how much workers got paid in total but *when* they got access to their money. One group was paid at the end of their two-week contract period, while the other group got paid in two installments, half of the pay in the middle of the contract period and the remainder at the end. Because these workers tended to live paycheck to paycheck and 86 percent were worried about their finances before they started working, the timing of the payment could substantially relieve their financial strain and worries.

Workers who got the money earlier were able to pay down debt and spend more on items such as food or fuel. They also reported thinking less about financial worries at work and were, as a result, more productive. Productivity was 7 percent higher than in the group who got paid at the very end. That is a substantial increase in productivity, made possible because the workers can actually focus on their work instead of worrying about their finances. What's more, the workers not only worked more, but they were also more attentive to their work. Quality of the output increased significantly. The study nicely demonstrated what is intuitively true: financial strain does reduce productivity and attentiveness. There's no question that being worried about money and living paycheck to paycheck kills motivation and engagement in workers. Schulman was right about that.

Many successful retailers are paying their employees more and reaping the benefits of increased productivity and profitability. As discussed before, companies like Costco and H-E-B pay their workers significantly more than their competitors, and as a result, they enjoy a more committed and motivated workforce. Even in industries with razor-thin margins, investing in employees is proving to be a smart strategy. One Fortune 500 company increased its own minimum wage to fifteen dollars per hour in 2019. A one dollar per hour increase in pay (which is a 5.5 percent bump) increased productivity by almost 6 percent. The increase in workers' productivity fully compensated for the increased costs. It was win-win! It might be a surprising outcome for people who think wages and profits are a zero-sum game, but in fact, such results are an old story in business. Something similar happened at Ford a century ago. In 1914, Henry Ford introduced a daily wage of five dollars, almost double what competitors would pay, for an eight-hour shift (down from the traditional nine hours). According to Ford: "The payment of $5 a day for an eight-hour day was one of the finest cost-cutting moves we ever made." With the boost in productivity and a reduction in turnover, Ford's strategy was a resounding success, and the company managed to double its profits in under two years.

Schulman, of course, is the CEO of a very successful company with a lot of resources. Is paying higher wages to give financial stability just for high-flying tech companies who are making tons of money? At a news event at the World Economic Forum in Davos, a CNBC host commented on Schulman's multistakeholder approach: "It's going to be expensive. I hope it's all justified and doable. You need a successful business, which you have, before you can become a *just* business." The subtext was clear: Schulman had the privilege to spend a lot of money to do the right thing, but many others do not. But the reality is that companies in a wide range of industries are paying higher wages, and the higher pay is having a positive effect for them.

An additional way to provide financial stability for workers is to provide stock options. Many of the companies that make sure their workers have financial stability are not only raising wages but issuing stock options to their employees. PayPal does it, as does H-E-B, the Texas grocery store with the cult following. So does HEICO. You might have never heard of HEICO, but chances are you've relied on its products without even realizing it. Whenever you fly on a plane, HEICO is with you. The manufacturing company produces critical components for air- and space-crafts, making it an essential player in the aerospace industry. HEICO also produces four crucial components for NASA's Perseverance rover, the vehicle that touched down on Mars in February 2021. Not many companies have such a literally universal reach. On top of this, it does all of its manufacturing in the United States—not in China or Mexico.

Larry Mendelson and his two sons, Eric and Victor, bought the company in 1990 and have been running it ever since. During that time, they have increased revenue by more than eighty times and made close to one hundred acquisitions. During a fireside chat near their Miami head-quarters, Larry Mendelson shared with me a core tenet of their business strategy: placing trust and respect for their team members at the forefront. Instead of referring to them as employees, they called them team members, highlighting their value as essential parts of the organization. They would, Mendelson told me, walk away from an acquisition if they got the feeling that the management of that company would not treat their employees with respect and trust. Inside HEICO, the Mendelsons have empowered their employees with stock options. They match whatever employees put into their 401(k) plans with HEICO stock (up to 5 percent of their wage). It is a core principle of Mendelson's to ensure that his team members have ownership as well. These practices have lowered turnover and made employees more productive and engaged and have made the company better financially too. The HEICO stock increased 47,500 percent from when the Mendelsons took over to the beginning of the pandemic, according to Forbes. That makes it one of the best-performing stocks in the United States. And guess who is also benefiting from this? HEICO employees on every level of the organization. Mendelson said: "It makes me very happy to know that these people who have worked so hard and done good things and made millions for shareholders are making millions for themselves."

Offering stock options to employees is a win-win scenario for both the company and its workers. Not only do stock options provide employees with financial security and an opportunity to create wealth, but they also foster a sense of shared ownership and commitment to the company's success. By aligning the interests of employees and employers, stock options can incentivize workers to go above and beyond, driving innovation and growth while benefiting both the individual and the organization as a whole. Investors are taking notice that this works. Spearheaded by Pete Stavros, a partner at the private equity firm Kohlberg, Kravis & Roberts (KKR), this idea is part of a new nonprofit he founded called Ownership Works. Stavros applies this idea to his own investment strategy and promotes it through his nonprofit organization. Stavros is convinced that "it's a superior way to operate a business in every respect. It is better for workers, it's better for companies in corporate cultures, and in the end, it delivers better results."

Providing financial stability and ownership as Dan Schulman has done at PayPal does really work. PayPal's turnover fell from 19.4 percent in 2019 to 7.3 percent in 2020 and engagement levels (in particular in customer-service operations) reached an all-time high. PayPal is also having some of its best years in growth and profits. Many companies and investors such as KKR are taking notice. Chipotle, Chobani, Prudential Financial, and Verizon are taking a page from PayPal's playbook to secure the financial health of their workforce. Hopefully more companies will continue to see that it's a win-win. At the lower end of the income distribution, paying wages that provide financial stability to workers and allow them to build wealth is important to increase morale and productivity.

However, it is crucial to distinguish between providing financial stability and empowering employees, as opposed to using monetary incentives as a simple carrot-and-stick approach to motivate or assuming that workers are solely driven by their paycheck. Regrettably, many companies fall into the trap of the latter perspective. Monetary incentives can prove ineffective or even counterproductive if not combined with other incentives. Why? Because our paycheck is not the only thing that motivates us to work. Monetary compensation alone does not create the employee advantage. Let's explore some situations in which money might fail to yield the desired results or even lead to negative outcomes.

Money Doesn't Work!

The belief that money is the ultimate motivator in business is deeply entrenched. In a survey from 2021, 99 percent of publicly listed companies employed short-term rewards, such as one-off bonus payments for achieving specific targets. These incentives might be tied to meeting sales goals, generating innovative ideas, maintaining consistent attendance, or assisting colleagues in other departments. Companies and managers operate under the conviction that financial incentives are if not the primary than at least an important driver of employee performance.

Yet, a growing body of research and empirical evidence suggests that the way money motivates us is much more complicated. It's undeniably true that monetary compensation provides financial stability and that this is important to employees. But it is also true that monetary incentives often fail to ensure sustained effort, innovation, and genuine commitment. In many scenarios, the allure of monetary rewards can even backfire, leading to decreased motivation, diminished creativity, and a culture that values short-term gains over long-term growth and collaboration. The question then arises: Why does the myth of money as the ultimate motivator persist, and when and why does money as a motivator not work?

Managers often lean toward monetary incentives as a primary tool for motivation, largely because they are straightforward to implement and offer immediate tangible rewards. From a managerial perspective, attaching a clear financial benefit to a task or goal provides a concrete measure that is easily understood by all. However, ease of implementation doesn't necessarily equate to it being the correct motivator.

This belief that money can unequivocally drive behavior and performance is reinforced by the immediate positive reactions employees often display when presented with a financial reward, which lead managers to overestimate the long-term motivational impact of such incentives. Studies have shown that people acclimate rapidly to increased financial means, unlike other forms of motivation such as autonomy. Even those who win the lottery don't maintain elevated happiness levels beyond an initial spike. Similarly, while employees quickly adjust to a salary increase in jobs with a longer commute, they don't grow accustomed to the extended commuting time and the consequent reduction in social interactions. A comprehensive meta-analysis of numerous studies involving more than fifteen thousand individuals revealed a notably weak correlation between wages and job satisfaction. Even the correlation with pay satisfaction turns out to be very weak. Yet, the belief in the power of monetary incentives persists.

In 2004, two researchers devised a study on the hidden costs and benefits of monetary incentives and also on the role of trust and trustworthiness in working partnerships. The researchers assembled two subject groups, one group of 126 undergraduate students and another of 76 CEOs. Each group was divided into pairs: with one taking on the role of principal (i.e., employer) and the other as agent (i.e., employee). Pairs were asked to collaborate with each other with no guarantee that their partners could be trusted to contribute equitably to the partnership. The principal managed a budget and had the power to fine or punish the agent if the principal decided the agent was not performing as desired. The findings were eye-opening. The study showed that people often collaborate willingly and do not need financial incentives. In fact, when principals introduced penalties for not meeting collaboration goals, things got worse: agents did less when they were threatened with money loss. This approach not only resulted in lower earnings for agents but also cost the principals money. Interestingly, despite the negative effects of these money-based incentives that the study revealed, many managers at companies continue to use them, leading to financial losses. Managers overestimate the importance of money and underestimate how well people can work together without it. The study suggests that managers need to rethink their view of money as a motivator and consider other ways to encourage teamwork and productivity.

A day-care center in Israel learned the negative effect of financial incentives the hard way. The center was fed up with parents picking up their kids too late, which forced staff to stay longer. The day care introduced a monetary fine for late pickup. The result was not what they were hoping for: parents picked up their kids even later than without the monetary disincentive.

A German retailer had a similar experience with financial incentives. They introduced a monetary bonus system for perfect attendance, in which employees would get 60 euros for every three months of perfect attendance. That's 240 euros for twelve months of perfect attendance. Instead of creating less absenteeism, however, the employees who were offered the money incentive were absent five days *more* per year than the employees who did not get an incentive. As we can see, all too often incentives don't have any impact. New York City, for instance, tried a $75 million program to incentivize teachers and schools to improve student performance. The incentive program had no effect on student performance, attendance, graduation rate, or any student or teacher behavior; if anything, it reduced student achievements.

These and other examples illustrate three key issues that arise when relying solely on monetary incentives.

Monetary incentives affect other motivators. The first issue with monetary incentives is that they are often not just in addition to other motivators but might interact or even destroy those other motivators. For instance, if I asked you whether you could bring me a printout from the photocopier on your way back from the coffee machine, I would hope that you would do it. After all, that's what colleagues do for each other. But what if I offered you five cents for this favor? You did it for free before, so now you should be even more motivated because you're getting some money for it, right? Nope.

People might be less likely to help when a monetary incentive is added to a behavior that was done as a social favor. Humans will interpret the incentive as a signal that the person giving the incentive has a particular view of them. We all know that monetary incentives are given for a reason, and receivers try to figure out what that reason is. The incentive would therefore result in questions like: Does this person think I'm so cheap that I would only get the copy if I'm paid five cents? Do they think I would not have done it before? Do they really think I care about five cents? Incentives can sometimes backfire by sending mixed signals.

Now let's go back to the study about collaboration and monetary incentives discussed before and ask what the penalty for not reaching the goal is signaling and how it causes the incentives to backfire. Adding a monetary fine in case a target is not reached signals that the manager does not trust the worker—and feeling controlled is very detrimental to human motivation. Monetary incentives or pay-for-performance policies signal, however, an underlying distrust and can therefore backfire. Workers who receive the threat of a bonus reduction may decide to do the absolute minimum—which is less than the trustworthy behavior they exhibited without the incentive.

But incentives can send other signals beyond distrust. In the case of paying a bonus for workplace attendance or exacting a fine for picking up a child late from day care, the incentive signals that, first, absenteeism or a late pickup is much more common than people thought. Once they conclude the problem is common, people feel less guilty about picking up their kids late or missing a day at work ("oh, everyone is doing it, so it's OK if I do it too"). Second, incentives put a price on behaviors that were originally guided by social norms. People begin to calibrate their behavior based on monetary calculations: "Only three dollars for being late? That's a great deal." "I'll only lose twenty dollars if I miss work a few days in a month? That's worth it to me."

There are many ways in which incentives can interact with and potentially destroy other motivators. Humans are motivated by their peers and by how their actions are perceived. Some employees like to go the extra mile to signal that they are particularly cooperative and helpful. If they get paid for that behavior, however, it will be less clear to an observer whether the behavior was selfless or whether the employee just did it for the money. Dan Ariely, Anat Bracha, and I investigated how monetary incentives can affect behavior in a situation in which humans behave nicely to signal to others that they are nice guys. The monetary incentive destroys that signal and as a result negatively affects behavior. There are many other ways in which monetary incentives can backfire by affecting no-pay motivational factors. This is another reason for looking beyond money: not only to leverage those factors to humanize work but to better understand how monetary incentives might affect them.

Monetary incentives focus too much on the wrong dimensions. Incentives can be a double-edged sword. They can be ineffective or even counterproductive as we just saw. But they can also work too well when they are only applied to the specific behavior that is incentivized. For example, Wells Fargo faced major repercussions for its incentive system. They paid $3 billion in 2020 to settle investigations after admitting employees opened two million unauthorized accounts. This was driven by pressure and incentives to meet aggressive quotas based on new accounts opened. The conundrum of incentives working too well is also very visible in the health-care industry and the debate about the fee-for-service system. Under this system, physicians are paid based on the number of procedures and products they prescribe. When it was first introduced, it worked like a charm. It led doctors to do a lot of incentivized procedures—especially the lucrative ones. If doctors get paid more for cesarean compared to vaginal delivery of babies, which they often do, they are incentivized to perform more C-sections. This explains the high C-section rates in certain countries whose health-care systems function this way.

The problem of the fee-for-service model is that it worked too well. Doctors became so focused on performing lucrative procedures that they neglected the quality of care and overprescribed products and services to their patients. The incentives did change the behavior of doctors but ultimately made the problem worse. This is a well-known phenomenon in which incentivizing quantity can lead to a decrease in quality. In health care, policymakers and hospital managers are now searching for more meaningful outcome measures than the volume of products and services delivered. Unfortunately, the most important outputs are often difficult to measure—in health care and in organizations in general. Vital aspects such as innovation, sharing information, and helping colleagues may be overlooked or undervalued because they cannot be quantified and incentivized. Bengt Holmström of MIT, who got a Nobel Prize in economics in 2016 for studying this problem of incentives, said in his Nobel Prize speech that "high-powered financial incentives can be very dysfunctional [...]. Typically, it is best to avoid high-powered incentives and sometimes not use pay-for-performance at all." In today's rapidly changing business environment, innovation and agility are crucial for companies to stay competitive. But strong monetary incentives and pay for performance can actually act as barriers to transformation.

Another problem is that it's hard to incentivize innovation. Some of my colleagues experienced this in a large research project they conducted in Sialkot, a region in Pakistan. While many Pakistanis are obsessed with cricket, the Sialkot region produces most of the world's hand-stitched soccer balls. To produce soccer balls, you have to cut twenty hexagonal and twelve pentagonal leather panels and stitch them together. The research team invented a new cutting technology that reduces the waste of raw material by around 7 percent. They then gave this technology to a random set of thirty-five companies in the Sialkot region to see how quickly it would be adopted.

To their great surprise, fifteen months later, only six companies were using the new technology. This was not what they expected. Maybe the technology was flawed? No, they confirmed that one company, the largest in the cluster, had ordered forty dies and leveraged the efficiency gains. The new technology did work, but for some reason its adoption by other soccer-ball makers was very low.

It turned out the reasons behind these low adoption numbers were monetary incentives. The scholars discovered that employees were sabotaging the new technology. The cutters in particular were less than thrilled about the innovation. They had strong pay-for-performance incentives (cut more panels equaled get more money) and had no interest in switching to another die method. Why should they learn something new, even if the training costs were minimal, if the old system was working for them and they were not benefiting from any efficiencies? The company that had adopted the new technology, however, paid much higher base salaries and had lower pay-for-performance incentives. It was only after the other companies changed their incentive structure that they were able to benefit from the new technology.

As this example shows, monetary incentives can work so well that they divert the focus too narrowly on measurable dimensions.

Organizations must be careful when using monetary incentives to drive innovation and change as strong pay-for-performance incentives can actually hinder agility and transformation. This becomes even more of a problem when, in today's world, innovation and constant change are becoming more and more important for an organization's survival and success.

Using monetary incentives, while sometimes effective, can be very tricky. It is undeniably important to give workers a decent salary to provide financial stability. But it can be dangerous to use monetary incentives as a control mechanism. Sometimes money works, and sometimes it does not or even backfires. If you want workers to be really engaged, money is not the most important motivator. Leaders need to internalize that their team members are doing their work for more than a paycheck.

More Than a Paycheck

At the heart of our thinking about how to motivate humans is the question of why humans put in effort at work in the first place. Adam Smith took up this question in *The Wealth of Nations* when he wrote about motivation: "It is not from the benevolence of the butcher, the brewer, or the baker that we expect our dinner, but from their regard to their own self-interest." Smith's famous quote has defined the predominant view in economics ever since: that financial incentives are the fundamental driver of human labor. It is this view that has led to the perception of work as necessary drudgery, a source of discomfort and futility, that most of us only do for financial compensation.

The paycheck allows us to do what we really want to do: have leisure time. Right? In this (and Mark Twain's) view, "work is a necessary evil to be avoided." Based on such a view of human motivation, the use of monitoring and financial incentives are logical solutions to make sure the work effort of employees is aligned with the interest of the bosses.

But there are many indicators that work provides a psychological value beyond pure income generation. Consider retirement. It is common for people to speak of the decades they are forced to work as an unavoidable drudge, with retirement as a final salvation. But the truth is, the transition to retirement is difficult for many workers, and this difficulty isn't only about the loss of a regular paycheck. We may think that people's health would improve after they are released from the stresses of work, but analysis shows that health outcomes after retirement are not always positive and, in the case of mandatory or involuntary retirement, often negative. Some studies even show that mortality rates among men increase after early retirement. For many workers, the routine and a meaningful activity are lost. In losing a job, they have lost more than just income.

The importance of employment to our mental well-being was studied in a refugee camp in Bangladesh. In 2017, researchers selected over seven hundred people from the camp and divided them into two groups: a cash group and a work group. (There was also a third control group.) The researchers randomly assigned the work group to do a part-time job in which individuals had to go around the camp and document the different activities other refugees in the camp were involved in. For this work, the group was paid a salary for eight weeks. Researchers then compared those refugees to the cash group, which got the same salary as the work group but whose members were only required to answer a weekly survey. All the participants were measured using indicators for depression, levels of stress, life satisfaction, self-worth, sociability, locus of control, and sense of stability.

If work is just a chore and wage compensation is the only benefit, then people would want to be in the second group, which got money for doing nothing. But that's not what the researchers found. The results showed that employment had substantial positive benefits on all those mental health indicators—way beyond receiving a salary alone. People who were employed enjoyed mental health benefits four times higher than the nonworking group. This shows that employment gives a particularly strong boost to self-worth, with jobs significantly affecting people's perception of how valuable they are to their families. The perception of a job's value clearly plays a significant role, but even a relatively straightforward task can offer a sense of self-worth. And indeed, after the eight weeks of employment came to an end, the researchers asked how many would be willing to work an extra week for zero pay. Sixty-nine percent said they were willing to be "employed" for no compensation. They had internalized the positive benefit of the employment activity.

The most robust findings regarding the importance of work for well-being (beyond income) come when looking at the psychological cost of losing a job. Getting fired and becoming unemployed is one of the most severe negative events that can happen to a person—which is supported in studies on people's life satisfaction or subjective well-being. For example, in Switzerland, the proportion of people who state that they are "completely satisfied" is 20.6 percentage points lower for unemployed than employed individuals. This is a massive drop. The difference between healthy and unhealthy individuals is "only" 13.3 percentage points. Similar results can be found across the globe, and they are the result of more than just lost income. Even in more conservative estimates, the psychological costs are a third to twice as important as the monetary cost.

Is this news? I have never met an executive or emerging leader who would publicly disagree with the observation that there is more to work than a paycheck. But in the many discussions I have had with executives about remote work, the mind-set that employees are shirking whenever they can becomes apparent. And so these executives go back to using the familiar tool kit of monitoring or financial incentives to make sure employees are working enough. Front-line workers are aware of this employee-management disconnect. In a survey of front-line workers and their managers, the authors of the study noted that "employers simply don't know enough of what matters most to their lowest-paid employees."

Maybe educators at business schools (that would be me) are partly to blame. As I mentioned before, business books about strategy spend much less time talking about employees than customers. A recent study for the United States and Denmark showed that managers with a business school degree cut the share of profits that go to the workforce by 3 to 5 percent compared to managers without a business degree, and the former reduced wages by 6 percent compared to the latter group of leaders. Business schools seem to be doing a poor job in implementing the two mind-set shifts: first, that treating employees well is win-win and, second, that money is not the only motivator.

It can be hard to convince some people that more than income and extrinsic motivators drive people's decisions to work. I often hear—perhaps too often!—from leaders I teach that their employees—past, current, and future—are mainly chasing the best compensation package. In response, I ask them to reflect on their own choices: "Did you always pick the job and position with the best salary?" "Do you really believe that the best-paying companies are always the most attractive workplaces?"

To answer this question, we turn to a group of people who would know: those who switch jobs. If workers only cared about income, the companies who attract most job switchers should be the ones that pay the most. But that is not the case. In fact, there are a lot of moves from higher-paying employers to lower-paying employers. These moves only make sense if people get compensated for the lower pay with nonfinancial benefits, such as a better work culture or more employee-centric practices. If a company is not providing intrinsic value to its employees, then it needs to pay more to keep talent—but sometimes, despite the better compensation, people still leave.

When employees—at every level in organizations—are asked what the important attributes of a good job are, financial compensation is not the only one or even the most important one. Financial compensation is undoubtedly more critical in low-wage jobs, but even in those roles, other factors like career opportunities and autonomy hold significant importance. In addition to the indirect evidence that humans are motivated by more than a paycheck, we can also just ask employees directly. In a survey with around 110,000 people in forty-seven countries, people were asked what attributes are important for them in a job. Among the attributes were income, work that is interesting, job flexibility, and whether the job is useful to society. Income obviously matters but was not the most important job attribute. Around 80 percent responded that income is "very important" or "important." But an interesting job was important or very important to 92 percent of responders. That is a 10 percentage point difference. Similar results can be seen in studies across the board. Moving a US worker from the worst job to the best job in terms of experience (that is, schedule flexibility, remote work opportunities, autonomy, paid time off, working with others, job training opportunities, and impact on society) is equivalent to changing that person's wage by 55 percent. That is, people would take a huge pay cut to get those good job attributes.

Even Adam Smith understood that people are not just driven by monetary self-interest. In his other masterpiece, *The Theory of Moral Sentiments*, he writes: "How selfish soever man may be supposed, there are evidently some principles in his nature, which interest him in the fortunes of others, and render their happiness necessary to him, though he derives nothing from it, except the pleasure of seeing it." While recognizing that people care about more than just a paycheck and are motivated by more than monetary incentives is the first step, but knowing that people want an interesting job hardly gives a clear guidance on how to motivate. That is why we will now move on to talk about the behavioral science behind what really makes a job interesting and motivates people.

As we've seen, this doesn't mean that people do not care about a paycheck or incentives. People (and, I can attest from introspection, myself as well) care about money and react to incentives. As we have seen, monetary compensation provides the appropriate financial stability for people to be productive and serves as a recognition for good performance. But dangling a carrot won't cut it for long-term motivation and can even backfire. Tread lightly with cash incentives. Instead, you need to dive deep into other powerful motivators to truly make a difference in your employees' experience. Customer-centricity again provides a helpful analogy. Just as customers care about prices, employees care about their paychecks. But just as customer-centricity is about changing the customer experience beyond price, employee-centricity is about creating an employee experience beyond the paycheck. Lowering prices and increasing compensation are easy to do, but they eat into profit margins. For success, companies should enhance both the customer and employee experience in a different way. This could mean offering a smooth shopping journey or ensuring work is impactful and fulfilling. Making these changes is harder than just lowering prices or increasing wages. But that's good, as these employee-centric initiatives will also be harder for competitors to imitate.

So even if leaders still believe that people are partly or even mainly motivated by money, leveraging nonpay attributes can provide a competitive advantage. It is in fact the key to creating the employee advantage. It requires understanding the four fundamental factors that motivate employees beyond their paychecks. These factors are based on research in psychology and behavioral economics. Let's explore these four factors in detail and see how to leverage them to create an employee experience that truly sets your team or organization apart.

CHAPTER 6

Shoot for the Moon

O N SEPTEMBER 12, 1962, President John F. Kennedy gave a speech at Rice University in Houston, Texas, that would make history and set the stage for the National Aeronautics and Space Administration's Apollo mission. In his speech, Kennedy reiterated an ambition he had stated to the US Congress a year earlier: that NASA would land a human on the moon before the end of the decade. The location of the speech was no coincidence. Just a year earlier, Houston was chosen as the location for NASA's Manned Spacecraft Center (today's Johnson Space Center). It was a pivotal moment for the space program and for NASA. When NASA was formed in 1958, it originally had multiple missions, like improving space technology to meet national interest in space and advancing science by exploring the solar system. Now Kennedy was clarifying the organization's primary aim: "We choose to go to the moon in this decade…not because [this goal is] easy, but because [it is] hard, because that goal will serve to organize and measure the best of our energies and skills, because that challenge is one that we are willing to accept, one we are unwilling to postpone, and one which we intend to win."

It was a very ambitious goal to say the least, given the track record of NASA up to this point. Years later, Neil Armstrong would point out that at the moment Kennedy set his bold goal, NASA had sent only one man, Alan Shepard, into space, on a short, twenty-minute suborbital flight. "[NASA] never had a person in orbit and now the president was challenging us to go to the moon. The gap between…a 20 minutes up-and-down flight and going to the moon, was something that was almost beyond belief."

Kennedy's speech was clearly motivated by political considerations. His presidency had not started out well. The Soviet Union launched the first man into space on April 12, 1961, just months after he took office. Five days after that, a failed US-supported coup to overthrow Fidel Castro at Cuba's Bay of Pigs became an embarrassment on a global scale.

Though Kennedy would tragically not live to see the realization of his mission, instilling a clear purpose for NASA ended up making all the difference. The United States put a man on the moon on July 21, 1969. How, exactly, this played out was the subject of a fascinating research paper entitled "I'm Not Mopping the Floors, I'm Putting a Man on the Moon: How NASA Leaders Enhanced the Meaningfulness of Work by Changing the Meaning of Work." Its author analyzed thousands of pages of archived records and hundreds of videos and books to look at what motivated employees of NASA to achieve the unthinkable. The research showed that the goal of putting a man on the moon served as a common purpose that was extremely motivating—independent of the function in the organization. The title of the article, for instance, refers to a quote by a janitor who sees his job as more meaningful than just "mopping floors." Lola Parker, who at the time was a NASA secretary (or administrative assistant in today's terms), said: "I don't know of anybody who was a clock puncher. No matter what role they played, that was in the back of their mind: we've got that man to get to the moon." Without the coordinated effort around this common purpose, it is hard to imagine how they would have put those three men on the moon and returned them safely.

The leadership at NASA successfully instilled a common purpose throughout the organization. This shared motivating force provided meaning and inspiration to even the most mundane daily tasks, resulting in a coordinated, extra effort to achieve this extremely ambitious goal. It required narrowing the mission of NASA from broad aims like advancing science or achieving preeminence in space to one single, specific goal that was concrete but also ambitious enough without being too out of reach. And this goal was set in spite of the fact that putting massive amounts of funding into transporting a man to the moon did not enjoy widespread support in the population. Kennedy, after all, had run for president on a platform to fund education and social welfare. Now he was rerouting scarce resources into a lunar ambition with questionable benefits. A Gallup poll in May 1961 showed that only 42 percent of Americans endorsed the moon mission. But in the end, NASA was able to rally everybody in the organization, and eventually a whole nation, to achieve its goal. This story illustrates the power of having your organization's own "shoot for the moon" purpose statement.

Formulating and implementing a moonshot statement for your organization may not be an easy task, but the motivational benefits are undeniable. In fact, for employees, the mission and purpose of a company can be just as powerful a motivator as income, if not more so. In a recent survey, more than nine out of ten responders said they would take a pay cut to accept a more purposeful job, and this result supports numerous other studies about the importance of purpose for motivation. Undergraduates, for instance, reported that they would be willing to take a 50 percent pay cut as an ad copywriter to work for the American Cancer Society compared to Camel cigarettes.

MBA students at top schools like Columbia Business School place a high value on social impact when considering future job opportunities. In fact, many are willing to take a pay cut to work for a company with a strong purpose. This trend is reflected in the job market as well, with positions that have a clear social purpose attracting more applicants. For instance, when a job posting for a data-collecting job highlighted its social purpose of benefiting underprivileged children, the number of applicants increased by 26 percent. In addition to attracting talent, purpose has benefits on coordinating effort in an organization and increasing productivity. A study by Adam Grant with fundraising callers shows that making the social purpose of the caller's job more salient (by providing testimonials of two beneficiaries of the donations) increased the number of pledges earned by 124 percent and the amount of donations raised by 152 percent.

Consumer companies were actually ahead of the curve when it came to recognizing the power of purpose. The fastest-growing consumer brands are those that have a clear purpose beyond just selling products. Take Seventh Generation, which has built its brand around environmental sustainability. The name originates from an ancient Iroquois philosophy that emphasizes considering the consequences of each intentional choice on the following seven generations. Since its establishment in 1988 in Burlington, Vermont, Seventh Generation has remained dedicated to manufacturing and selling products with a strong focus on sustainability and environmental responsibility. This focus has helped the company grow at an impressive rate—and led it to being acquired in 2016 by Unilever. Leading consumer companies, such as Unilever and PepsiCo, understood that customers not only care about the quality of a product, but also care about its impact on the environment and society, including how the workers are treated. In fact, according to Unilever and independent research, brands within Unilever that communicate a strong environmental or social purpose are growing almost 70 percent faster than the rest of the company. Those large companies then started to build their own purpose-driven brands or acquire ones, such as Unilever's acquisition of Seventh Generation.

Indra Nooyi, former CEO of PepsiCo, transformed the entire organization in 2006 with her program Performance with Purpose, with a focus on health. This emphasis on purpose has helped the company stay relevant and competitive in a constantly evolving marketplace. Purpose has basically become the fifth p of marketing, with product, price, place, and promotion being the original four. Obviously, consumers who buy from purpose-driven companies are also employees who want to work for purpose-driven companies. This means that having a clear purpose is not only good for selling products, but also for attracting, retaining, and motivating talent.

It's not like companies aren't aware, at some level, that providing employees with meaning is important—after all, almost every company has some sort of purpose statement. But most of those purpose statements are not that useful. You can see this in action when two thousand CEOs across different industries and around the globe were asked about the purpose of their company. Ninety-three percent failed to even mention why their company is in business. Most of these "purpose" statements lacked any meaningful sense of purpose! Similarly, a McKinsey study of one thousand CEOs from American companies showed that while 82 percent of them felt that purpose is important to have, only 42 percent reported that their company's purpose has any effect. In a survey of European CEOs (also by McKinsey), "about 70 percent of them fail to reach their stated goals." A majority of leaders claim that purpose is important, but few say that purpose is guiding their leadership decisions.

Two obstacles are preventing leaders from unlocking the power of purpose. The first is that many leaders have been unable to change their deeply ingrained mind-set that business is only about the bottom line, and they also project this mind-set onto their employees. As an article in the *Harvard Business Review* summarizes: "Many executives avoid working on their firm's purpose. Why? Because it defies what they have learned in business school and, perhaps, in subsequent experiences: that work is fundamentally contractual, and employees will seek to minimize personal cost and effort." Those leaders basically still think that money is the only (or at least the most important) motivator of humans or do not believe that having a strong purpose that is guiding decisions in the organization will positively impact its profitability. But those leaders are wrong.

When it comes to work, humans are driven by something greater than just a paycheck. It is very motivating to contribute to a higher purpose, a shared mission that gives meaning to our daily tasks. This common purpose acts as a guiding light, aligning our behaviors and actions within our organization. It's like a North Star that keeps us on course and moving toward a greater goal. An analysis of half a million employees' perception of purpose across hundreds of organizations shows that companies with a clearly defined and communicated purpose have a stock return that is around 7.6 percent higher than other companies.

But the most important obstacle to making purpose an important force within an organization is that it is simply hard to do well. Just having a purpose statement on one's website or big posters in the hallways is about as effective as having a ping-pong table.

Creating a useful purpose strategy requires doing the hard work to answer three questions. First, ask yourself, what is your organization's "putting a man on the moon" purpose? *Why* does your company exist? Identifying the right purpose for an organization is no easy feat—it takes a great deal of effort and thoughtful consideration. Second, to truly have an impact, a purpose must guide decision-making throughout an organization. It should be an integral part of the company's culture and values, visible to all stakeholders, and be genuine and authentic. Ask yourself, what tangible changes have occurred within your organization as a result of your purpose? And third, for a purpose to truly inspire and motivate us, it must be both ambitious but also relevant to our daily work. Lofty but vague statements like "help make the world better" are meaningless. It should challenge us to strive for greatness, while also being deeply connected to the tasks we perform each day. So, ask yourself: Does everybody in your organization see their job, including mopping the floor, as helping put a man on the moon?

Fortunately, evidence from behavioral science and case studies of successful companies that found their purpose can guide leaders in their effort to create a powerful purpose that motivates employees. Let's first look at a hostile takeover bid by a ketchup company of a mayonnaise producer.

Beyond Profits

In 2017, Kraft Heinz, the American food giant known for its brands like Heinz Tomato Ketchup and Kraft Mac & Cheese, made a surprise bid to acquire Unilever, the Anglo-Dutch consumer goods company that owns brands like Hellmann's Real Mayonnaise, Dove soap, and Ben & Jerry's ice cream. The proposed deal would have been one of the largest in corporate history, with a value of $143 billion. The amount Kraft Heinz was offering to pay was an 18 percent premium over the market price. Share-holders and executives at Unilever would have made a lot of money from this deal, but they ultimately rejected the offer and successfully fought against the takeover.

At the core of the takeover battle were fundamental differences in the values and purpose of the two companies. Heinz Kraft had been acquired two years earlier by the American holding company Berkshire Hathaway and 3G, a Brazilian private equity company known for its ruthless cost-cutting measures. In contrast, Unilever had a long-standing commitment to its purpose, which went beyond just making profits. The battle highlighted the ongoing tension between shareholders and stakeholders in the corporate world, with 3G and Berkshire Hathaway prioritizing shareholder value over other considerations.

In 2010, Unilever's former CEO, Paul Polman, had famously stated that the company's purpose was not just about profits and that sacrificing that purpose for short-term gains would ultimately lead to its destruction. Polman started its ambitious Unilever Sustainable Living Plan (USLP) seven years prior to the takeover bid, which put purpose and enriching others' lives at the company's core. Polman said, "The goal of the USLP is financial gain *because* of sustainability, not despite it—not profits with a side of purpose, but profits *through* purpose." This dedication to long-term value was signaled early in Polman's tenure when he stopped reporting the company's results every quarter, which focuses investors on short-term stock performance, and moved to reporting annually instead.

The premium Kraft Heinz offered over Unilever's value was, in fact, based on a belief that Unilever was hurting shareholders with this purpose-driven mission and long-term value perspective. But Polman and Unilever were ultimately able to convince the company's board and shareholders that purpose and profit are not an either-or equation and that, in fact, putting purpose first and profit second is win-win. Kraft Heinz, 3G, and Berkshire Hathaway pulled the bid only a couple of days after making it. Interestingly, the stock valuation of the two corporations diverged after the failed bid in a surprising way, with Unilever yielding four times the shareholder return than Kraft Heinz did over the next few years. Polman concluded that Unilever "was creating long-term, reliable shareholder value, but as a result of its business model, not as the primary goal."

As we saw in the previous chapter, nobody gets out of bed to work for a company to increase shareholder value. Even increasing wages is not that motivating. This is something that many of the leaders of employee-centric organizations intuited or quickly figured out. As John Mackey, cofounder and CEO of Whole Foods, said: "Just as people cannot live without eating, so a business cannot live without profits. But most people don't live to eat, and neither must businesses live just to make profits."

This pattern is also clearly visible in the public sector. A long line of research shows that people are willing to accept a lower wage if they work at a nonprofit or public sector job whose purpose is to contribute to the public good, not just to be profitable. For for-profit organizations, making more money is obviously key to securing the long-term sustainability of the business. But, at least for Paul Polman, profits should come after purpose. He cites legendary management guru Peter Drucker, who said: "Profit for a company is like oxygen for a person. If you don't have enough of it, you are out of the game. But if you think your life is about breathing you're really missing something."

Behavioral research provides us with guidance on which *why* is most motivating. I have been studying what motivates people to cooperate with and help others for years. Based on the evidence I have seen, I am convinced that although there are few individuals who are completely selfless, most people are strongly driven by the desire to have a positive impact on others and to reduce inequality and unfairness. Social impact is powerful, and it's why many purpose statements are explicitly about others. Some good examples are the pharmaceutical company Merck, which commits itself to "save and improve lives around the world," and its competitor Bayer, another pharmaceutical company that also works on nutrition and farming, which pledges "Health for all, hunger for none." These goals have a motivational effect on the workers at these companies. My colleagues and I conducted a study in Sweden that showed that the level of meaning at work is significantly higher for jobs that rank higher on "beneficence," a measure that reflects concerns, caring, and helping others. This higher perceived meaning positively translates into job satisfaction and lower turnover. My colleague and coauthor Vanessa Burbano hired hundreds of workers for a data-entry job. Although all work paid the same piece rate, half of the jobs included a task that would trigger a donation to a charity. The jobs that included a social component received more applications, even though the workers were willing to accept a 44 percent lower wage. Ultimately, employees in positions with a social mission demonstrated greater effort. Various studies conducted across multiple environments have affirmed the inspirational influence of a job that has a positive impact on society. Apart from boosting motivation and engagement levels, a social impact also has the potential to attract a diverse range of talented individuals to a company. Studies have also shown that employees who are drawn to organizations with a social purpose tend to be more productive and driven in their work, resulting in increased productivity for the company.

At the core of any successful purpose strategy lies a clear and compelling reason for why the company exists. This reason, or *why*, must be rooted in a critical problem that affects humans in a significant way. Ask yourself: What major problem is my company aiming to solve? When the solution to this problem directly benefits people, the impact is more profound and resonates with our deepest motivations. However, not every organization is a children's hospital, where the beneficiaries are clearly defined. Take Unilever, for instance. Mayonnaise and ice cream are hardly essential for survival (although my kids would disagree). Yet, Unilever's purpose of "making sustainable living commonplace" speaks to a larger problem that affects us all. By addressing issues such as climate change, waste reduction, and ethical sourcing, Unilever is tackling problems that have far-reaching consequences for our planet and its inhabitants. Its products may not be necessities, but the way Unilever produces and markets them can make a significant difference in the world.

Ultimately, the why behind Unilever's purpose is about improving the quality of life for all of us. Given that more than 70 percent of individuals in advanced economies around the world are very concerned about climate change, this viewpoint not only strikes a chord with the customer but also resonates with the workforce. In this spirit, goals related to ESG (environmental, social, governance) have become an important source of purpose, encompassing a company's sustainability and ethical impact. In various businesses, ESG efforts clearly benefit company performance in both increased sales and enhanced employee motivation and productivity.

Some companies are indirectly helping others by eliminating inequality in access to services and technology. Google, for example, is about organizing the world's information and making it universally accessible and useful, and PayPal makes access to affordable and convenient financial services a right for all rather than a privilege for the few. Still others indirectly tap into a "David versus Goliath" mentality, like Dollar Shave Club, which provides affordable, high-quality grooming products through a hassle-free subscription service, unlike the industry incumbents. (The industry giant Unilever did briefly own Dollar Shave Club but sold it a few years following the acquisition.) Another is Casper, which disrupted the mattress industry by selling online, delivering for free, and having a generous return policy. But a strong purpose does not need to be prosocial in nature. Being about innovation (3M solves problems and improves lives through science and innovation) or excellence (DHL Express is about "Excellence. Simply Delivered") does not tap into prosocial or fairness values, but they can be invigorating because these goals fulfill a human need for achievement and personal growth.

In the end, a common purpose can be a very powerful way to attract, motivate, and retain employees. "Purpose-driven companies run by purpose-driven leaders are better for society, outperform their peers, and attract the best people like moths to a flame," according to Unilever's CEO. He goes on to add "both Patagonia and Unilever are among the most in-demand employers in the world."

With this in mind, ask yourself whether your employees know what the purpose of your company is (my guess is many do not know). Even more importantly, can they formulate the purpose in their own words? Is it inspiring? To articulate a powerful common purpose is no easy feat and, as I discuss at the end, should involve your employees. And that is just the beginning.

Avoid Purpose Washing

If a company's purpose statement is not authentically created, it may not only be ineffective, but it may also have adverse effects. One of the most egregious examples is when a company's actions contradict its communicated purpose, mission, or values. Greenwashing, in which companies falsely claim that their products or services are environmentally friendly or sustainable, is one of the most outrageous forms of such deceptive tactics. For example, Volkswagen was famously charged in 2016 by the Federal Trade Commission for deceiving consumers with its clean diesel campaign. It turned out that the company rigged the cars with devices that would deceive the emissions tests. It is difficult to quantify the full extent of greenwashing, but some estimates show that about 40 percent of green claims in 2021 were exaggerated, false, or deceptive, and about 58 percent of leaders admit that their companies were guilty of greenwashing. This number rises to 68 percent among US leaders.

Greenwashing also backfires within the company. Most studies focus on the negative effect on consumer perception, purchases, and brand trust, but greenwashing or purpose washing can also have a negative impact on employee motivation. When a company's purpose statement does not align with its actions, it leads to a perception of corporate hypocrisy, which has measurable negative effects on companies through decreased motivation and performance and increased turnover. This shouldn't be a surprise. After all, employees have an easier time figuring out whether purpose matches actions in an organization than consumers do. Employees are the ones who have insight into the intricacies and inner workings hidden beneath the surface visible to consumers. Therefore, avoiding purpose washing and genuinely living the purpose is crucial to creating an employee advantage.

It becomes even more challenging as companies not only need to take tangible steps to support their purpose, but they also must be doing it for the right reasons. Consider two companies that pledged to aid an education program for disadvantaged children with an equal amount of financial commitment. One company first conducted a market analysis to determine the program's potential impact on its employees before deciding to support the program, while the other firm pledged its support because it was the right thing to do, without conducting an evaluation. Although both companies have the same social outcome in mind, their motivations for supporting the program are clearly distinct. One company appears to be interested in whether supporting the educational program will have a positive effect on workers' motivation, while the other may not be making a decision based solely on the program's benefit to the company.

Would the different intentions of these two firms matter to you? My colleague and I spoke with three hundred potential employees to explore the significance of intentions. As it turned out, intentions do matter. We discovered that when a company engages in a corporate social responsibility program solely after ensuring it benefits their bottom line, potential hires find that company approximately 30 percent less appealing to work for. Moreover, self-reported motivation among candidates decreased by 20 percent compared to the company that acted socially responsible simply because it was the right thing to do.

The inherent challenge of aligning internal actions and intentions with purpose is a crucial aspect of harnessing purpose as a potent motivator. Indeed, if this alignment is not challenging, it suggests that the organization's purpose may not be the most fitting or inspiring one. It's important to emphasize that a purpose should transcend mere profit maximization and instead offer a tangible blueprint for why a company exists. The inherent tension between purpose and the profit motive makes this alignment difficult, yet it can also serve as a powerful source of motivation. In Paul Polman's words: "If a goal is not making you uncomfortable, it's not aggressive enough." Unilever and Polman faced their fair share of criticism from various parties, including the Heinz Kraft, 3G, and Berkshire Hathaway consortium and other investors. In its Unilever Sustainable Living Plan, the company pledged to improve its products and business practices to benefit both the environment and people. This involved shifting away from short-term thinking, which included discontinuing quarterly earnings calls. "For years, Unilever skeptics had been eager to see the company stumble. Many mainstream investors who preach shareholder primacy found the sustainability thing too hippie," Polman remembered. However, the company persevered. Ultimately, it was able to pursue its purpose strategy while remaining profitable, despite sidelong glances from the skeptics.

One thing to remember is that in order for your purpose strategy to work, much of the organization may need to change. Instead of being an afterthought or a separate initiative, purpose needs to be at the core of a company's strategy and operation and ultimately every decision. A common purpose can only be a North Star for leaders and employees if it helps them make difficult decisions. Consider this scenario: if your purpose is improving public health, should you discontinue the sale of cigarettes (CVS Pharmacy decided yes), decrease sugar levels in your products (PepsiCo decided yes), undertake new projects that align with your purpose but may not be profitable (Merck did by creating an Ebola vaccine), or take additional measures to safeguard your employees (as DHL Express did during the pandemic)? Unfortunately, numerous companies treat purpose and associated corporate social responsibility (CSR) strategies as supplementary elements rather than integral components. That is why only around 30 to 40 percent use purpose as their North Star when making decisions. Polman again: "The plan was not a CSR-style add-on, sitting to the side of the core business. It was, and is, the strategy, and it's hard-wired into the growth agenda. Because it wasn't separate, the company could not excel if the USLP was not successful, and vice versa."

Ultimately to make sure that purpose is at the heart of a business and not just a nice poster or website slogan, companies need metrics about their progress regarding their ambitious goals—and to be transparent about it. If, for example, your purpose is about inclusivity or diversity, as is the case for PayPal and Etsy, transparently provide metrics on how you are doing on that front. Companies need to show progress, and if they fall behind their projections to reach a promised goal, they should have concrete plans to improve. The same is true for any other purpose. For example, if environmental impact is a core part of a company's purpose (as it is with Unilever), it needs to provide detailed metrics about all of its emissions.

There is one more step that is crucial in making purpose an important part of the employee advantage. You need to answer the following question: How does your company's purpose invigorate the workforce *on a daily basis*? Does it do this even for people whose tasks seem tangential to the purpose? How do you get the person who mops the floor to see his or her job as a part of the company's moonshot mission? Leaders must adopt a distinct approach to establish a connection between a company's purpose and their employees' daily tasks, which differs from creating a purpose strategy for customers or other stakeholders. This is exemplified in an unexpected profession when it comes to purpose—an accounting firm.

Linked to Task

We don't generally think of accounting as a profession driven by an ambitious and far-reaching purpose. I mean, how can you feel a higher purpose when you are auditing financial statements? But KPMG, one of the Big Four accounting firms (in addition to Deloitte, Ernst & Young, and PricewaterhouseCoopers), explodes those stereotypes. What is remarkable about KPMG's purpose story is less about its purpose per se and more about how the company made its purpose come alive and become relevant for its workforce.

Obviously, professional service or accounting companies like KPMG are important for any type of organization—including the children's hospitals of the world. But do the KPMG accountants see their work in light of this higher purpose? In 1995, KPMG sought to strengthen the company's identity as an organization that has played a key role in larger achievements. To do this, KPMG launched an internal campaign to remind its employees how the people of KPMG "Inspire Confidence. Empower Change." KPMG was, for example, critically important in defeating Nazi Germany through the work of one of its partners, who was responsible for material procurement for the Lend-Lease Act in 1941. The campaign reminded employees that KPMG also certified the 1994 South African presidential election, which brought the nation's first Black president, Nelson Mandela, to power after the apartheid regime. To highlight such historical narratives, the company created some nice posters about "shaping history," which showed how KPMG helped change the lives of clients, communities, and society. But the company wanted all twenty-six thousand employees to feel their own impact, so they came up with an idea: the 10,000 Stories Challenge.

In June of that year, the company asked its employees to submit posters illustrating how their work made a personal impact. The company announced that if it received 10,000 posters by Thanksgiving, created and submitted by individuals or teams of employees, everybody at KPMG would get two extra vacation days. That was a pretty ambitious threshold, but by the beginning of July, the 10,000 posters had been submitted. The kicker: though the employees had reached the goal and gotten the extra vacation days, thousands of posters continued to come in. Clearly, it was not just the vacation-day incentive that had gotten people to submit their stories. By Thanksgiving, the company had received 42,000 posters with employees' personal impact stories. The program had hit a nerve and was extremely successful—not just in the number of submitted stories but in how the corporate purpose had come alive.

Bruce Pfau, a partner at KPMG and vice chair of human resources and communications, remembered that on all metrics of employee engagement, the challenge was a tremendous success, with scores on engagement levels at all-time highs. In the end, 89 percent of employees said that KPMG is a great place to work (up from 82 percent a year earlier). KPMG rose seventeen spots on the *Fortune* 100 Best Companies to Work For list, making it the number-one ranked firm among the Big Four accounting companies for the first time ever. Perhaps best of all, turnover at KPMG plummeted. According to Pfau, the company figured out that "we needed to do more than simply announce our purpose and expect it to take hold. We needed employees to experience it for *themselves*."

The 10,000 Stories Challenge addresses a common problem with purpose as a motivator. Purpose and meaning are crucial for motivating people at work, but it can be difficult for a corporate purpose to be effectively conveyed and felt by employees in their day-to-day tasks. When seeking to motivate employees, companies need to take a completely different approach from the purpose-led initiatives instituted to build a strong and appealing consumer brand. Most of those initiatives are top-down: a purpose statement is decided upon and then the executive team communicates the purpose through many channels to the consumer. But that does nothing to invigorate the workforce and create a common purpose. Each employee needs to be actively involved.

Consider the following analogy: if you've ever gone to therapy, you have probably come across the concept of gratitude intervention. Maybe you don't use that exact term, but the idea is to reflect on a few things each day that you are thankful for. Studies show this helps improve happiness and overall mental health, but the gratitude intervention only works if people think of very concrete and personal things to be grateful for (for example, I am personally grateful for my daily bike ride to work—especially when there is no headwind). A therapist can offer guidance, but it is really up to the individual to make it personal. The same is true for a company's purpose. Employees need to grasp the concrete implications of their company's purpose in their own work and become passionate about it. That is why KPMG's 10,000 Story Challenge was so impactful and why it is important that employees can formulate a company's purpose in their own words. Employees saw their own impact at work.

A workplace intervention aimed at promoting purpose, which involves prompting employees to reflect on their impact on a daily basis, has the potential to be highly effective. In addition to such private reflections, conversations are critically important—and emerging leaders play an important role. In KPMG, employees who report that their managers discuss purposes with them are 30 percent more likely to be proud to work at KPMG. They are more likely to stay and more motivated to thrive.

Unilever goes even one step further. All their top leaders go through a weeklong purpose workshop to learn about the company's purpose goals but also to reflect on their own personal purpose. And it's not just the leadership team but everybody in the company (we are talking about 150,000 employees) who attends a Discover Your Purpose Workshop. So far more than 60,000 employees have attended it. The workshop is not really about communicating Unilever's purpose but for employees to find their own and see how they can leverage their personal mission in their job. This mission can be to work at Unilever for the next thirty years but does not need to be. Unilever will help find other opportunities (inside or outside the company) to help people find personal purpose with their jobs. Leena Nair, the former chief HR officer at Unilever and now CEO of Chanel, was overseeing the introduction of the program and really saw the impact: "I'm so pleased because so much of the data is saying that people who have been through these workshops and have discovered there and are living their purpose and action at Unilever are 49 percent more intrinsically motivated, have 25 percent more job satisfaction, and are 40 percent more likely to stick with the company. So, there's a real, real importance to doing some of this work around purpose."

Are there other ways for purpose to come alive in our work? I recently spoke with an executive from a prominent emergency room network located in the southern United States. The company manages these rooms, including the physicians working within them, but was finding that the doctors (and probably the staff in general) lacked motivation and a sense of higher purpose. It's difficult to imagine how these employees could experience a disconnect between their daily tasks and the purpose of their jobs! They literally are saving lives and still don't experience a higher purpose? As we'll see later in Chapter 7, a missing link between purpose and task might only be one of the issues in such a setting that can lead to disengagement. But the executive wanted to focus on the missing purpose link. He read an academic study that showed that donating to a good cause for a certain abstract task has an impact. In fact, it was one of the studies I cited earlier. He asked, "Can we create a study to demonstrate the motivating effect of donation to charity for each medical procedure (such as repairing an injured knee), with the hospital making the donation in the doctor's name? That will increase the doctors' motivation, right?" He was very excited about the idea and disappointed when I told him in no uncertain terms, "No, it will not."

There are many companies that provide opportunities to have impact, often social, outside the workplace or as an add-on to the tasks. For example, Comcast NBCUniversal, one of the largest broadcasting and cable television companies in the world, organizes its annual Comcast Cares Day. Thousands of Comcast employees volunteer their time for a good cause on that day, making it one of the largest corporate volunteer initiatives in the United States. And those programs certainly have a positive effect on the charities that they support and are probably also attractive for the employees. Similarly, a study of ten thousand management consultants shows that those who got assigned to pro bono projects are more likely to stay at the company. The meaningful work outside their normal work seems to have a positive spillover to their overall motivation. But while those add-on activities have some benefit, they are no substitute for making the daily job meaningful itself. So, while nobody will object when the emergency room executive makes a donation to a charity for every injured knee, it will not increase the doctors' motivation or make them feel they have a meaningful job. Merely making a donation won't establish the essential direct connection between the work people do and the positive impact it creates. But if, for example, a doctor can recognize that an injured knee is more than just a body part that they repaired or replaced and know that their work has enabled the patient to continue dancing or gardening, the doctor can have a greater sense of purpose and the job feels more meaningful. The motivational effects of a higher purpose are most impactful when the purpose is directly linked to activities and is personally felt by employees. Supplying the doctor with updates on the patient's life and recovery progress or setting up a channel through which patients can personally express their gratitude with thank-you notes will establish that connection. While establishing such a system is more difficult to implement than simply initiating a donation, it will be much more motivating and meaningful.

And then we come back full circle to where we started this chapter: What is a company's purpose? To discover the answer and create a connection between purpose and day-to-day work, it is necessary to involve your employees. When Nordea, a large bank in Scandinavia recently reevaluated its purpose, an executive explained that management spent time "listening to more than 7,000 people in and around our organization over a period of six months…in workshops…online with surveys…[and] in more than 1,500 coffee-corner discussions.…We discussed deeply why people had joined us, why they stayed, and what they see as impact for a financial institution." Those conversations informed the new purpose and as such were more than just slogans or hallway posters dreamed up by the branding team.

When Sam Palmisano took over as CEO of IBM, the company was struggling, and Palmisano wanted to instill a new purpose and values. In this time of crisis for the company, he opted for a bottom-up, risky strategy, which turned out to be successful: he asked for feedback from his massive workforce. Over three days, the intranet served as a forum for discussion about what values IBM should pursue. About fifty thousand employees checked out the discussion, dubbed ValuesJam, and left around ten thousand comments. In the first twenty-four hours, criticism and cynicism were dominant. One post read: "The only value in IBM today is the stock price." Some of Palmisano's executives urged him to pull the plug given the negative mood, but he prevailed. By day two, the mood on ValuesJam had changed and the discussion had become constructive. People began discussing what IBM's purpose should be and which values to embrace or strengthen. The set of values developed during the ValuesJam turned out to be very meaningful for IBM employees. Sam Palmisano knew: "We had to come up with a way to get the employees to create the value system, to determine the company's principles." By listening to them, IBM created exactly that.

If done right, providing a purpose for employees is very powerful. It can create meaningful work *and* make the world a better place. But it is difficult to do—and that is exactly why it is powerful. If a company just comes up with a nice slogan or an add-on volunteer program because it wants to make more money, the strategy will not work. But genuinely providing purposeful jobs will lead to an employee advantage. Or in Leena Nair's words: "Companies with purpose last, brands with purpose grow, and people with purpose thrive in uncertain times."

Of course, having a sense of purpose in work, while undoubtedly important, is not the only element that drives people at work. Merely working at a children's hospital, for instance, will not guarantee an engaging and motivating experience. If other essential factors are absent, even the most meaningful job can become unbearable. And when that is the case, the root of the problem is often trust, or the absence of it.

CHAPTER 7

A Matter of Trust

F REDERICK W. TAYLOR, the turn-of-the-century industrial efficiency guru famous for his investigations into "scientific management," would have had a field day with modern technological tools. When he was consulting at the end of the nineteenth century (he was alive from 1856 to 1915), he was limited to collecting data in the steel mill in which he worked using paper and pencil. Taylor was convinced that if workers were better managed, efficiency could be increased and labor cost reduced. So, he would observe people at work, meticulously recording what they were doing and how long it would take them to do a certain task. Based on those observations of time and motion in the production processes, he would suggest to management that they cut jobs into smaller tasks, and then monitor and control the performance of those tasks to increase productivity. In spite of his limited tools, his approach had an enormous impact. Taylor is today remembered as the first and most prominent management consultant and is the author of *The Principles of Scientific Management*, one of the most influential management books of all time.

Taylorism, as his approach was later called, involved a clear division of responsibilities between management and workers. Management used scientific management principles to design work plans and oversee performance, while workers were responsible for executing the assigned tasks. The measurement of workers' performance served as a vital tool to continuously optimize work processes, leading to enhanced productivity and reduced labor costs. This engineering-oriented approach to human management, aimed at optimizing individuals much like machines, had a profound influence on people management philosophies for many years to come. It also laid the foundation for various other approaches, including Jack Welch's favored Six Sigma methodology.

Traditional Taylorism seems like child's play today, when the wealth of data accessible to managers regarding workforce performance is enormous. Consider what can be known about a delivery driver at UPS, the renowned logistics company with a global workforce of over half a million individuals. A UPS delivery truck alone has about two hundred sensors that record everything: the speed of the vehicle, when the brakes are used, how closely the driver is following other vehicles, and whether a driver is buckled up. The handheld scanners used by drivers also collect information, such as when and where a driver drops off a package. All the data is reported back to UPS headquarters in real time for analysis. The insights have led to recommendations on how to improve efficiency in delivery, captured in a seventy-four-page guidebook for drivers. For example, backing up must be avoided as much as possible as it leads to a higher proportion of accidents. Driver behavior data is of significant value when it comes to driver feedback and performance reviews.

The amount of data we can collect on the performance of employees in all types of jobs is overwhelming, and it's being used in more and more invasive ways. The patents filed by Amazon for technology to be used in their fulfillment centers describe machines explicitly designed to collect more data—which is intended, as one analyst puts it, to "increase worker surveillance and work rhythms." The transition to remote and hybrid work arrangements has brought significant attention to the level of surveillance managers still have on their office workers' activities. Beyond monitoring email exchanges, Slack conversations, and shared document collaboration, certain software solutions (called "bossware") are now capable of measuring a range of other factors pertaining to employee engagement and productivity. Programs such as Time Doctor or Veriato track not just email and chat activity but can also capture how often a computer is idle or active and what documents are being created and changed. The programs can also take screenshots to see what the employees are working on, either randomly or continuously. The program uses AI to figure out if workers are satisfied at work by analyzing language or keywords used. Employees' use of keywords such as *interview* or their visits to job search sites can alert their employer. Some programs use a computer's camera to take pictures of employees while they are at work. All that data is then shared with managers.

The emergence of Digital Taylorism, which employs data as a means of command and control, presents new opportunities for contemporary efficiency experts. But while there is no doubt that this data enables new approaches to scientific management, leaders must be extremely careful when using it. There is a reason why Taylorism has fallen out of favor in recent years.

Humans do not like being treated like cogs in a machine, a fact that we can see as far back as 1936, when Charlie Chaplin's movie *Modern Times* was released. Chaplin's satire poked fun at Taylorism by showing his iconic Tramp character trying to keep up with the relentless push for efficiency in a factory job overseen by a humorless management expert. The Tramp is shown being chastised on an assembly line for falling behind when he stops to scratch an itch or shoo a fly away. The management guru is intrigued when he is told that a new machine, designed to shove food into employees' mouths while they work, can eliminate the need for lunch breaks.

The fact is some jobs can be repetitive and boring, and when you add to that an invasive level of monitoring, workers will rebel. We've seen this over and over again in studies of human motivation. Taylorism is the opposite of human-centric.

One of the most important motivational factors for humans is discretion and autonomy. Given the freedom to figure something out, it sparks creativity and allows people to do it in the way that best fits their personality and working style. In fact, the search for autonomy often leads people to leave organizations completely and start their own business—despite the fact that for the vast majority of workers it is less financially rewarding to be self-employed or start their own company.

Despite earning less money, people who are self-employed often experience significantly higher levels of job satisfaction. Two of my coauthors, Matthias Benz and Bruno S. Frey, looked into the job satisfaction gap between self-employed individuals and those who are employed by others. Their study of workers in twenty-three countries revealed that the substantial disparity in job satisfaction is primarily attributed to the greater autonomy of people who are self-employed. "Being your own boss" is valuable.

This kind of empowerment can be applied to people working within organizations as well, and there is compelling evidence of its positive impact. One comprehensive study revealed that when leaders delegate authority, actively seek employee inputs, and foster a culture of autonomy, employees are free to be more creative, develop innovative problem-solving approaches, and demonstrate exemplary corporate citizenship. Above and beyond their work, they will participate in corporate volunteer projects, assist other coworkers who might need help, and overall go above and beyond their contractual obligations.

Taylorism also proves insufficient in a rapidly evolving world. The hierarchical and bureaucratic methods inherent in Taylorism don't work in an era where businesses must continuously adapt in unpredictable ways. Just as autonomy is the antithesis of control, agility is the antithesis of a command-and-control system.

Providing autonomy in the workplace is a critical piece of creating the employee advantage, but implementing it can be challenging. First, leaders must view employees as inherently motivated and capable individuals who can contribute significantly to the organization's success. This shift in perspective requires a departure from traditional hierarchical structures and a move toward fostering a collaborative and empowering environment. It demands that leaders relinquish some of their power and authority, which can be a difficult adjustment for some. But it's not about letting employees do what they want. It requires engaged autonomy. Leaders must shift from being managers to being coaches. Ask yourself: When you grant your team members greater autonomy and discretion, do you also provide more (rather than less) engagement and support? As elaborated below, this is the only way it will succeed.

Second, building autonomy and discretion requires a foundation of trust between leaders and employees. Trust is absolutely essential. It can be hard for managers to trust their employees—it makes them vulnerable and creates the potential for violations. However, embracing this vulnerability is precisely what is needed to cultivate a workplace that values autonomy and enables individuals to thrive and contribute to their fullest potential. Finally, employees' inputs should be heard and taken seriously, and employees should be encouraged to voice their opinions to their managers about their work.

Looking at the rise in surveillance technology after the pandemic shows that we are even further away from empowering our employees. The use of bossware such as Veriato doubled from the start of the pandemic in early 2020 to 2022. Sixty percent of companies employing fifty or more full-time workers use such tools today, and that number is expected to increase to at least 70 percent according to the research. In 2022, there was 100 percent growth of Veriato's business across the Asia Pacific region.

Rather than improving worker performance, the surveillance prompts workers to get creative and engage in unproductive efforts to manipulate surveillance systems. Various models of undetectable mouse movers or jigglers for purchase on platforms like Amazon are indicative of this response. It is difficult to envision a practical purpose for a mouse jiggler—which makes it appear that someone is actively at work on their computer—beyond potentially deceiving a surveillance system. Trying to control employees can lead to a self-fulfilling prophecy in which monitoring lowers trust and motivation and triggers counterproductive behavior, which in turn justifies the surveillance in the first place.

Monitoring software is booming today, but even before the pandemic, worker autonomy was already declining. In a 2019 study by consulting firm PwC, which surveyed twelve hundred business and HR leaders from seventy-nine countries, only 45 percent responded that their "employees have a high degree of autonomy over how they work." Managers appear to be increasingly unwilling to give up their control and trust their employees. But that is exactly what they need to be doing. As we navigate the evolving landscape of technology in the workplace, it is essential to strike a delicate balance between leveraging its benefits to foster autonomy and empower employees to work flexibly and independently while safeguarding against the potential pitfalls of excessive control and surveillance. Ask yourself: Do you have enough trust in your team to unleash the potential of autonomy?

In order to create autonomy in the workplace that works, leaders need to become engaged coaches, and they need to trust and listen.

Engaged Autonomy

As we know, in the quest for growth, innovation, and constant improvement, it is essential to recognize that great ideas can emerge from the most unexpected corners of an organization. By providing autonomy and fostering an environment of widespread ideation and encouraging creativity, companies have the potential to unlock a treasure trove of unconventional ideas that can revolutionize their industries. Think about 3M's Post-it note and Google's Gmail app, which were dreamed up by employees when they were encouraged to work on their own personal projects. Those and other innovations stand as a testament to the transformative power of giving individuals the opportunity to contribute their unique perspectives and unleash their creative potential.

The benefit of empowering employees goes beyond fostering product innovation; it also plays a vital role in process improvement and in elevating customer service to new heights. A study comparing two Mexican manufacturers of Nike T-shirts provides an excellent illustration of this. The two plants basically produce the same T-shirts but with very different models of autonomy for their workers. One (Plant A) uses the Toyota model and provides workers with greater autonomy and power on the shop floor. Workers are trained to stop production when they see defects, and they work in autonomous units that participate in decisions affecting performance targets and work techniques. Plant B, on the other hand, uses a more conventional management structure and workers have no voice in production decisions or any other part of their work. The productivity results are stark: Plant A uses only six workers per assembly line compared to ten in Plant B. Workers in those lines in Plant A produce 150 shirts per worker per day compared to only 80 in Plant B. Labor costs per T-shirt are eleven cents for Plant A compared to eighteen cents for Plant B. Autonomy works and is a win-win for workers (who can also be paid more) in the T-shirt plant.

Organizations such as Southwest Airlines and Zappos.com have embraced the philosophy of empowering their employees to deliver exceptional customer experiences. Both give their employees (cabin crew or call center staff) a lot of autonomy to do whatever it takes to wow their customers. The often improvised safety announcements that cabin crews at Southwest come up with (which sometimes go viral) are very funny examples of the benefit of tapping into employee creativity. The high customer service ratings and customer loyalty scores show the overall benefit. By trusting their front-line staff to make autonomous decisions and go the extra mile for customers, these companies have created a culture of exceptional service that sets them apart from their competitors.

Remember, though, that empowering employees does not diminish the need for effective leadership. Leaders must play an engaged coaching role to ensure that empowerment aligns with their organizations' goals and values, which involves both organizational-level adjustments and shifts in individual leadership styles.

GE Appliances (GEA), the division of GE that produces refrigerators, air conditioners, and washing machines (called "white goods" because of their typical color), has an interest in encouraging innovation. After all, that is one of the keys to success in its industry. Undoubtedly, the leadership always believed that they provided their employees with the freedom to generate innovative ideas. But there was a problem: their approach was not working.

In 2016, GEA was bought by Haier, a successful Chinese white goods producer that had transitioned from producing small refrigerators (think cheap mini-fridges for dorm rooms) to dominance of the global white goods industry. But while Haier was globally dominant in 2016, it had not yet achieved much penetration in the US market. That came to an end with the $5.6 billion acquisition of GEA, which raised the question: Would Haier be able to continue to grow in this new arena? It didn't take long for investors to discover the answer: Haier changed the way GEA was run and achieved double-digit growth in the first four years that Haier owned it—all by providing real autonomy.

At the core of the Haier model is the concept of RenDanHeYi. *Ren* (人) means "human" or "employee," *dan* (单) means "user," *he* (合) means "integrate" or "together," and *yi* (一) means "unity" or "becoming one." The management concept that Haier's founder, chairman, and CEO, Zhang Ruimin, established in 2005 is about empowering its employees to please its customers and users without any distance between them; that is, no middle managers or top management who tell the different business units how to do their job. Zhang Ruimin realized that in today's fast-moving and highly uncertain market environments, top-down and command-and-control management cannot keep up with the speed and can even kill motivation and innovation.

To create RenDanHeYi, Haier is all about autonomous teams. It is organized into four thousand microenterprises (ME) that each have a small number of employees. Some of them are market facing and are concerned with selling the final product to a consumer, such as refrigerators to college kids. Others are internal focused and produce and sell components or services to ME within the organization. The company sets ambitious leading targets, but each ME has full autonomy to do whatever is required to achieve these targets. By doing so, Haier got rid of bureaucracy and middle managers. In return, according to the *Harvard Business Review*, this new management approach "makes employees energetic entrepreneurs directly accountable to customers and organizes them in an open ecosystem of users, inventors, and partners."

Haier introduced this approach to GEA, leading to a complete transformation of the organization. GEA adopted a structure with multiple MEs, where each ME was granted full autonomy. The outcomes of this transformation serve as evidence of the model's success, highlighting the power of harnessing human motivation. However, implementing such a model is not easy. It contradicts traditional management models that rely on top-down and command-and-control structures that have been in place for decades. Zhang Ruimin said: "Companies try to learn from us and say it is quite difficult to replicate our model. I reply that adopting our model requires giving up powers, including decision making, hiring and firing, and setting compensation. You must delegate all those powers to the microenterprises themselves. One boss asked me how he could control his employees without those three powers. Well, I believe that giving up that control is actually an important part of the model." Providing autonomy requires structural changes that shift the power from management to employees.

To empower employees requires more involvement from leaders instead of less. Leadership has two dimensions: how frequently a leader checks in and how much guidance a leader offers. The right amount of each determines whether a leader empowers the employees.

A leader who is frequently involved *and* controlling, providing too much guidance and direction, is the much-hated but very common micromanager. You might, as an employer, have some micromanager tendencies yourself or have worked in the past for a boss who has them. These leaders need to be involved in every decision and use their engagement to control their employees. This leadership style kills motivation and is closest to Taylorism. For these managers, the increased availability of detailed data about employees is a micromanager dream come true: it allows them to better control and micromanage their workforce. The result is that employees are even less motivated.

McKinsey has a term for the manager type who provides autonomy but is not frequently involved: a cheerleader. Under cheerleaders, employees have a lot of autonomy but lack sufficient guidance, and as a result, the manager needs to intervene, not only to offer motivation but also to address issues when they arise—and they will. Interactions between leaders and employees primarily revolve around dealing with mistakes and can become problematic and even toxic. The notion that granting autonomy equates to disengagement is a misconception. The danger lies in leaders transitioning from micromanagers to mere cheerleaders who provide motivation but only infrequently check in on progress. This approach can potentially lead to disaster, as it lacks the necessary guidance and support that employees need to excel.

Effective leadership in an empowered environment requires clear communication of goals, allowing employees the freedom to execute their roles while providing support when needed. Leaders need to step up and be engaged. They need to be very open and transparent. At Google, empowering employees is central to their people strategy—in addition to their 20 percent rule. And transparency is key. In his book *Work Rules!*, Google's former HR chief, or "Head of People," Lazlo Bock describes the virtues of transparency: "Openness demonstrates to your employees that you believe they are trustworthy and have good judgment. And giving them more context about what is happening (and how and why) will enable them to do their jobs more effectively and contribute in ways a top-down manager couldn't anticipate."

Empowering employees and setting them up for success requires more frequent check-ins and feedback. It involves redefining job descriptions to be broader, altering organizational structures to remove bureaucratic obstacles, and focusing on enabling employees to excel in their roles. A leader's role then becomes that of a coach, who provides guidance and constant feedback and removes barriers that hinder productivity, without being controlling. By taking on this coaching role, leaders can unleash the full potential of their employees and drive exceptional performance.

The distinction between a leader who acts as a coach, rather than just a cheerleader, lies in consistently providing feedback to all employees, not just those who are facing performance challenges. Since cheerleaders check in infrequently, they inevitably need to step in when things go sour. As a result, they will mainly talk to underperforming employees. A large spa and massage chain in China conducted a six-month experiment with more than ten thousand workers to assess the effects of two distinct types of conversations held between managers and employees. Managers were required to engage in individual conversations, lasting fifteen to twenty minutes, once a week with a specific group of employees selected from their regular team of approximately forty-five workers. In one condition (which I call the coach condition), managers were given names that were randomly selected from their team. Employees who got selected got some extra attention from their manager. In the other condition (which I call cheerleader), the employees were selected based on their low level of motivation. Under this condition, only the problematic employees got to have a talk. Then, both of these conditions were compared to a third group in which no extra manager-employee conversations were implemented.

The results support the view that a coaching approach is more motivating. In the stores in which random employees got special attention from the manager, store revenue increased 6.6 percent and employee attrition dropped by 13.9 percent compared to the control group. Targeting lower-performing employees has no effect on revenue or attrition. Struggling employees in the cheerleader group still expressed appreciation in surveys for the extra attention they received compared to the control stores where no extra conversations between managers and employees were initiated. But compared to the coaching approach, they had fewer positive views about the manager. Having a coach as a manager who supports everybody was very motivating and impacted performance positively.

Technology can play a valuable role in fostering engaged autonomy by empowering employees while simultaneously offering regular feedback and guidance. The abundance of available data enables leaders to provide the necessary feedback for autonomous employees to continually enhance their performance, all without feeling controlling. The largest home health-care provider in the Netherlands shows how it can be done. The company, Buurtzorg, employs more than ten thousand nurses who provide home health-care services ranging from taking blood and administering medication to helping clients with daily tasks such as eating or personal hygiene. The home care market is estimated to be globally a $362 billion revenue market and is expected to grow by almost 8 percent in the coming years. A number of trends, such as an aging population and a rise in telehealth opportunities, have contributed to its growth. But the market also faces challenges, particularly rising costs and scarcity in nursing staff. Buurtzorg, established in 2006, employs a management model in this market that is now seen globally as a potential solution for addressing these challenges. Buurtzorg has been able to create a client satisfaction rate that is 30 percent higher than its competitors. At the same time its absenteeism, overhead, turnover, and required hours of care per clients is one-third to two-thirds lower. Buurtzorg accomplishes these achievements by leveraging technology to facilitate engaged autonomy.

At the core of the organization is an IT system called Buurtzorg Web, through which the company collects all kinds of data. In addition to patient data and medical history, the system captures detailed performance metrics of the different teams and individual nurses, such as patient satisfaction and number of cases by teams. All the information is available to both nurses and Buurtzorg's headquarters. Crucially, the information of other teams is also shared so that everybody has transparency into their performance—even relative to other teams.

Importantly, management does not use the system to monitor or supervise nurses. Quite the opposite: nurses are organized into self-managed teams of around twelve. They are fully autonomous and are responsible for everything related to care, but they also engage in personnel management, such as hiring, training, or firing staff. For Buurtzorg, autonomy is key. Jos de Blok, one of the founders of the company, said: "It is important that these nurses feel the autonomy to do what they think is needed at the moment that problems occur, and that they also have autonomy to share it with their colleagues." And providing such autonomy is motivating. Mijiam de Leede, a nurse practitioner, said: "Because I had this enormous freedom, [...] the creativity was just out of the box. It is amazing. You can get so much out of a person, they bring so much to the table, and it is so innovative to work this way. I wish lots of other people had that, too."

The self-management model relies on both Buurtzorg Web to provide real-time feedback and a channel for teams to share information and provide one another with support. At the same time, the fifty people in the back office see their role as supporting instead of controlling or managing the teams. Gonnie Kronenberg, another founder and codirector, said, "I like to make procedures as easy as possible," and sees giving this support as her role. This is engaged autonomy in action. Autonomy without the feedback and support system would not work. It is the combination that creates superior performance and high motivation.

Leaders must ask themselves whether they empower their employees with autonomy, which is a vital driver of work motivation. In doing so, they must also fulfill the role of engaged coaches who provide support, transparency, clarity, and frequent feedback to their employees, all while avoiding being controlling. You need to be the type of leader who checks in frequently and offers feedback to ensure your team members thrive while enjoying autonomy.

Striking the right balance between offering feedback, being an engaged leader, and avoiding a sense of control is a delicate endeavor—especially in a world in which availability of an enormous amount of data would make micromanaging easier. And the crux of the issue is trust, or more precisely, the lack thereof.

Trust Is Good, Period

The biggest obstacle to providing autonomy is that it requires trust. And trust is a scarce resource in many organizations. Who hasn't met a leader who jokingly (but maybe not so jokingly) cites the famous quote attributed to Lenin that "trust is good but control is better"? This sentiment was widespread after the move to remote and hybrid work during the pandemic. A survey by Microsoft of twenty thousand people in eleven countries found that "85 percent of leaders say the shift to hybrid work has made it challenging to have confidence that employees are being productive." That explains the soaring adaptation of surveillance technology such as Time Doctor or Veriato.

But trust and control do not square well. Research shows, unsurprisingly, that control and extensive monitoring destroy trust. And a lack of trust can have a substantial negative impact on motivation and performance. Indeed, studies show that people working in high-trust companies had a remarkable reduction of 74 percent in stress levels, an impressive increase of 106 percent in workplace energy, a 50 percent boost in productivity, 13 percent fewer instances of sick leave, a remarkable 76 percent increase in engagement, a 29 percent rise in overall life satisfaction, and a substantial 40 percent decrease in burnout compared to their counterparts in low-trust companies. Trust plays a crucial role both in the relationship between employees and employers, as well as in the confidence consumers have in brands. It is estimated that once a brand loses trust due to a scandal, it loses 20 to 56 percent of its stock market value. Similarly, the absence of trust within an organization can have equally damaging consequences.

Companies that trust their employees are more efficient than those that don't. They can decentralize and grant autonomy to different teams, akin to Haier's extreme approach. Of course, local culture plays an important role in how easily a company can implement a decentralized structure. An analysis of four thousand companies in twelve countries in Europe, North America, and Asia shows that companies in regions with high trust (controlling for many other factors) provide more decision-making rights to local managers. And they do so even if they expand globally. Trust levels vary significantly among countries, with wealthier nations that possess robust institutions like legal systems generally exhibiting higher trust levels. Additionally, historical events, such as civil wars and ethnic conflicts, can diminish trust levels, the distrust sometimes persisting for centuries. As Haier comes from a relatively low-trust country, the company is the exception that proves the rule.

Instilling trust can also create a virtuous cycle. Trust will be reciprocated with trustworthiness, which will reward being trusting in the first place. To examine this causal effect, my team and I conducted an experiment aimed at instilling trust. In a group task, we showed some teams an example of trustworthy behavior before the team worked. Instilling some trust into a team was enough to change behavior: controlling behavior reduced by 60 percent and earnings increased by 9 percent.

Does this mean we should blindly trust? Absolutely not. Fostering a corporate culture built on trust and autonomy means placing even greater importance on carefully selecting your employees, and then being crystal clear about the performance metrics and transparency in general. It is also crucial not only for managers to trust their team members, but also for employees to have trust in one another. Engaged autonomy and clear expectations are again crucial to create such a mutually trusting atmosphere.

Think about remote work and the temptation to use surveillance technology to monitor employees. The urge is rooted in a lack of trust of the manager. But the real problem might be a lack of clear performance metrics. It is obvious that organizations should only care about clearly defined output (what employees achieve) instead of inputs (how they get there). There is no need to track the number of keystrokes on the keyboard if the goal is clear. If an employee delivers the required results with fewer keystrokes and in less time (even if they are doing it in an unconventional way), managers should not care. Let's be honest: even if bosses see their employees in their chairs in the office, they do not know how engaged they are at work. If it is required to be in the chair for X hours a day, they will fill the time even if they could achieve the goal in less time. As long as employees have clear goals and performance (output) metrics, remote work can provide them with the flexibility and autonomy to achieve results in the best possible way. If you find yourself wanting to implement some of these surveillance techniques, ask yourself: Are my employees' performance measures clear?

Moreover, it is important to understand that remote workdays should not mirror in-person office days. The fundamental purpose of providing autonomy and remote work opportunities is to empower workers to engage in different tasks and approaches when working remotely. For example, more focus time at home that requires less coordination with others can provide individuals the autonomy to time and space out tasks in a way that fits their personality and circumstances. Surveillance systems are then not only a breach of trust but are completely missing the point of providing individual autonomy to allow for creativity, flexibility, and the fulfillment of the true potential of remote work.

New research conducted after the pandemic is trickling in showing the benefits of giving workers flexibility in where and when to work. One of those studies was conducted in an Italian company with a mix of blue- and white-collar workers. One randomly selected group of workers was allowed one day per week to decide where and when to work—giving them extreme flexibility about how to structure their day. Compared to a control group who had to come into the office five days a week during specific hours, the randomly selected group was more satisfied with both their job and their work-life balance. These workers could organize their remote day according to their own needs and personalities while the control group workers were constrained and had difficulty organizing their life outside work. For example, male workers increased their domestic work significantly when given more flexibility. As a result, the number of absentee days decreased for workers who got flexibility, an important metric for the company, and productivity in general increased. The result was so positive that the company introduced hybrid work company-wide. Different field studies have yielded positive outcomes when it comes to providing remote work flexibility. These studies have been conducted in various settings and industries, showcasing the benefits of flexible work arrangements, with some studies exploring scenarios where workers had flexibility on a substantial number of days per week.

Another study focused on engineers and marketing and finance employees at Trip.com, the third-largest global travel agent, after Expedia.com and Bookings.com, with headquarters in Shanghai, China. Hybrid work was highly valued by employees and reduced attrition by 33 percent and increased motivation significantly—without any negative impact on productivity. The results also showed that managers and nonmanagers evaluate hybrid work very differently. Managers expect negative productivity effects, are less likely to volunteer to work from home, and are more likely to quit when selected to work hybrid. The evidence in general shows that, when performance goals are clear, providing flexibility to workers on how to organize their day and their work is very powerful. Managers and leaders who are still skeptical should take notice.

Creating clear performance metrics goes hand in hand with trust. The same is true for selecting the right employees. As mentioned previously, companies such as Zappos.com or Southwest place great importance on carefully selecting their employees. This is a vital factor that enables them to grant significant autonomy and freedom to their call center staff. It may seem obvious, but it is worth noting that having trustworthy employees makes trust building easier; it's almost a tautological statement. On the other hand, if you find yourself lacking trust in your employees' ability to be productive and engaged without constant supervision, it suggests that you have an issue with either the selection process or the performance metrics in place.

Trust serves as the foundational element in cultivating an empowered and motivated workforce. However, it should not be viewed as a stand-alone solution. Clear performance targets, coupled with accountability and a rigorous selection process, are indispensable components. It remains crucial to establish output targets while fostering trust and selecting the right employees. This approach not only reinforces a leader's trust but also cultivates an environment where peers can trust one another. The allure of promoting autonomy through trust lies in its contagious nature. When leaders trust their employees and peers trust one another, it sets the stage for a virtuous cycle, further enhancing collaboration and success within the organization.

Ask yourself if you are providing the necessary support and guidance for autonomy to thrive within your organization. By assuming the role of an engaged coach, establishing transparent standards, and trusting your workforce, you can create a space where employees can excel and leverage their full potential.

Raise Their Voice

Many organizations are engaged in the annual ritual of conducting employee-engagement surveys. It usually goes like this: HR distributes a survey and encourages employees to participate. However, due to the prevailing belief that these surveys hold no significant influence, only a small number of employees actually fill them out. Their skepticism is often proven right, as little to no action or change occurs as a result of the survey findings. In a survey among three thousand HR professionals, around 60 percent of companies admitted that they basically ignore the results of employee surveys. Research supports the notion that the primary reason employees refrain from participating in annual surveys is their perception that the surveys will have no meaningful impact. If you asked someone whether it is a good idea to get customer feedback once a year only to ignore it, they would rightly tell you it is foolish to ignore a crucial stakeholder. But that is what many companies do with their employees.

A substantial part of providing autonomy and trust is to actively listen to employees. According to Laszlo Bock: "Voice means giving employees a real say in how the company is run. Either you believe people are good and you welcome their input, or you don't." A significant portion of employees wish to have a say in various matters. It's obvious that employees want to have a voice when it comes to their work. But the findings from a large 2017 survey offer more detail and context. Employees want to have a say in how they work, the conditions of their employment, the quality of the products or services they contribute to, and the values upheld by their organization. About half of the responders report having a "voice gap" and less input than they would like. It still seems that the prevailing view from managers is that they know best and that employees will have unrealistic demands. Why poke the bear by really involving employees? Bock warns managers that this is a mistake: "For many organizations this [providing voice] is terrifying, but it is the only way to live in adherence to your values."

There are many reasons why raising your employees' voices is beneficial. First, innovative ideas for new products, process improvements, or detecting and dealing with various forms of failure come from the bottom up within an organization. The andon cord only works if managers provide a safe space for employees to raise problems and employees' suggestions are taken seriously. Second, providing a place for employees to voice their problems can help to channel dissatisfaction. The renowned social scientist Albert Hirschman famously pointed out in 1970 that consumers and employees have two options if they are unsatisfied with a brand or company: they can either leave (exit) or they can express (voice) their dissatisfaction. If they do not have an option to voice, they will exit. Third, being heard is inherently valuable and affects job satisfaction. Studies consistently show that interventions that increase opportunities for workers' voices and participation increase worker well-being.

But how does listening to employees' voices affect outcomes for organizations and teams? A Chinese car manufacturing company examined the effects of providing employees with a voice on turnover rates, management practices, and key performance indicators (KPIs). It is worth noting that the automobile manufacturing industry holds significant importance in China and has emerged as one of the largest industries in the country. In fact, China surpassed the United States as the world's largest producer and consumer of cars in 2009. The company would assign seventy-six production teams (with 1,250 workers) randomly into two conditions: a voice condition and a control condition.

Workers who were provided voice could evaluate their managers in five areas: production organization, fairness, openness to suggestions, adaptability, and empathy. Over an eight-month period, those evaluations were publicly posted, and for the first six months, they influenced 20 percent of a manager's monthly evaluation score. This score is important for monthly bonuses, annual raises, and promotions. So workers in the voice condition were able to give regular feedback options with real consequences for managers. For many managers, this might sound terrifying, and as somebody who constantly gets evaluated by my students, I understand the anxiety. But the effect of providing a voice option was overwhelmingly positive for everybody. Workers' well-being increased, and the all-important concern—worker turnover—was reduced by more than 50 percent for workers with voice. The lower turnover rates not only reduced hiring and training costs but also increased consistency on teams, which improved team KPIs by 2.3 percent.

Managers were aware that turnover is a key barrier to firm growth. Before the intervention their top suggestions to solve the problem were to raise wages (favored by 52.8 percent of managers) or improve training (favored by 33 percent), but few expected that voice would help. In fact, only 8 percent thought this would be helpful to reduce turnover. This impression changed dramatically after the intervention. Managers in the voice condition were 37 percentage points more likely to state that worker feedback is a solution.

The results of this study had even more beneficial effects. For one, managers improved their treatment of workers. After the voice condition, workers reported that managers encouraged them more instead of criticizing them and observed that managers began socializing more with workers. Sounds like they became more engaged coaches. The improved management style was present even when feedback was not affecting the managers' scores. Without any observable downside, providing voice was positive for workers (who are happier and less likely to quit), for managers (who have better-performing teams), and for the company (who cares about the increased KPIs). After the company heard about the results of the experiment, they rolled the voice option out to all its twenty thousand employees. This is win-win and the employee advantage in action.

Jensen Huang, the cofounder and CEO of Nvidia, strongly advocates for granting autonomy to his employees and listening to each one of them—a philosophy that has shaped a flat organizational structure with a democratic culture greatly appreciated by the employees. As one Nvidia worker described it: "When you're in a meeting there is no hierarchy. It's a free flow of ideas from everybody." During a talk I helped organized at Columbia Business School, Huang highlighted his employee-centric approach and that "companies are all about people." His management approach has proven instrumental in achieving outstanding performance and pioneering innovations. Nvidia is one of the fastest-growing companies in the world, and Huang was not only voted to be one of *Time* magazine's one hundred most influential people in 2023 but also the world's best CEO by *Harvard Business Review* (in 2019) and Brand Finance (in 2023). Listening to employees and trusting them with autonomy works well.

How about more formal representation of workers on either boards or on work councils? The concept of granting workers formal representation has gained attention in discussions surrounding worker empowerment. These practices, known as codetermination laws, are prevalent in several European countries and have been proposed in US policy debates as a means to enhance worker voice. An examination of evidence from European studies reveals that board representation typically yields minimal or only slightly positive effects on working conditions and company performance. On the other hand, work councils, which involve workers in decision-making processes related to work design, have shown positive impacts on both job quality and productivity. Therefore, while board representation may have limited effects, involving workers in decision-making through work councils appears to be a promising approach to improve overall work conditions and enhance productivity. The evidence is also clear that codetermination only works if workers are given real authority and not just minimal representation. As such, the German work councils that have real power show stronger positive effects on job quality and company performance.

To capture the employee advantage, providing voice to employees is critically important. It goes hand in hand with engaged autonomy and trust. All of these options stem from the fundamental human motivation to have a voice in shaping how work is carried out. As Lazlo Bock points out: "If you believe people are fundamentally good, and if your organization is able to hire well, there is nothing to fear from giving your people freedom." He continues: "Give people slightly more trust, freedom, and authority than you are comfortable giving them. If you're not nervous, you haven't given them enough."

This represents a significant departure from the principles of (digital) Taylorism, emphasizing the importance of resisting excessive control and embracing bottom-up autonomy with engaged leaders acting as coaches. The other part of Taylorism is that tasks got repetitive and boring, which leads me to the next factor that motivates humans. I can best illustrate this motivator by talking about My Weird School.

CHAPTER 8

Just Right Tasks

J ANUARY 7, 2019, WAS A BIG day in my house: it was the first time my son bought a book. He was eight years old and hadn't been an avid reader. (To be perfectly honest, I wasn't either at his age. I was more into Legos.) He was passionate about soccer and basketball and cars, but it was a struggle to get him to read for thirty minutes each day. This became a source of a lot of mutual frustration for us. Then, out of nowhere on that particular day, he dragged me into a bookstore that he had previously avoided like the plague. As if this wasn't surprising enough, he then used some precious birthday money he'd saved up to buy not just one book but a boxed set of several books from a series. And these weren't graphic novels or books about soccer stars but legitimate chapter books with lots of words. The moment we got home, he immediately started reading.

It was remarkable—nobody forced him to read or shamed him into using his birthday money for books. It was as if, overnight, he just turned into a bibliophile. I soon learned what was going on. He'd learned about the series—called My Weird School—from a classmate and quickly became obsessed. He was so drawn into the world of these books that it took him only a couple of days to read twelve of them. We returned to that bookshop, and I was happy to supply him with more. So, in addition to my modest contributions to the royalty checks of Dan Gutman, the author of the My Weird School series, I would like to take this opportunity to personally thank him for writing something my son absolutely loved. His stories have not only unlocked his and countless other kids' love of reading, but they are also perfect examples of "just right" books, a concept that can tell us a lot about how motivation works for people of any age.

The idea behind "just right" books is that when kids learn to read, they need to have books that are "just right" for their reading skills at the moment. If the book is too easy, then it is a "baby book" (quoting my son here). If it is too sophisticated, it can frustrate kids who aren't yet able to understand the nuances. I learned this the hard way when my son wanted to read the Harry Potter books by himself before he was ready.

The most motivating level for reading is "just right." That's when kids are optimally challenged—the book is within their reading skills but challenging enough that it pushes them to stretch their abilities. Finishing books like this gives kids a sense of personal pride: they don't need a gold star to be motivated. And the best part is, there is always another "just right" book waiting for kids—or adults—when the old ones are no longer challenging them (or they read all the books!). So while I am thanking people, let me also acknowledge Stuart Gibbs, who wrote the series that my son read after he finished the My Weird School series. This was the bestselling Spy School series, and it represented the second time that my son would buy a book with his own money. The level of what is just right is constantly changing and rising.

Obviously, kids learn very differently from one another, and some enjoy reading books more than others. But being motivated by just right tasks is universal—and not just for kids. Motivational psychologists call this motivational factor competence, which refers to the inclination to derive satisfaction from our abilities and employ them to their fullest potential while striving for continual improvement in our pursuits. Feeling competent is a very human and powerful motivator. Alternatively, if our skills are not optimally used and constantly enhanced, we will experience boredom or frustration in our attempts to attain our objectives. And as with just right books, the level of demanded skills and challenges at work is constantly changing and rising.

Providing just right tasks at work and delivering appropriate recognition for achievements is crucially important for having an engaged, motivated, and productive workforce, and research shows that skill utilization is associated with higher job satisfaction and engagement. Engaging in an activity that one is good at is generally pleasant. But if the skill level of the task doesn't match that of the employee, they'll get frustrated or bored, which is associated with all kinds of bad outcomes, including elevated turnover rates, greater intentions to retire, and adverse health outcomes such as depression, increased stress, anxiety, and insomnia. This skills mismatch can mean the task isn't challenging enough for the employee, but it might also be too challenging. In 2022, Starbucks's baristas complained to Howard Schultz (when he briefly took over as CEO again that year) that they were not well trained and did not feel competent. The lack of training prevented the baristas from feeling good about their competence in the job. As a result, Schultz promised to double training to make sure Starbucks's employees felt competent in their jobs.

In general, companies have been doing a terrible job in creating just right tasks. A substantial portion of employees feel either that their skills are underutilized or that they do not have opportunities within the company to grow and develop. Surveys in the UK and Australia among representative samples of employees show that between 12 and 19 percent of workers report that their skills are "much higher" than needed in their present job. An additional 31 to 33 percent of employees report that they feel "moderately over-skilled." That is a lot of people whose skills are not optimally calibrated—and as a result, they don't feel competent. Indeed, workers who report being overskilled are not only reporting lower job satisfaction and engagement levels but are also more likely to leave the company. In fact, the number-one reason why employees leave a job is not the compensation but the lack of career and growth opportunities within a company. While their perception of what they find optimally challenging, that is, just right, has evolved, their current job and the opportunities they see within their company have not kept pace. In a survey by McKinsey of more than thirteen thousand employees in Australia, Canada, India, Singapore, the UK, and the United States, more than 40 percent stated a lack of growth opportunities as the number-one reason they quit their job.

In LinkedIn's 2023 Workplace Learning Report, around a third of responders reported that "opportunities to learn and develop new skills" is the most important factor when they are considering a new job opportunity. Companies should take this very seriously when designing development and retention strategies. At the moment, many of them aren't because only 26 percent report that "their organization challenged them to learn a new skill"—despite the fact that employees want to learn and feel good about their new skills. Marc Cenedella, founder and CEO of the career platform The Ladders, remarked in an interview with Business Insider that "if you haven't picked up a new skill, viewpoint, or way of doing things in the past six months, it could be a sign that it's time to go." Indeed, many employees are not happy with learning and development at their companies and/or their growth opportunities and leave. In a study quoted in the *Harvard Business Review*, 75 percent of fifteen hundred managers surveyed from across fifty organizations were dissatisfied with their company's learning and development (L&D) function, 70 percent of employees in the same study reported that they hadn't mastered the skills needed to do their jobs, and only 12 percent of employees had applied new skills learned in L&D programs to their jobs. Not surprisingly, employees are leaving, and retention has become a substantial problem.

The analogy with just right books provides three key insights for corporate learning and development. First, everyone, not just kids, can struggle with motivation. If people are not feeling challenged and provided with the right opportunities, they will become disengaged at work. Second, everybody is different in their skill level, their interest, and their ambition. A one-size-fits-all approach does not work for kids or for employees. And third, due to rapid technological change, learned skills are getting obsolete faster and new skills are more frequently required. Just right books become baby books faster than ever before.

Ask yourself if your organization offers tasks that are tailored to each individual's just right level of challenge. Since these tasks are highly individual and subject to change, it's crucial to establish a mechanism for personalization and ongoing updates. This can be achieved through individual skills plans that are regularly reviewed and updated.

To address those three insights and provide just right tasks, companies need to rethink their approach to providing opportunities in an employee-centric way. This will give power to the employee. While not every leader will feel comfortable ceding this to his or her employees, it is the only way to the employee advantage.

The Grass Is Greener in Your Own Backyard

Who would have thought that making ventilators could help in developing an all-electric HUMMER—and in the process create exciting opportunities for workers *within* the same company? But that is what happened at General Motors (GM). It all started with the desperate need for more ventilators in the first year of the COVID-19 pandemic. Before vaccines were developed, access to ventilators was often the deciding factor between life and death at overwhelmed hospitals, and there were not enough of them. The companies who could build them could not scale up fast enough. Ventec Life, a Seattle-based company, is one of those specialized companies that produces these complicated machines. Ventec Life produces around two hundred to three hundred ventilators a month—even at full capacity. That is not enough in a pandemic when tens of thousands of ventilators are needed.

In the early months of the pandemic, Mary Barra, CEO of GM, thought that maybe she could help out and initiated a conversation with the team at Ventec Life. The car maker knew a thing or two about production at scale and how to deal with supply chains. But cars are pretty different from ventilators, and the goal of ten thousand ventilators per month was extremely ambitious—after all, you cannot simply put ventilators on a car assembly line. Nevertheless, Barra believed that across the large 167,000 employee company, there were people with the skills to solve this difficult problem. The pivot was definitely no easy feat and required training hundreds of employees, figuring out supply chain challenges, and doing all this while following strict manufacturing guidelines for medical equipment that differ markedly from cars. Oh, and all of this within a couple of weeks.

GM needed to organize differently to achieve its goal. There is no ventilator division (and never will be), and nobody was hired as an expert in ventilator production. Project V, the code name for a venture to convert a GM plant in Kokomo, Indiana, into a ventilator plant, relied on the expertise of volunteers from across the entire organization. It created an internal talent marketplace where employees were not only invited but encouraged to apply for the opportunity to work on the project. By leveraging this approach, GM was able to identify qualified and enthusiastic individuals within the organization to work on ventilator production at an accelerated pace. Marcelo Conti, a director of purchasing, was part of the team. He later pointed out how access to this diverse range of skills and the experience of working in a highly competitive industry were all factors that helped GM "leverage our engineering, manufacturing, supply management and program management expertise (to cite a few) to do things better, faster, at lower costs. It also pushe[d] us to 'think on our feet.'" For GM, job titles or the reason people were originally hired or what team they belonged to or what they were doing before did not matter. What mattered was whether they had the skills and ambition to pull Project V off the ground at speed.

Blake Rollins, a GM worker for thirty years, is the facilities manager for the Kokomo plant. He stepped up and oversaw all the steps of the ventilator production. In an interview with CNN, he noted that his job now "is completely different from what [he] had been doing before." Across the whole organization, employees would get involved in this endeavor— and find it very engaging and interesting because they could use their skills to help people. Debbie Hollis had worked at GM for twenty-five years making circuit boards. She volunteered to be involved in Project V—and absolutely loved it. Making car parts is extremely different from assembling a ventilator. "It's more assembly than I've ever done," said

Hollis. "There are a lot more tools and screws than we usually use. It's been pretty intense, but interesting."

In just 154 days, GM would produce thirty thousand ventilators—that is one ventilator every seven minutes. Though President Trump complained on Twitter about the speed of production ("as usual with 'this' General Motors, things just never seem to work out. […] Always a mess with Mary B"), it was actually an astonishing result for a car company that has often been accused of being too slow because of its unionized workforce to switch so quickly to produce a new product at a massive scale. So, Mary Barra ("Mary B") is right to be proud and commented that "the willingness of employees to contribute has been inspiring."

Project V had two long-lasting effects on GM that illustrate the upside of providing opportunities within the company. First, a project like Project V, or any other engagement that allows employees to use their skills in a new way, can be engaging and thrilling. In a study with seventeen hundred engineers across many companies, being "intellectually challenged" and having "independence" were not only the most important job attributes (before salary), but they also led to more innovation if the workers were indeed challenged. Giving employees new and interesting opportunities sparks engagement. Humans want to use and develop their skills, and the opportunity to work on a project like Project V was extremely motivating. Barra observed: "When you engage your team and then set them free to do what they can do, they can accomplish amazing things." Other companies—such as Unilever, Mastercard, or Seagate in the private sector or the army or NASA among government organizations—have provided similar experiences by formally creating internal talent marketplaces. These internal talent marketplaces are dynamic digital platforms, much like an internal job board on steroids, where employees can showcase their skills and career aspirations and managers can post short-term projects, temporary roles, or even permanent positions. As a result of such engagement, employees are not leaving for other companies. For example, Seagate Technology, a Silicon

Valley firm that provides data storage, avoided the Great Resignation by harnessing the power of an internal talent marketplace to give their employees full transparency into all of the available jobs inside the company and to take career development into their own hands. Patricia Frost, CHRO at Seagate, explains that through "career discovery," the internal name for its marketplace, employees are able to gain access to vertical and lateral movement within their organization. Employees are encouraged to find their just right tasks within the firm and as a result are staying to work for Seagate.

One would imagine that companies already provide plenty of internal opportunities, but they do not. In fact, several companies have clear guidelines that prohibit internal transfers for a period of one to three years. Even when the restriction is lifted or in the absence of such a policy, a significant obstacle remains: the incentives of the managers. They do not want their best team members to leave their team. Evidence for this—what is called "talent hoarding"—is substantial. In Germany, for example, 83 percent of the top publicly traded companies report that manager talent hoarding is a major problem internally. A large and insightful study in 2023 provided further evidence of widespread talent hoarding in one of the largest manufacturing companies in Germany, which employs around two hundred thousand employees in Germany and across the globe.

In a survey of around thirty thousand of the company's employees, many responded that management's limited support for career progression was one of the main challenges to their development in the company. One employee responded: "Career development is not supported by direct supervisors, instead it is actively blocked with the goal of keeping people in their current position." Forty-one percent reported that they are afraid to apply to positions internally because they fear retaliation if their manager finds out about the application. Researchers have estimated that if internal opportunities existed, employees would apply to those instead of looking beyond the company, to the tune of 123 percent more internal applications.

Internal talent marketplaces can help provide ample opportunities and just right tasks for employees. But at the minimum, employee-centric companies need to provide active career advice to their employees. Every job in an organization should have a clearly defined and communicated career plan, so that employees know exactly what job performance metrics and skills are required to qualify for the next opportunity within the company. Such a career plan is extremely important for all levels in the organization. Sixty-two percent of front-line workers indicate that they would stay at the current employer if provided with a prospect of upward mobility. Costco clearly communicates such career paths for all employees and helps workers reach those goals. It does this by cross-training their employees so that they are not just doing simple and standardized tasks, such as shelving, but are also getting other opportunities. Costco even has an internal rule that 86 percent of positions need to be internally filled, but "in truth, it turns out to be 98 percent," according to its founder and former CEO, James Sinegal.

Another benefit of implementing an internal talent marketplace, as exemplified by GM's approach to ramping up ventilator production, is that it can provide advantages to the company beyond simply engaging and retaining workers. And here is where the EV HUMMER comes into play. For innovative projects that need to move at speed, organizations need employees with the potential for acquiring skills they don't have yet or for which they were not hired. The traditional way of organizing the workforce based on existing roles and skills, by keeping a record of what workers already know in some centralized database, does not capture their potential.

Creating internal talent marketplaces helps companies get the talent they need using the people they already have. Workers are empowered to assess their own skills and aspirations, and then offer them to address the specific needs communicated by the company. Companies become more agile as a result and use their skilled employees in the just right way. For Mary Barra, "doing the ventilator project was kind of a game changer from a General Motors perspective, from a culture-change perspective." And she continues: "One of the most important lessons that I've taken away from the pandemic is the limitless potential of our people when we set them free and remove barriers and bureaucracy. Projects that used to take weeks were completed in days." The experience during the ventilator project changed the company and was most importantly implemented in their ambitious goal of being all-electric by 2035. The first success is their HUMMER EV. When the model was revealed, Barra tweeted: "The new chapter in the #GMCHummerEV story brings us one step closer to an all-electric future. I am so proud of the team that continues working at 'ventilator speed' to achieve our ambitious goals."

In light of all this, employers should look at their organizations and ask themselves: Are we providing clear growth opportunities for all employees on every level? Providing exciting opportunities for existing employees, either through internal marketplaces or clear career paths, benefits everyone: employees can find their just right tasks and will not leave, and companies benefit with greater innovation and agility. As with most employee-centric changes, offering growth opportunities gives employees more autonomy and requires a mind-set shift among leaders. But offering opportunities is not enough on its own. Employers must also provide learning and development.

Empower Employees' Own Growth

"Train people well enough so they can leave, treat them well enough so they don't want to." The famous quote by serial entrepreneur Richard Branson, the founder of everything Virgin (such as Virgin Atlantic, Virgin Active, or Virgin Galactic), hints at what employee-centric corporate learning and development should look like. The quote has two parts, which are both important for future-oriented and employee-centric learning.

The first is about providing training and teaching skills that are valuable even outside an organization. Very few companies are in doubt about the importance of learning and development (L&D). Most large organizations have L&D functions and programs, and their leaders are committed to investing large sums into their workforce's learning. There are probably hundreds of books talking about corporate learning, and it seems that there are even more learning consultants. The speed of innovation and the need for new skills makes the need for L&D even more critical. The World Economic Forum calls this a "reskill revolution," in which more than one billion people will need reskilling in the next decade. To meet the challenge, leaders need to be willing to empower their employees' learning journey and adopt an employee-centric way of training. The approach moves away from job-based to skill-based learning and puts employees in the center. It requires finding the just right level of learning and opportunities, which are different for every employee.

In 2016, Unilever was completely rethinking how to develop its workforce given the trends of technological advancement and longer lives— which mean longer careers. "No organizations can offer jobs for life anymore," according to its learning and innovation director Nicola Braden. "But we can offer skills for life." This realization and insights from the science of learning lead to one of three pillars in Unilever's future of work strategy: "Ignite Lifelong Learning and Critical Skills."

The core of its strategy is about empowering employees to find their own journey. We already talked about Unilever's purpose workshops. The goal of those workshops went beyond helping employees find their purpose and meaning in life. The workshop should inform an employee's individual development plan. That means that employees get clarity about their next potential role and what skills are needed to reach it. Unilever actively works together with employees to develop personalized plans, a "future fit plan." The process is an explicit collaboration between workers and the company in which employees are empowered to make choices about their journey, and Unilever provides data on what skills are required for the next role. Employees can then choose from a menu of different options to reskill and upskill. Those can be more traditional learning modules, but also include mentoring options or flex assignments that provide workers with experiences that let them learn new skills, all tailored to the employee's individual future fit plan—and driven by their initiatives.

Unilever is taking a proactive approach in empowering its employees by shifting the focus from job-based training to skill-based learning. Recognizing the rapidly evolving nature of the business landscape and the changing nature of jobs and roles, the company understands the importance of equipping its workforce with versatile skills that can adapt to changing demands. By emphasizing skill-based learning, Unilever and other companies encourage employees to cultivate a broad range of capabilities that transcend specific roles, enabling them to navigate various tasks and challenges effectively. This forward-thinking approach not only promotes professional growth and development but also fosters a culture of continuous learning, innovation, and adaptability within the organization and recognizes the changing nature of work.

And Unilever goes a step further "to train them so that they can leave" by partnering with Degreed, a learning platform. The platform provides endless learning options but also gives the employees agency in their learning journeys. And everybody in the organization has access. According to Nicola Braden, director of Unilever's Global Learning Innovation team: "We wanted to move away from seeing learning as just a reward for people who reached a new work level. We wanted to empower the learners to take charge of their own learning, with some guidance from the business of course. Numbers now show that more people do more training more frequently." The Degreed certifications allow employees to take their skills anywhere. "So, even if you leave Unilever," Braden said, "the learning record belongs to you. You can take your credentials with you wherever you go next."

To foster the employee advantage requires shifting away from seeing training as an investment in firm-specific capital, that is, skills that are only valuable for the specific company and that will, the old thinking goes, tie employees to the company and make it more likely they will stay. Instead, the knowledge and learned skills taught should be more general and transferable to other settings and organizations. These are skills that are valuable to both the organization and its employee, and because employees are given opportunities to grow on their own terms, they do not leave. According to Unilever's assessment, employees who have access to lifelong learning and upskilling opportunities are 35 percent less likely to leave the company, which leads to a potential savings of 6.6 million euros for every seven hundred employees trained.

Independent of the size of the company, empowering employees' growth journey is critical to creating the employee advantage. Unilever is large enough to create its own enormous program. Smaller companies also need to support their employees' growth opportunities by working with learning partners. If an organization does not empower its employees, they will leave.

But what if not everybody wants to learn and grow? It's absolutely essential to make learning part of your culture.

Learn to Learn

When Satya Nadella took the helm at Microsoft, the software giant was still generating insane amounts of revenue selling its operating system and office suite. But there was a sense that the company had stagnated and was no longer as innovative as it had once been. It was also falling behind its multiple competitors, most prominently in the rapidly evolving mobile device market, which includes smartphones and tablets, along with associated services and technologies. Over the years, Nadella determined that the culture of Microsoft had become very bureaucratic and not particularly open to learning. "Our culture had been rigid," he later wrote. "Each employee had to prove to everyone that he or she knew it all and was the smartest person in the room." This cut-throat culture was not supportive of learning, and Nadella knew that this would ultimately stifle innovation. So he decided to "hit refresh" (also the title of his book) and instill a culture focused on learning. This decision would ultimately reinvent Microsoft with a new emphasis on its cloud computing and gaming businesses and its industry-leading work on artificial intelligence. The latter focus would lead, for example, to the much-praised early investment in OpenAI, the company behind ChatGPT.

Satya Nadella was an unconventional choice to lead a cultural transformation at Microsoft. He had spent his entire career within the traditional framework of the company's operations. However, outside work, Nadella had had an experience that taught him the value and necessity of constant learning. It began when he and his wife, Anu Nadella, had their first child, Zain. Their son was born with a severe disability. "After Zain, things started to change for me," Nadella wrote. "It has had a profound impact on how I think, lead and relate to people." Two daughters followed, and it was soon clear that one of them had some learning difficulties that the local schools could not deal with properly. These unexpected challenges forced the Nadellas to confront the limits of their knowledge and embrace the unfamiliar.

It was during this time of personal transformation that Anu Nadella introduced her husband to Carol Dweck's book *Growth Mindset.* The book's teachings resonated deeply with him, as it emphasized the power of adopting a growth mind-set—believing in the capacity to learn and grow throughout life. This mind-set shift became a guiding principle for Nadella, both personally and professionally.

Armed with his newfound understanding, Nadella set out to reshape Microsoft's culture. He recognized that a rigid, know-it-all mentality stifled innovation and limited the company's ability to adapt to new technologies and market demands. Nadella's vision was to foster a learning culture—one where employees would embrace continuous learning, collaboration, and the courage to embrace change.

Under Nadella's leadership, Microsoft began a remarkable transformation. The company started embracing openness, promoting cross-team collaboration and encouraging employees to take risks and learn from failure. Learning initiatives were implemented across the organization, providing employees with opportunities to develop new skills, explore emerging technologies, and stay ahead of industry trends. Nadella told his employees at a conference: "We can have all the bold ambitions. We can have all the bold goals. We can aspire to our new mission. But it's only going to happen if we live our culture, if we teach our culture. And to me that model of culture is not a static thing. It is about a dynamic learning culture. In fact, the phrase we use to describe our emerging culture is 'growth mindset,' because it's about every individual, every one of us having that attitude—that mindset—of being able to overcome any constraint, stand up to any challenge, making it possible for us to grow and, thereby, for the company to grow." And he emphasized that "I was not talking bottom-line growth. I was talking about our individual growth. We will grow as a company if everyone, individually, grows in their roles and in their lives."

The transformation of Microsoft's culture wasn't an easy feat, but Nadella's unwavering commitment to fostering a growth mind-set helped drive the change. He also led by example, showing how he, the CEO, was also constantly learning from mistakes. This was exemplified by his handling of an awkward moment at a women's tech event in 2014 (the Grace Hopper Conference), when he was asked what advice he would give women who are not comfortable asking for a pay raise. His initial, tone-deaf answer—that women need to trust "karma" if they are not getting a raise—was not helped when he continued "that might be one of the initial 'super powers,' that quite frankly, women who don't ask for a raise have." So he means that women should not ask for a raise and all will be good eventually?

You can imagine the backlash from this comment. Some CEOs might have doubled down or laughed it off, but Nadella quickly sent a memo of apology to all his employees and took it as a learning opportunity. The memo ended: "I said I was looking forward to the Grace Hopper Conference to learn, and I certainly learned a valuable lesson." By changing the culture from a "know-it-all to a learn-it-all culture" (as he says), Microsoft unleashed the potential of its employees, spurring innovation and enabling the company to stay competitive in a rapidly evolving tech landscape. Microsoft became cool again.

In times of constant and uncertain change in which the half-life of knowledge and skills is getting shorter and shorter, it is important to instill a learning culture. That means encouraging people to ask critical questions, be curious, and never give up on learning. More often than not, it is the organization that is stifling learning and growth. In a fixed mind-set environment in which everybody is expected to know already, learning is suppressed as employees are not allowed to struggle or to fail. "The fixed mindset doesn't allow people the luxury of becoming. They have to already be."

Creating a learning culture that fosters curiosity and continuous learning requires leaders to prioritize learning as a top organizational goal. In addition to investing in employees' learning and development, they must serve as role models by investing time and effort into their own development, demonstrating that leaders are learners too. This shift challenges the traditional notion of a leader as the know-it-all figure. Leaders who, instead, model learning behavior have a profound impact on shaping the culture. Recognizing that no one has all the answers, leaders who embrace a learning mind-set empower their teams to embrace the same attitude. Learning how to learn becomes a fundamental skill that holds increasing importance in today's rapidly evolving world. Companies that understand the significance of this skill and actively encourage their employees to develop and leverage it will gain an employee advantage. By embracing learning as a shared value, these organizations create a competitive advantage that fuels growth and innovation.

Trophies and Gold Stars

To ensure that a just right task is motivating, it is crucial to create opportunities to acknowledge and celebrate exceptional performances. Using awards can be an effective means to attain this objective as it can boost productivity and lower employee turnover. Think about editors on Wikipedia, our modern-day Encyclopedia Britannica. Wikipedia relies entirely on volunteer editors, which they call Wikipedians, who check and correct entries and write their own content for articles. Talk about motivation beyond a paycheck! While Wikipedians are not officially employed by Wikipedia and thus not on its payroll, they undeniably constitute a vital part of its workforce, and their engagement is crucial for Wikipedia's success. Even though those volunteers are motivated by the mission of Wikipedia and find their tasks just right and motivating, retention of editors is still a challenge for the company. Many newcomer editors do not remain active over a long period of time. Can awards help keep them motivated?

Research in collaboration with Wikipedia tested the effect of a purely symbolic award. Because it was on the Wikipedia site in Switzerland, the name of the award had a Swiss touch: "Edelweiss with a Star." To make certain the award was seen as a legitimate honor, it was designed in collaboration with researchers and a group of senior Wikipedians. At regular intervals, a set of around four thousand newcomer Wikipedians would receive an Edelweiss with a Star as an appreciation. The editors had the choice of whether to showcase their award on their personal user page. This purely symbolic award had a substantial impact on motivation: the group who received an award was 20 percent more likely to be active the following months, and the share of editors who directly contributed content to articles increased by 13 percent. Even better, one could still observe the positive effect of the Edelweiss award a year after the virtual giving of the award. A very impressive impact of an award that is purely symbolic.

If you have ever gotten an award or recognition that you cared about, you know how this can feel. I am personally very proud of the teaching award I received for my consistently good instruction in our mandatory strategy class for our incoming MBA students. There is no direct material value attached to it, but even years later, it still makes me proud. Another example: after my research was cited in the *Economic Report of the President*, I received, in the spring of 2023, a personally addressed email from the Executive Office of the President of the United States congratulating me. The report discussed my article on the meaning of work, which formed the foundation for this book. It was not even an award but just a standard message that many of my cited colleagues at other universities received as well. But the acknowledgment made me proud of my work. I felt I was making a difference with my research, and the acknowledgment reminded me that I am in the right profession. My job is "just right."

Not surprisingly, awards are one of the nonmonetary ways of rewarding employees most frequently used by organizations, and employee-centric companies are leading the way. Truck driver Danny Guerro Jr. received one such award at H-E-B, the Texas grocer with the cult following. His accomplishment: driving four million consecutive miles without an accident. This was something only one other truck driver at H-E-B had achieved before him. The event honoring his amazing achievement was celebrated appropriately with his family and members of H-E-B's executive team. Guerro received four gold stars, which he can wear proudly on his shoulder. Carson Landsgard, H-E-B executive vice president of manufacturing, supply chain and logistics, who attended the celebration said: "We're super proud of all our drivers. We truly have the best team in all the industry. But it takes individuals like Danny to take the bar and set it high. In certain professions there are individuals who are superstars, who you admire and respect for doing the impossible. Danny gets to be in that elite status today." Guerro was already a member of the truck driver hall of fame at H-E-B. Every year, at the annual celebration, drivers who achieved one million safety miles would be honored to be part of it. It is a very important honor to be part of the hall of fame for the drivers. That is just one way, H-E-B acknowledges its workers' achievements and celebrates them.

But you have to make sure the awards mean something. My son, for instance, did not even want to take the "trophy for participation" he received at his soccer camp back home with him. For him, this trophy was code for "everybody who got this did not get more meaningful awards." Research supports that awards sometimes do not work or even backfire. And there is no one-size-fits-all solution for how companies can implement effective awards programs. Many companies do get it wrong because they either think about awards as a cheap form of incentives or are not designing them with a human-centric mind-set. Fortunately, research in behavioral science provides guidance on how to use "trophies and gold stars" in an employee-centric way.

Let's start with the question: What behavior is worthy of celebration? Awards and recognition should not be awarded for something that is easy to achieve. Employees need to be rewarded with an award for a skill or performance that is exceptional. The recognition that comes with the award should allow one to feel proud and provide an opportunity to show off to others. However, there are too many awards that are about relatively easy tasks. For example, awards for attendance are often used in companies or in other settings such as schools. Shouldn't we expect near-perfect attendance, anyway? The evidence about the effect of attendance awards is therefore mixed at best. A number of studies show that they actually backfire. Especially for employees who already have near-perfect attendance, the awards show that either the company does not expect perfect attendance and/or it suggests that absenteeism is more common than the employees with perfect attendance thought.

It is understandable that many awards are about easy-to-measure behavior such as attendance. But though attendance awards are very objective and easy to implement, they often exactly miss the point of what awards should do compared to other types of incentives. Keep in mind that awards should be used to heighten the feeling of competence through recognizing skills in just right tasks.

Awards cannot and should not replace monetary compensation, but they can serve as a supplement. Certain actions, such as achieving sales targets, are easily quantifiable and should be financially rewarded. However, other actions are more complex and harder to measure, and this is where awards can be effective in acknowledging them. The selection process for awardees of such hard-to-measure skills often involves a degree of subjectivity, but as long as it is considered fair, it is acceptable and the only way to celebrate an amazing performance. Prestigious awards like the Nobel Prize or manager of the year are typically granted for exceptional achievements that are difficult to measure. So ask yourself whether you have a comprehensive system of incentives, from monetary bonuses to nonmonetary rewards, such as trophies and gold stars. Think about whether there are some exceptional employees or skills in your company that should be rewarded but aren't.

It's important for companies to exercise caution when assigning a monetary worth to awards. For instance, combining symbolic rewards like trophies and gold stars with tangible rewards such as gift cards can be risky because it can create the impression that the company is trying to substitute the award for a bonus, which can be perceived as cheap. Additionally, offering a monetary incentive alongside a public recognition can actually decrease the value of the award as a form of signaling. If employees are recognized for being amazing corporate citizens by helping others, giving an award with money attached makes it less clear whether the employee actually is doing good or is just behaving in a certain way to do well. This is how these recognitions can backfire.

The final and most crucial factor to consider is that awards must be accompanied by genuine praise, recognition, and a personal touch. When managers and peers take time out of their busy schedules to participate in an award ceremony, they signal that the recognition is genuine and the awardee's performance is exceptional. The purpose of presenting trophies and gold stars is to acknowledge outstanding performance and encourage the ideal level of just right effort. This entails a genuine investment from the organization and its managers in valuing and celebrating the awards. While the monetary value of the awards may be low, the attention and recognition they convey should be perceived as invaluable. As a leader, you demonstrate recognition by allocating one of the most valuable resources: your time. Investing time in acknowledging and spending time with your team members can be profoundly motivating. Carve out time in your calendar to recognize your team members on a regular basis.

Ultimately, a simple recognition and acknowledgment from managers and peers is valuable and motivating. In surveys of around sixteen thousand professionals in more than four thousand companies, 85 percent would actually prefer a thank-you over a celebration or gift for day-to-day accomplishments. One responder answered: "Sometimes a simple 'thank you' and acknowledgement of effort and results achieved is enough—never underestimate the power of 'thank you.'" Well, unfortunately, research also shows that many actually underestimate the power of a thank-you and recognition. Once you get the thank-you culture going in your team, you can think about regular events. But while it is a good idea to award trophies and gold stars with some regularity, companies and teams need to think carefully about the frequency. A yearly event, like H-E-B's annual award ceremony for its truck driver hall of fame, can become something that everybody looks forward to within the firm. But an employee of the month or week, though it sounds like a good idea, may present problems if you run out of employees worthy of the award. If employees sense you are just circling through people, the award will soon lose its relevance and any potential to motivate.

The employee advantage can be achieved by focusing on providing and celebrating just right tasks. This requires a shift to empowering employees to be in charge of their career journey and learning. In the end, it will lead to engaged employees who will be motivated to grow. And as a result, there will be many instances to celebrate successes—for both employees and organizations.

CHAPTER 9

Working Together Works

O N MY EIGHTEENTH BIRTHDAY, I received a summons for military service. Every Swiss male receives this summons (for females it is optional). The Swiss government requires recruits to attend basic training sometime within the next six years. The requirements for basic training have evolved over time, but currently, it spans eighteen weeks, followed by six three-week refresher courses, spread out over the next nine years. I opted to go to basic training (seventeen weeks at that time) when I was twenty-one, and while I learned all the fundamental skills, like marching and using a gun, I specialized as a paramedic working in military hospitals. After basic training, I had to return to an army base every other year, for a couple of weeks at a time, to take refresher courses. To be perfectly honest, I was not crazy about the whole experience, but while doing one of the refresher courses on a large training site, I observed firsthand the power—and dark side—of organizational identity. This lesson would later inform one of my research studies.

At the time I was serving in a military hospital on a site that provided basic training to two of the Swiss army's elite branches, the Grenadier and Reconnaissance Forces. Both of these branches are very selective, accepting only the most dedicated and physically fit Swiss. While I worked through my shifts, I would observe how these two branches created strong identities through rituals such as songs and strong bonding experiences. Many of their tasks were physical in nature and occasionally led to injuries and accidents, which brought these people to the hospital I worked at.

It is well known that group identity and bonding are critically important to motivate soldiers to risk their lives. After all, they are preparing to defend their home country. (Yes, even the Swiss, who have not been involved in any active combat since 1847, must be prepared to defend themselves from aggressors.) A strong sense of identity and a feeling of belonging are essential if an organization wants to motivate its members to do extraordinary things.

At some point during my posting, I noticed something curious: the leaders of the training site would never allow members of the two branches to have their free evenings at the same time. When I asked why, I was told that if members of these two groups encountered one another in local bars, they would often get into fights.

This seemed strange. They were all training hard to fight for the same thing: their country. Why would they so frequently fight with each other? This seemed counterproductive to the ultimate goal of the Swiss army, which is to defend Switzerland. It turns out this is unremarkable in military organizations. My MBA students who have served in the US armed forces are unsurprised when I tell this story. In fact, they are all too ready to describe the ways in which other branches are different (or inferior) to the one they served in.

In 2005, I decided to investigate what makes those patterns of behavior more or less extreme. With my coauthors, I worked with the Swiss army to explore those patterns in an officer training program. For the study, the officers were randomly assigned to different learning groups, with which they would study, exercise, and accomplish other tasks together. The purpose was to break the bigger group into smaller ones (think breakout groups). The groupings were completely random and not based on the officers' background or their branch of service. We had the officers participate in various activities and games that mimicked two crucial aspects of group interactions: team collaboration (how much individuals are willing to cooperate with one another) and enforcement of group norms (the way individuals uphold implicit expectations for group behavior).

The most important aspect of the functioning of groups is how much individuals are willing to cooperate with one another. All organizations or communities in general rely on people voluntarily contributing to the common cause by doing things like helping organize community events, contributing to a culture of sharing information, or providing constructive feedback to others' work. Trash day in Switzerland (and probably in many other countries) can illustrate the importance (and problem) with cooperation. If trash is collected on Thursday, nobody should put their trash on the streets on any other day. This behavioral norm keeps the neighborhood looking nice and prevents problems like attracting raccoons and rats. It is, however, a little cumbersome to keep the trash in the house for a week and remember to take it out on the correct day. Doing this requires individuals to put the common good above their private benefit and cost.

In general, humans are surprisingly compliant when it comes to cooperating: research shows that most individuals will not take advantage of others, even if they could do so anonymously, but will contribute their share to the common good, at least initially. Problems arise when a few individuals become free riders. These people think to themselves: "If I put out just my one garbage bag a few days early, that won't create a problem, will it?" And this might be true, especially if everybody else adheres to the norm. But as more and more people free ride, the critical common good in a community or organization is compromised.

This leads to the second important aspect of group interactions: individuals' willingness to enforce group norms to prevent free riding. The Swiss are masters in this. If somebody puts out the trash on a nontrash day, their neighbors will let them know that this is not right. Somebody has to be willing to take on the burden (and the possibility of an unpleasant argument) of enforcing the behavioral norm. Research around the globe shows that for organizations and communities to function, it is crucial that peers take on the burden of letting others know when they are not contributing to the common good. Research confirms that the Swiss are very good at such norm enforcement. When observing obvious littering, for example, they react and let the violator know. (Much more so than New Yorkers—my casual observation in both places confirms the rigorous research.) Effective enforcement also requires that only those who are not playing nice are targeted. Shaming becomes ineffective when it indiscriminately targets even those who comply with the established norms. Unfortunately, it is too often the case that these two conditions are not met. Even among Swiss army officers—as we will later see.

But first, the positive results of our study. We found that having a group identity, even if that identity is the result of a randomly formed group, increases cooperation among team members. They are more willing to help and trust their members. And when it comes to enforcing a norm of being cooperative, group members will protect other group members. If one of them is treated badly, others in the group will step up and "punish" the individual who behaved selfishly toward their team member. So while the officer training we observed was not even trying to create strong group bonding, the mere fact that candidates were put into groups was enough to create a group identity. Add into the mix common rituals, group building exercises, and strong organizational culture, such as I observed in the two elite branches in the Swiss army, and the effect is even stronger on cohesion, group identity, cooperation, and norm enforcement.

It is a very human tendency to help other humans in a group that we identify with. It is a critical aspect of why people help others in organizations. (And, as we will see later, it can also be the source of trouble.) In general, interpersonal interactions play a vital role in the engagement and effectiveness of organizations, as humans are inherently social beings. Remarkably, humans have the capacity to extend their assistance and support to individuals who are not genetically related to them under favorable circumstances. Recognizing and comprehending these interactions within an organizational context is of paramount importance as it allows for leveraging them to create the employee advantage. Embracing and harnessing the power of social connections and group identity within an organization can lead to enhanced collaboration, motivation, and overall success.

Evidence about the drawbacks of remote work shows how much employees need other employees. The move to remote work during the pandemic, which suddenly took people from shared office spaces to improvised work stations in their living rooms or bedrooms, also led to widespread feelings of isolation. This was especially true for employees who lived alone. Most humans do not do well in isolation. There is a reason, after all, why solitary confinement is considered an extreme punishment. Many argue that remote work was one of the main contributors to the dramatic increase in mental health issues that emerged after the pandemic. Arthur Brooks of Harvard University calls it the "Hidden Toll of Remote Work."

When asked about the most important benefits of coming to the office, around 50 percent of employees mention face-to-face collaborations and 50 percent put socializing into the top three reasons. The downsides of remote work don't necessarily imply that leaders should strip employees of their autonomy, but they should still offer flexibility and independence. However, it's important to note that the primary advantage of the office is the opportunity for social interactions. When employees can freely choose which three days to come into the office, they tend to coordinate to be in at the same time. There is for sure nothing more depressing than a half-empty office. And, on the other side, a buzzing workplace creates energy.

Professor Alex "Sandy" Pentland from MIT's Media Lab and his team examined workplace connections using smart badges capable of tracking individuals' whereabouts and interactions. They show that people who interact more with others at work report higher job satisfaction and are more productive. That is even true if the employees are not chatting about work issues but, for example, sports or their life outside work. From his research, Pentland has concluded that "we are part of a social fabric, and our basic human nature is to pay attention to other people and to share mood and attitudes. That's really the core of who humans are."

In another study at a call center for Bank of America, Pentland and his team were able to convince the bank to change its workers' break schedules. The bank had previously used staggered breaks for their call center employees to make sure that there was continuous coverage. This neglected the benefit of interpersonal interactions. Based on the researcher team's recommendation, the bank began to make sure that all employees in one of their call centers took their coffee break at the same time. This small change unlocked the power of working together: employee satisfaction increased 10 percent and average handling time (the gold standard for call center efficiency) increased 8 percent on average and 20 percent for lower-performing teams. It was such a success that the bank decided to roll it out to all ten of its call centers (which employed twenty-five thousand people), resulting in an estimated productivity increase of $15 million a year. Think about this the next time you are not having coffee with your team or when you see all your team members having lunch alone.

Embracing and leveraging the power of social connections within an organization can result in amplified collaboration, motivation, and overall achievement. Beyond the influence of identity and interpersonal energy, interpersonal relationships facilitate essential information sharing, mentoring, innovation, and positive peer effects, as well as norm enforcement. Working together can really work magic, and it is key for an organization's success. I think everybody who ever worked in an organization, played on a sports team, or was part of a community knows what I am talking about.

Unsurprisingly, personal interactions are at the center of the battle to return to office—as this is where interactions happened in the past. When engaging in conversations with executives regarding personal interactions and remote work, concerns often arise regarding the potential loss of the intangible magic that occurs when individuals are physically present in the same location at the same time (in addition that they are worried about slacking off, as discussed in Chapter 7). I am constantly hearing: "Collaborations, watercooler moments, and fostering a corporate culture is impossible without people being in the office together."

Bob Iger, CEO of Disney, said in 2023 in a memo to his employees: "I've been reminded of the tremendous value in being together with the people you work with. In a creative business like ours, nothing can replace the ability to connect, observe, and create with peers that comes from being physically together, nor the opportunity to grow professionally by learning from leaders and mentors." Jamie Dimon, CEO of J.P. Morgan, mentioned at the World Economic Forum in Davos in 2023 that working remotely "doesn't work for young kids or [for] spontaneity or management." And even in the tech sector, which originally embraced remote work, executives are voicing concerns. Mark Zuckerberg of Meta wrote in a memo to his employees: "In-person time helps build relationships and get more done." Some go even as far as claiming that the collapse of Silicon Valley Bank in 2023, the largest US bank failure since 2008, was partly due to remote work. The bank's annual report claimed that the bank "may experience negative effects of a prolonged work-from-home arrangement."

So, does just being physically next to each other unlock the "working together works" magic? If only it were that easy.

The Dark Side of Human Interactions

There is certainly something very powerful about personal interactions. And the magic of personal interactions often thrives in the realm of physical proximity, which enables a profound level of engagement and shared experience. But let's be honest: personal interactions can also lead to terrible relationships and ugly human behavior. Toxic work cultures are not a new phenomenon. Just because your team is physically together does not mean that all the good things that can come out of interpersonal relations will materialize. In fact, employees have been leaving workplaces in droves because of the toxicity of workplace relationships. In a survey in 2019, 49 percent of responders say they have thought about leaving a job in the last five years because of toxic work cultures. Twenty percent actually have. The Society of Human Resource Management, who conducted the survey, estimates that toxic work cultures costs about a quarter trillion dollars over a five-year period.

A lot can go wrong and turn toxic in interpersonal interactions. Hostility, sabotage, or even violence against people who are not considered a part of an in-group are just some of the darker aspects of working together. In teams that lack proper support and mentoring, toxic behavior is widespread. Workplace ostracism, where employees get explicitly ignored and marginalized, is well documented and very common. According to recent studies, a significant percentage of employees (around 70 percent) have reported experiencing instances of ostracism in the workplace. Sexual harassment is also shockingly common. It has been estimated that about 13 percent of women in Swedish workplaces reported sexual harassment over a twelve-month period. That number almost doubles in male-dominated industries. These examples are just the tip of a very ugly iceberg.

So, just because people are working side by side does not make an office an inspiring, creative, supportive, and inclusive environment. Nor should we be surprised that in surveys about how many remote workdays people want, minorities are less keen to spend more time in the office—for them, the office was never a welcoming place before the pandemic. As a Black, woman vice president said in a survey conducted by McKinsey and the LeanIn organization in 2022, "some microaggressions just 100 percent don't happen when I'm remote."

William Golding's classic 1954 novel *Lord of the Flies* dramatizes how quickly group dynamics can unravel into something ugly—when not intentionally managed. The novel tells the story of a group of young boys stranded on a deserted island. The boys initially attempt to establish order and work together for survival. However, as their situation becomes more challenging and their primal instincts take over, conflicts arise, and they descend into chaos and violence.

While there are certainly a few individuals who exhibit negative behaviors or selfish tendencies (which we will discuss later), they are outnumbered by the majority who embrace cooperative and helpful attitudes. However, there are certain group dynamics that can impact the effectiveness and value of working together—and turn even the best human into a horrible coworker and manager. These challenges arise from three things: our natural inclination to prioritize our own groups, our aversion to inequality, and the way we are perceived by others.

We have a natural inclination to prioritize our own groups—and conversely be potentially hostile toward members of other groups. Ethnic conflicts are just the ugliest form of those group dynamics. But in the Swiss army study, the pattern of favoring one's own group compared to others happened in completely randomly assigned groups: there was no history between the groups or differences between the members.

It is almost impossible to prevent competition between groups, divisions, and departments completely. Often it is used as a tactic to increase group cohesion and motivation. When we added a small bonus for each member of the best team in the army experiment, the behavior of favoring one's own group members turned into outright hostility toward others. Additionally, patterns of norm enforcement became dysfunctional. It didn't matter if members of an opposing group behaved well; their behavior was always perceived as negative and punished. So even if a member of a group (or, in a company context, a division, department, or team) was inclined to help someone in another group, the negative atmosphere and responses discouraged this behavior. Even the stereotypically well-behaved Swiss, who were all together in the Swiss army, would behave dysfunctionally and hurt the overall goal of the organization.

Second, humans possess a profound concern for fairness and are averse to inequality. This critically affects intracompany dynamics. For example, although a certain percentage of individuals are initially willing to contribute to a common good, research reveals a significant decline in their contributions over time if left to their own devices. This decline occurs because nobody wants to be perceived as the one who is making a substantial effort while others take advantage without reciprocation. Employees might help other team members even if they are not incentivized to do so. It's also hard to quantify and document such helping behavior in their annual review: they just contribute to a general atmosphere of stepping in for others. However, if people figure out that they are the only ones doing so—even if the number of free riders is initially small—over time cooperation will deteriorate if not managed. If left unmanaged, everybody will eventually start to look out only for themselves.

Finally, people care a lot about others' opinions and their image. This is especially true in organizations. In fact, people care so much about what others think that they will behave the way they *think* they are expected to. For example, if workers believe that asking for help signals that they are weak or lack expertise and should only be done as a last resort, they will not ask for help. This tendency was characteristic of Microsoft's know-it-all culture before Satya Nadella took over. There is a silver lining here. It's true that when employees change their behavior to meet expectations, it can potentially lead to negative dynamics. But it can also open up opportunities for leaders to change the wrong beliefs.

Just as negative group dynamics can be shaped by leadership and environment, so can positive interpersonal interactions. Serendipitous "watercooler moments" and automatic mentoring do not materialize on their own. Trust and bonding don't happen just because we are in the same organization or commiserate about office life. Likewise, the flow of information cannot be assumed, even when individuals share the same physical office space. Leaders, whether overseeing teams or entire organizations, have the power to enhance these interactions and be deliberate about it. Failing to do so not only squanders the potential for fostering positive dynamics but also risks the emergence of destructive behaviors, reminiscent of the troubling dynamics portrayed in *Lord of the Flies*.

But creating the right group dynamics is no easy task for leaders. The pandemic and the experiment with remote work underscored how team dynamics have to be managed deliberately. This is true not just in virtual, remote, or distributed teams, but also when people are working in the same physical office. Insights from behavioral science show that creating positive group dynamics boils down to thinking about where, what, and who. *Where* should connection happen, *what* should the nature of interactions be, and *who* should be on the team?

Let's first look at how leaders can be deliberate about where people meet different colleagues before discussing how we as leaders can create the right environment for positive interactions.

Actively Facilitate Connections—In-Person or Remote

As we have all experienced, something is lost in virtual interactions and teleconferenced meetings. I certainly experienced this teaching my classes on Zoom during the pandemic. Teaching a full classroom can be very energizing. I have found teaching in a Zoom room, on the other hand, to be draining. The presence of other humans in the same space creates energy, and you can assess the engagement of the classroom based on students' body language. When that body language is missing, it can make it difficult to manage a discussion.

Classroom formats (in-person, hybrid, or virtual) also affect where people meet and how they work together, and this also affects networking. When my colleagues and I analyzed whether online teaching would affect which students in a class would become close, it was clear that in virtual classes (although classes were the same), they would make fewer connections. This is a big loss for students because networking is a crucial benefit of the MBA program. Analyzing the collaboration patterns and connections of more than sixty thousand Microsoft employees shows a similar pattern. Based on data from emails, calendars, instant messages, and video and audio calls, remote work reduces collaboration networks and makes them more siloed. While remote work does not significantly impact collaborations within existing teams, it leads to decreased connections with individuals outside these established work groups. This poses a challenge, especially since many innovations and vital new information often rely on connections forged beyond established networks. Furthermore, Melanie Brucks, my colleague and literal office neighbor, along with her coauthor, have demonstrated that individuals tend to generate more creative ideas when engaging in face-to-face meetings as opposed to virtual meetings conducted via platforms like Zoom or Microsoft Teams. There certainly is something special about face-to-face interactions. Ask yourself which tasks your team or you are doing as part of your job that truly necessitate face-to-face interactions and which are better suited for uninterrupted, solitary work without social interactions. When crafting return-to-office policies and determining the structure of remote and in-person days, consider the proportion of tasks that are better suited to each environment.

But even being in the same location does not guarantee that workers will enjoy the full benefits of social interaction. If left to their own devices, people will form cliques and gravitate toward people who are similar. This is known as homophily, a well-studied and documented phenomenon. For example, at mixers and networking events, humans tend to gravitate toward people they already know—despite participants' stated goal to meet new people at those events. So much for hoping that people will meet new people and come up with great new ideas at the watercooler or kombucha tap. In a large Southeast Asian bank, researchers observed that many employees met not just at the watercooler but in the smoking area. Analysis of data for almost fifteen thousand employees and thirteen hundred managers showed that face-to-face meetings of smoking employees with their (also smoking) managers increased the probability of promotion significantly. The problem: only 4 percent of female employees smoked compared to 31 percent of their male coworkers. The study estimated that these spontaneous personal interactions accounted for about one-third of the gender gap in promotions in this commercial bank—indicating that such spontaneous personal interactions led to a negative outcome, contrary to the organization's ideal of equitable and inclusive advancement.

Meaningful connections have to be deliberately facilitated and sometimes mandated. Mentoring, for example, is an important benefit of working together. About half the companies surveyed in 2022 do have formal mentoring programs. In a majority (60 percent) of those programs, participation is voluntary, the logic being that forcing employees into a program against their will might backfire as employees might resent it, or at least roll their eyes at it. But in the end, only 27 percent participate in those voluntary mentoring programs. A sales call center conducted an experiment in collaboration with scholars to test the impact of making mentoring a mandatory practice as opposed to a voluntary one. New sales agents were either mandated to have a mentor or could volunteer for the program. All mentors were more experienced peers (aka nonsupervisory sales agents), and mentor-mentee pairs were asked to meet thirty minutes every week for four weeks to discuss work-related questions. Mandating the mentoring program improved both productivity and retention (two of the most important metrics in this job). Daily revenue increased 17 percent for agents mandated to be mentored. The higher productivity remained well beyond the four-week experiment period. Even after the sales agents' first six months, 80 percent of the mentoring effect remained. Agents personally benefited from the increased productivity as they were paid by sales commissions. While turnover in the first 30 days was normally high in this job, it was significantly lower for the "forced" mentees. The net present value of mandating mentoring for the 114 workers in the experiment was estimated to be around $578,000 for the company over the first six months of the agent's tenure. The deliberate implementation of a policy aimed at fostering connections yielded substantial benefits for both the company and its agents.

Facilitating relationships that would not happen organically is especially important across groups and between teams. Even conflict between hostile groups can be minimized or eliminated through carefully managed interactions. For example, in the city of Mostar, located in Bosnia and Herzegovina, students of two ethnic groups, Catholic Croats and Muslim Bosniaks, had long been segregated. When the Yugoslav Wars ended in the 1990s, two of four schools became integrated. According to a study published in *Science*, the ethnoreligious groups in the integrated schools exhibited cooperation levels and norm enforcement patterns akin to a single unified group. In contrast, segregated schools presented a different scenario, with students displaying a strong preference for members of their own group and exhibiting pronounced hostility toward individuals from other groups.

Random encounters—especially among different groups—can help. And here comes the bright side of videoconference teaching: random breakout groups. Many videoconference programs offer a feature that instantly places participants into random groups, effectively disrupting naturally occurring groupings and fostering new connections. The participant's appearance on the screens is not ordered by hierarchy or status, which allows for more diverse voices to be heard. Starting videoconference meetings in my department with random breakout groups is much easier and more effective in bringing different members together than anything I tried to do during in-person meetings.

However, deliberate efforts can also yield similar effects in face-to-face gatherings. Umbrex, a company that establishes a network of independent consultants, has embraced this concept. Founder and CEO Will Bachman organizes Umbrex networking events with intentional activities and random seating arrangements to counteract humans' inclination to gravitate toward familiar or similar individuals. This approach encourages attendees to interact with new people and broaden their professional networks. Think about organizing an event with the most introverted member in mind.

Merely being in the same building or office does not create all those encounters. In fact, the physicality of workplaces creates constraints that make random encounters difficult. The advertising department of a German bank was having trouble successfully launching campaigns of the bank's new products. The bank looked at who was talking to whom. It turned out that no one in the advertising department was communicating with the customer service department. As a result, the bank would launch ad campaigns that were not supported by customer service. The physical separation of the two departments, which were located on different floors, largely caused this lack of interaction. The bank found that simply moving part of the customer service department to the ad department floor helped—but in the end physical proximity alone was not enough to ensure that the right people talked to one another.

Surprisingly, companies that are mostly remote often do a better job facilitating interaction because they have to be deliberate about it. Take Doximity, a professional medical network for physicians that helps doctors be more productive. Since its founding in 2010, the company has mostly operated remotely. Right from the start, the cofounder and CEO, Jeff Tangney, emphasized the significance of in-person meetings for fostering robust interpersonal connections within a remote organization. The company has quarterly offsites in which social activities and community building are an important part—more so than in normal retreats. Those deliberate off-site activities, in locations like Palm Springs, California, and Stanford Sierra Camp near Lake Tahoe—might have a stronger impact on community building than random encounters next to the coffee machine.

Being deliberate about creating connections and intrapersonal interactions shapes decisions about what requires a meeting and what the format of it will be. Obviously, not every meeting is productive. In fact, as we all know, many are not and just take away from important, uninterrupted focus time. Leaders need to think carefully about when workers need a meeting and when they can work asynchronously, such as by email. In addition, leaders need to decide when working together needs to be synchronous, that is, requiring people to work together at the same time. An employee might have a question that requires an immediate answer from a colleague before more work can get done. That doesn't mean that these employees need to be working in the same place, but it does mean that they have to be working at the same time. But certain tasks do not require the whole team to be present. Leaders need to set the norms on when synchronous working together is not required or even discouraged. Providing employees with the flexibility to work at times and in places of their choosing, where they can focus, is important—especially but not only in a hybrid work setting.

It should be obvious that remote days should not look like in-person days. One of the main benefits of remote days is that employees can focus on their work uninterrupted by meetings (scheduled or drive-by) and have the flexibility to schedule a day that fits their style and personality. I am very productive from 6 to 10 a.m. but less so late in the afternoon, so it is unproductive for my boss to force me to be at my desk from 9 a.m. to late afternoon. Remote workdays should allow for that. But in-person days should also take advantage of the benefits of the office. When I am in the office, I should not spend most of my time on Zoom or in my cubicle. The benefit of being together should be leveraged by having more group and brainstorming sessions and random meetings. The benefit of in-person days, being together with others, will be maximized if leaders recognize these different dynamics and plan accordingly. It will additionally require coordination among team members.

The concept of a weekend should give us hope that companies can make the necessary cultural adjustments to accommodate remote work. Today, the majority of companies have reached a consensus that two specific days (typically Saturday and Sunday in the Western world) should be designated as nonworking days, free from in-person meetings and synchronous remote interactions, such as Slack or emails. These days are meant for rest and rejuvenation. Similarly, by setting consistent norms regarding both remote and in-person workdays, organizations can optimize overall happiness and productivity for their employees.

Finally, managers should give careful consideration to the physical spaces in offices where interactions will occur. This means creating conducive environments, such as communal areas, breakout rooms, or designated collaboration zones that cultivate a sense of openness and encourage individuals to connect on a deeper level. By thoughtfully considering both the type of interactions and the optimal locations, organizations can actively foster meaningful connections among individuals, leading to increased collaboration, engagement, and overall team success.

LEGO, the renowned Danish toy brick maker, showcased its forward-thinking approach by embarking on the design of a new headquarters in Billund, Denmark, optimized for hybrid work even before the pandemic. The architects collaborated closely with an in-house anthropologist to determine the right mix of spaces for collaboration, social interaction, and focused work. This comprehensive approach involved analyzing job roles and breaking them down into distinct tasks, while also considering the frequency of employee engagement in activities requiring direct collaboration with colleagues. By understanding the specific work patterns of their workforce, they could then design spaces that best facilitate and support these tasks. The incorporation of flexible spaces was particularly focused on fostering connections and promoting interaction among employees, reinforcing the value of bringing people together within the organization. "Employees told us that they wanted the freedom to choose an environment that suited them best for whatever they were working on, but also liked to stay close to teammates," explains LEGO's senior workplace anthropologist Anneke Beerkens. "So we built team 'neighbourhoods' which are a mix of individual and collaborative workspaces designed to create a caring environment where people can do great quality work."

Employee-centric companies around the globe are redesigning their workspaces, as LEGO did, to optimize their spaces for working together. The redesign is centered on the needs of the employees and their tasks. As a result, working together works better, and employees are happy to come back to the office. As head of Workplace Experience at LEGO, Tim Ahrensbach comments about their efforts: "We've done [the redesign] in a really exciting way that makes our colleagues, when they come into LEGO campus, realize there's a reason why [they've] gone into the office today. I'm not just doing it out of habit or because there's this policy."

In employee-centric companies, careful attention is given to the dynamics of interactions within the organization. Merely having teams in the same physical location does not automatically ensure positive or productive collaborations. Employee-centric leaders recognize this and take deliberate steps to foster positive interactions by matching the right individuals in the right spaces. They understand that creating optimal interactions is not a one-size-fits-all approach, but rather requires a personalized understanding of what is meaningful to each employee for collaborating and cultivating a sense of community. While not every organization has the ability to completely overhaul its workspaces, it can still be intentional about optimizing social interactions. So ask yourself: What are you doing to explicitly facilitate meaningful connections? Are you playing a crucial role in cultivating a cohesive and motivating work environment where employees can thrive and contribute to the organization's success?

The initial step involves recognizing the significance of interpersonal interactions in the workplace. Next, leaders need to facilitate appropriate interactions among employees, managers, and team members. This requires an in-depth understanding of what truly matters to each individual employee on a personal level. By acknowledging and catering to these unique preferences and needs, organizations can foster a more supportive and engaging work environment. Taking the time to understand and respond to employees' needs can transform the performance of a company. To illustrate this point, let's look at a story that Howard Schultz, the founder and CEO of Starbucks, likes to tell about how Jack Ma, the founder and CEO of Alibaba, helped turn around the coffee giant's fortunes in China.

Make It Personal

When Starbucks expanded their operations into China in 1999, their executives hoped to continue the same run of success they had enjoyed in North America. But though the Seattle coffee chain entered China with big fanfare, it almost immediately ran into cultural problems. Store after store reported low sales and low morale and high turnover among its baristas. As Howard Schultz would later admit, Starbucks struggled for nine years to understand what was going wrong. As its Chinese coffee shops floundered, Starbucks sent one talented manager after another from Seattle to try to turn the China business around. One problem was obvious: changing a tea-drinking culture to a coffee-drinking one is not an easy endeavor. But there was another problem: US executives, Schultz realized and admitted in his master class, "did not understand [...] the sensibility of the Chinese consumer, the Chinese employee, and the marketplace." Figuring out what kind of personal relationships matter for Chinese employees was an important part of the turnaround. And everything started with a talk Schultz gave at an event at Alibaba, the Chinese tech giant.

Jack Ma, Alibaba's CEO, had invited the Starbucks founder to give a keynote address to his employees. As Schultz addressed the packed auditorium, Schultz noticed that the audience of Alibaba workers seemed very old. Schultz asked Ma directly why this was the case. To Schultz's big surprise, Ma answered that the elderly audience members were not his employees but the parents of his employees. Schultz was baffled by the answer. Ma went on to explain the importance of family and parents for Chinese workers, especially because of the one-child policy that had been in effect in China for many years. "So," he explained, "the child is devoted to the parents and the grandparents and vice versa. So, we create this family atmosphere." It was Alibaba's way of fostering and respecting its employees' sense of community and meaningful personal connections. It illustrates not only how important personal relationships inside and outside an organization are for people's motivation but also that it is not trivial to figure out what employees care about. Starbucks didn't get this for almost ten years.

It took some effort for Howard Schultz to convince his team in Seattle that parent events are important in China. They originally had the same reaction that Schultz had when he first heard from Ma about this. But since 2012, Starbucks has held an annual parent event. The first event was a breakthrough. "We had an annual meeting of parents in Beijing and Shanghai," Schultz said, "and we had about 90 percent participation. We did not know who or how many would come. In most cases, there were whole families. There were parents, grandparents, aunts, and uncles. It was unbelievable… it was a breakthrough for the company and a milestone for local relevancy and sensitivity." A few years later, Schultz further solidified the significance of family in motivating workers by introducing health insurance coverage for the parents of his employees.

It is important to understand not only that social connections within the company are critically important but also what matters to individual members and how to foster a sense of community for them. That requires leaders spending time and effort to actually get to know employees on an individual level and provide a safe space to voice any concerns regarding interpersonal behavior.

Sandoz, a division of the Swiss pharmaceutical firm Novartis, tested how best to "get personal" with around a thousand teams, which comprise about seven thousand employees. They conducted a six-week experiment in 2021, with two treatment groups and one control group. The main goal of the experiment was to test how treating employees as unique individuals would improve the working atmosphere and lower the barriers to provide feedback to others and increase psychological safety in general.

For the first treatment group, a group of managers in the Novartis division received an email encouraging them to have regular one-on-one meetings with team members. But they were not only asked to meet regularly but also to focus on the individual needs of their team members. They were asked to encourage the employees to use the meeting to share what was important to them and where they needed support. The focus was on prioritizing individual needs and recognizing each person as a unique individual as a way to create a more supportive and inclusive culture. A second treatment group of managers was encouraged to have one-on-one meetings but to focus more generally on how to remove obstacles that would slow down teams, while a control group was simply told that meeting habits were being studied during the next six weeks and was given no additional guidance. After the six weeks, the company evaluated the effect of the different approaches.

Focusing on individual needs of employees had a strong positive effect on interpersonal interactions. Over the six weeks, employees in the first treatment group increased their score by 12 percent compared to the control group on questions such as whether "different perspectives are valued in my team" and "I feel safe sharing feedback with colleagues." This was double the increase of the second group, tasked only with removing obstacles, whose score rose just 6 percent compared to the control group. For teams that were low on those scores to begin with, the effects were even more pronounced: their score improved 19 percent in the first group. In addition, perception of career development and progress improved 21 percent and perception of managers as role models increased by 15 percent. So getting personal does pay off by creating better interpersonal relationships. The increased psychological safety can then uncover problems within the organizations and allow for healthy norm enforcement—between managers and the team and among team members.

In addition to cultivating a psychologically safe environment and establishing the right connections, leaders must actively facilitate positive interactions within their teams. This requires once more understanding the behavioral barriers to unlocking the full potential of personal connections. Often concerns about one's image are at the core of those limitations. Research in a US sales call center that sells television, phone, and internet services showed that just pairing team members for learning is not enough. When the company provided a structured protocol for what the pairs should discuss during their weekly meetings, revenue increased 24 percent. The protocol explicitly guided members to discuss strengths and challenges and to actively seek advice. It eliminated any fear of being intimidated to ask for advice and actively encouraged information flow. The research showed that it is not the knowledge providers who do not want to share any tips and tricks. Rather, the knowledge seekers—the team members who need to ask questions—need to be assured that it is perfectly OK to ask questions and encouraged to get advice. The research further found that providing monetary incentives to share information doesn't have any impact.

Leaders have a pivotal position as role models, shaping the standards and norms for personal interactions within their organizations. The workplace climate is an important factor in promoting effective collaboration, and in many companies, managers could do a much better job improving that climate. In the United States, 76 percent of employees say their manager sets the culture, yet 36 percent say their manager does a terrible job. Fifty-eight percent of employees who quit because of poor workplace culture blame their manager. This is common around the world. In a study in Turkey, 50 percent of professionals put "toxic relationships and antisocial behavior" in the top three problems they face. For 47 percent of employees, "difficult leaders" also make the top three. According to McKinsey: "In most organizations, the average manager has neither the incentives nor the skills to focus on employee happiness." It should, however, not be that difficult to treat employees with respect as unique individuals and to encourage teamwork. But it only happens if the employee advantage is top of mind.

A training program in Turkey helps illustrate the huge benefits of humane leaders. Turkey is no exception when it comes to toxic work culture, and twenty of some of the largest Turkish corporations wanted to change that. They worked together with a group of behavioral economists to evaluate the effectiveness of a training program designed to enhance the relational climate within organizations. Involving approximately three thousand employees across those twenty companies, the program promotes prosocial behavior and emphasizes the use of professional language among leaders. In a series of online workshops, professionals were trained to focus on three things: respectful communications and avoiding condescending and toxic language; understanding and respecting differences in opinions and preferences; and learning from others by accepting vulnerability. All the modules and activities were, according to the study, about "encouraging professional and humane treatment of one another."

When leaders are trained to treat others humanely, the positive effects on the organization are remarkable, when compared to a control group of organizations that do not implement the training program. Workplace satisfaction increases significantly, for one. Employees see leaders as much more professional and empathetic and are more likely to see them as a professional and personal support. Furthermore, all the potential negative effects of working together are mitigated and become positive: collegial behavior increases, connections in the organizations become much less siloed, helping behavior increases, and sabotaging is reduced. The proportion of subordinates who report a lack of support drops 41 percent. Turnover is significantly reduced. Facilitating healthy relationships at work and being a role model has a huge effect on how working together works. The percentage of people who prefer to work from home also drops by 6 percentage points. This suggests that, for many, part of not wanting to come to the office is less about wanting to stay at home and more about avoiding toxic workplaces. If the office is a welcoming place, people are more likely to want to return to the office and to work together in the same physical space.

The power of being nice, treating everybody with respect and as unique individuals, and encouraging a culture of teamwork pays off in higher motivation and productivity. Teamwork is only going to become more important in the future, as work becomes more challenging. Studies from around the globe on workers of all types (from less educated to highly educated) show that tasks are becoming less routine and more complex. Cognitive routine tasks, for example, have declined more than one-half since the 1950s, and routine manual tasks have declined even more. The increase in complex tasks goes hand in hand with an increase in team production and the importance of working together. The share of jobs that require a high level of social interactions, such as coordinating ("adjusting actions in relation to others' action"), negotiating ("bring others together and trying to reconcile differences"), or being socially perceptive ("being aware of others' reactions and understanding why they react as they do"), grew by 12 percentage points from 1980 to 2012 in the United States.

So, organizations definitely need to figure out what makes teams smarter and how working together works even better. But what increases a team's IQ?

Hire and Promote Prosocial Team Players

As we are all aware, IQ, or intelligence quotient, is a measure, normally based around an average score of 100, that is derived from a series of standardized tasks used to assess a person's cognitive abilities and intellectual potential. While there is a lot of controversy about IQ as a measure of cognitive ability, it is still widely used.

In 2009, researchers began to look into the question of whether we can similarly measure collective intelligence and determine if groups have their own IQ. Are there groups that do better in not just one task but consistently outperform other groups in a variety of tasks? And is the composition of high IQ individuals the key to building better teams? The idea of success being solely dependent on hiring the smartest individuals assumes that teams with a higher number of intelligent members are inherently superior.

The resulting study, published in the journal *Science*, looked for collective intelligence and found it, but not in the form you might expect. The first, very intuitive result is that some (randomly formed) teams are actually smarter. That means that those groups consistently outperform other teams in a variety of tasks, which are similar to IQ tasks but tailored for group work. But what makes those teams perform better? The researchers had a lot of information about the individual members of the teams, including their individual IQ scores and other skills related to the task performed. But the average IQ scores of the individuals, or the cumulative intelligence quotient of the group based on these measures, was only weakly correlated with the collective intelligence the study found. Just having all the smartest people in a group is not enough to outperform other groups.

So what was highly predictive of whether teams are smart? Answer: the percentage of individuals within the group who are better in assessing someone's emotions solely based on observing their eyes, that is, the ones who got the highest scores on the "Reading the Mind in the Eyes" test, a diagnostic tool originally developed by University of Cambridge professor Sir Simon Baron-Cohen for his research on autism. In the test, individuals are shown images of people's eyes (including the skin around them) and have to match the eyes to the emotions they are expressing. In hundreds of studies, this measure turns out to capture individuals' empathic abilities very reliably.

So it turns out that the higher the number of group members who are empathetic and socially intelligent, the smarter the group. It is not really about the eyes per se but about empathy in general. And it doesn't matter if you are working in an office or remotely. Even in online interactions, in which nobody sees anybody's eyes at all, more socially intelligent members, who score higher on the eye test, make groups smarter. Interestingly, women do better on that measure in general, and so another conclusion to draw from the results is that groups with a higher proportion of women are likely smarter than those with a lower proportion. Besides having team members who demonstrate empathy, smarter groups also exhibit a more equitable distribution of participation during team discussions.

Social skills are not just important collectively for groups but also determine who is a good team player. Team players make every team better. Obviously, skills do matter and have an impact on a team's performance. For instance, if you are in a hackathon team competition, where computer programmers collaborate intensively over a short period of time, you probably want Gennady Korotkevich on your team. He is one of the best competitive programmers in the world, having won all major programming competitions. He has the highest score on many programmer rankings and clearly would make a big difference on any hackathon team. But would he, alone, make the collective better? Do his individual talents elevate the collective to superior performance? And if you can't count on one talented individual to elevate the team, are there team players who can make the collective better and what are their attributes?

Research by a team of Harvard behavioral economists shows that team players who consistently make different teams better do exist. And it's not a minor difference. The effect of these team players is about 65 percent as large as individual task-specific skills. Such team players do not have higher IQs or more education; they have more empathy and score high on the eye test.

Social intelligence and empathy are critical skills in employees. Empathic team members not only create a more enjoyable work atmosphere; they also make teams more productive. This puts a different spin on Southwest Airlines founder Herb Kelleher's famous quote: "Hire for attitudes and train for skills." Hiring people with the highest IQ or those who do well on brain teaser tests does not cut it. Significant weight should be given to social skills or "attitudes." How does a candidate respect and treat people independent of their job title? How do they function in groups? How do they handle group tasks?

Some companies already employ such practices. HEICO CEO Larry Mendelson told me that before HEICO acquires a company, he tours the company with its executive team. He is looking for how the executives respect and treat their workforce and will walk away from an acquisition if those executives do not show empathy toward their workforce. In my division at Columbia University, candidates for professor positions will have lunch with our PhD students. We then interview our PhD students to see how the candidate treats people who will be lower in rank and are not voting in the hiring process. I have found that sometimes the candidates who seem the nicest when I, the chair of the division, interview them, can be really disrespectful to those they think have no say in the process. As at HEICO, how a candidate interacts can influence whether or not we hire that person.

But hiring on this basis does require being deliberate about how to measure those social skills or attitudes and weighting them appropriately against the "hard" metrics of IQ, degrees, and aptitude tests. Jensen Huang, the cofounder and CEO of the $1 trillion company Nvidia, expressed this vision eloquently: "It is the company's choice to decide what kind of engineers irrespective of their talent but also their character and their personalities and the value systems to let into the company. [...] We try to figure out whether this person has brains, guts, and heart in the process of the interview." When reevaluating your hiring process, you might add team activities and group interviews to one-on-one interviews and skill evaluations. In general, you have to ask yourself whether you give enough weight to the social skills of candidates who are being evaluated for a position.

Social skills are also critically important for managers. Arguably, it might even be more important for leaders to have social skills. So why then, you might wonder, are so many bosses apparently bad at this? Because the skills that lead to a promotion are not necessarily the ones that make great leaders. The best salesperson, for example, often gets promoted to lead the sales team. But being a great salesperson doesn't make one a great leader. Research with around forty thousand sales workers across 131 companies indicated that the majority of those organizations prioritize an employee's current job performance when making promotion decisions. They tend to assign lesser significance to other observable characteristics, such as how successfully the salesperson collaborates with others to make a sale, which are more accurate predictors of managerial performance. Management positions are bestowed like awards for high performance and are not seen as jobs that require a specific skill set. Consequently, the quality of managers suffers. If these companies were to adopt a promotion policy that expected managerial quality by, for example, taking collaborative skills into account, managerial quality would increase by 30 percent. This lack of managerial quality is a very common problem.

In addition to criteria for hiring, promotion decisions need to take social skills very seriously in order to create the employee advantage. This requires different metrics for evaluating leaders—and taking those metrics into account. Indra Nooyi, in her last five years as CEO at PepsiCo, actively changed the metrics for how leaders were evaluated. They used to base 75 percent of a candidate's annual bonus score on business outcomes and only 25 percent on how the candidate's team was doing. "We changed it to 50-50, and that was a big sign to people that people management is a very important aspect of your job as a leader. . . . The key is to make sure that the three or four metrics that you are tracking are clearly articulated so that you are rewarding people only if they move the needle on the people agenda."

Positive social interactions are the fourth factor and one of the most important human motivators. How to foster a team that works well together—how to make working together work—needs to be one of the priorities of any leader. Human relations at work need to be deliberately encouraged and steered in the right direction. If done right, working together really works and will lead to the employee advantage.

While social connections and positive interactions at work are undeniably crucial motivators, they are just one of the four critical factors that contribute to a thriving workplace: having a purpose that aims high (shoot for the moon), providing autonomy based on trust (a matter of trust), ensuring tasks suit the employees and providing the right challenge to individuals (just right tasks), and promoting effective teamwork (working together works). These factors are distinct and of equal importance and cannot be substituted for one another. For instance, having a lofty purpose does not compensate for a toxic work culture.

Effective leaders understand the significance of incorporating all four factors into their organizational design. Achieving this, however, is not an easy feat and demands unwavering commitment to creating an employee-centric environment. It necessitates careful attention to all human motivators and a thorough redesign of work processes accordingly.

Much like being consumer-centric requires more than mere lip service to caring about customers, being employee-centric demands more than empty declarations of concern for employees. And there is one more step copied from customer-centricity: a truly employee-centric organization acknowledges the uniqueness of each individual within its workforce, just as customer-centric companies recognize the diversity among their customers.

PART III

Workforce of One

CHAPTER 10

Customize EX

I F YOU WANT TO BENEFIT from the employee advantage at your company, it is crucial to understand the four behavioral factors of how humans work, discussed in Part II—purpose, autonomy, just right tasks, and social connections. Guided by them, managers can stop obsessing only on monetary compensation and begin creating a workplace that is motivating and engaging. But how, exactly, does one go about doing that? The first step is by implementing tools that have long been the staple of every successful marketer.

The customer-centric revolution started with the availability of massive amounts of data that allowed us to understand and serve the customers better—to improve the customer experience (CX). But customer-centricity did not stop there. The data showed that people are very different from one another in their needs, emotional reactions, and attitudes. Thus, customer segmentation, which involves categorizing customers into distinct groups based on behavioral and aspirational traits and tailoring marketing strategies accordingly, has become the bread-and-butter of every marketer.

Over time, the tools and approaches used for customer segmentation have evolved and became increasingly sophisticated, enabling marketers to personalize their targeting efforts to a remarkable degree. That means that the segments become smaller and smaller. Ideally, we would have "segments of one," which would give businesses the ability to create highly personalized experiences for individual customers based on their unique preferences and characteristics. This level of granularity in customer segmentation and targeting has revolutionized the way businesses engage with their customers and drives marketing success. This is at the core of customer-centricity.

To make the shift to being an employee-centric organization, you also must start with insights about who an organization's employees are, and what they want, to improve the employee experience (EX). Every person has different wants and motivations. Although almost everyone is influenced by the four behavioral motivators discussed in Part II, there exists considerable variability in the importance people assign to each of them. Maybe one worker values a company's core purpose over the ability to connect with others. Perhaps another employee values autonomy much more than a feeling of competence. A majority of employees appreciate the flexibility of being able to work from home on certain days. But surveys showed that people differ significantly in how much. While roughly 25 percent want to only work remotely, 25 percent want to fully work on premises, and the rest of the 50 percent differ in how many days they prefer to work remotely. Some prefer one day at home while others want to be only one day in the office. And so on. Those preferences are driven by differences in people's motivations, personality traits, and situational factors at home and in their life in general.

It is crucial for workers to feel that their differences are taken seriously. As one Amazon employee put it: "It is very important that area managers understand that associates are more than just numbers. We are human beings." Hence, just as personalization is vital in consumer marketing, the personal recognition and a personalized approach to employees has demonstrated an impact on effort and motivation. And it's not just the behavioral science that supports this. Neuroscientists, for example, have shown that people exhibit unique brain activities when they hear their own name versus hearing other first names. It's no wonder that, as we have all gotten used to hyperpersonalized experiences as consumers, we are now expecting the same in the workplace. The traditional one-size-fits-all approach in treating employees is not cutting it anymore.

The goal of employee-centric organizations is to understand who cares about which aspect of work. Traditional HR data (such as age, tenure, position, education) is inadequate to achieve this goal. Commonly used segments based on demographics such as age or generation do not capture the differences among workers adequately, as an individual's preferences and needs are also shaped by personal factors such as personality traits or personal experience. For instance, we know that the macroeconomic condition that existed when a person was growing up influences the importance for them of meaning at work and how much they make. People who experience relatively bad macroeconomic conditions during their formative years (between the ages of eighteen and twenty-five) are more likely to value income over meaning at work, a mind-set that can last for the rest of their lives. We can see major differences within the same age group and certainly within a single generation, due to regional disparities in labor markets. Failing to recognize the diversity within different sociodemographic groups overlooks the significant differences among people. To effectively segment employees, it is crucial to consider their unique motivations and behaviors.

Employee segmentation is still in its infancy compared to customer segmentation. Even when companies decide to segment their workforce, they often use crude categories like demographics. According to a survey conducted by Deloitte in 2020, 53 percent of leaders identified work-related demographics, such as tenure and level, as one of the top three attributes they use to segment their workforce. Personal demographics, such as generations, were considered among the top three attributes by 44 percent of leaders. Surprisingly, only 27 percent of leaders based their segmentation on work behavior, and an even smaller percentage (22 percent) took personal behavior into account, including factors like personality traits or preferred working style.

Today, most companies know more about their customers than they know about their employees. This is even more surprising when you consider how easy it has become to gather information about employees. The sheer amount of data on employees is increasing by the day. Only a fraction comes from traditional HR databases; the majority comes from channels that we have long analyzed for customers, such as click behavior on webpages or email metadata. Collecting and analyzing email metadata, for example, can reveal the social network of an organization and provide insights on how to improve collaboration patterns.

There are many sources of available employee data and right and wrong ways of using employee data to personalize EX. Ensuring transparency, trust, and a collaborative relationship with employees is key to this effort. The goal of gathering data should never be about surveillance. Employee data is about improving EX, not about implementing new ways of monitoring.

Segment by Behavior

Until I decided to study the company closely, I had a lot of misconceptions about what it meant to be a typical Uber driver. I thought, for instance, that a driver got into their car whenever they felt like it, opened the app, and then selected from the dispatches that would come in, going from passenger to passenger until they decided they'd worked long enough. And while it's true that drivers can do that, what I didn't understand was that taking such a passive approach would result in them making very little money. In order to have higher earnings per hour (EPH), drivers need to make critical decisions, in particular when and where to drive. If you are opening your app on a weekday afternoon in the suburbs, you are going to make very little money. If you open it instead on a weekend at 1 a.m. in the nightlife district of an urban area, you are going to make much more.

And then there are decisions about whether you should accept every dispatch or instead be strategic about where you drive. Should you wait at the airport for potential passengers (airport pickups are normally longer rides but also require longer wait times)? After you've dropped an airport passenger off, should you return to the airport with an empty car for another airport pickup? There is much more skill involved in making those decisions than I originally thought. According to estimates, even after driving for up to twenty-five hundred hours, drivers are still learning how to become better. Ask your next Uber driver about their strategy, and you will see how each driver thinks about this challenge very differently. One of the drivers I met had an Excel sheet in which he optimized his earnings and analyzed his choices. Very impressive!

I became a consultant at Uber during my sabbatical from Columbia Business School in the spring of 2018. I wanted to look at whether and how drivers differ in their motivation and in their skills in knowing how to optimally drive. The understanding of human motivation that informs the design of the Uber app essentially assumes that all drivers aim to maximize their earnings and that each one possesses a comprehensive understanding of how to optimize their EPH. The driver I met with the Excel sheet is a perfect example of what the Uber software designers had in mind. But not everybody is that organized and motivated to earn top dollar.

While it is evident that all Uber drivers engage in the gig for monetary reasons, the value and importance of other aspects of the job—such as the flexibility to choose the time and number of working hours or the social aspect of interacting with passengers—vary from driver to driver. In that regard, a passenger pickup at 2 a.m. in the bar district is very different from one in the afternoon in the suburbs. My previous research on attitudes toward various nonmonetary aspects of a job demonstrated significant differences among workers in different contexts.

In addition to differences among drivers in what they appreciate in a job in general and driving for Uber in particular, not everybody knows what the best way is to optimize earnings. My research on financial literacy and credit and mortgage decisions showed that there are substantial differences in how good people are with numbers—which affects the financial outcome of those individuals. There might be a similar "driver literacy" in which some drivers are better than others at knowing when and where to drive—and to make money as a result. Understanding the differences among the drivers is critically important. It matters a lot whether drivers are not optimizing their earnings because they do not know where and when to drive or whether they know but choose to avoid certain times and areas because they value other aspects of the job beyond maximizing earnings.

To analyze whether there are different segments of Uber drivers, I worked with a senior economist at Uber and conducted a survey of drivers in Los Angeles. We measured their driver literacy (based on their knowledge of when and where one should drive if one wants to maximize earnings) and elicited what, beyond monetary compensation, they care about in a job in general and at Uber in particular. The results showed that there are different segments within the Uber driver workforce that can explain different driving behaviors and earnings. In terms of driver literacy, for instance, there are drivers who have trouble determining which neighborhoods would make them the most money.

But when it came to what time to drive, it turns out most drivers are aware when the best times to drive are: "Bar hours: good, afternoon suburbs: bad." So what explained the reasons for drivers who chose to drive during the least profitable times of day? We discovered that attitudes on what is important in a job, generally, explain significantly when drivers are active—and as a result how much they earn. If drivers care about flexibility and the quality of their interactions with passengers, they are less likely to drive at night because that's when they are most likely to pick up rude, drunk passengers.

So if Uber wants to understand what motivates their drivers, merely examining driving data (i.e., where drivers drive and how much money they make) is not sufficient because different driving patterns have entirely different motivations. The behavior of drivers does not provide enough information to reveal what their motivation is, in the first place.

Segmentation based on behavior and attitudes allows Uber to target its different drivers in different ways. For the drivers who want to maximize their earnings but do not know what the optimal neighborhoods are, the company can support them in their decision-making process. But for those who value other aspects of the job—like flexibility or convenience—Uber can provide nonmonetary incentives that support them. For example, Uber could create options on its app to only dispatch rides that are close to the driver's home address so that drivers have the flexibility to undertake other activities before and after driving.

The behavioral factors discussed earlier can help create meaningful segments to use the right tactics to motivate and engage individual employees. Let's look at another example. We know that purpose matters for many employees—but how much differs from employee to employee. Survey evidence from Net Impact's *Talent Report: What Workers Want in 2012* found that 52 percent of workers consider making an impact as essential for a job and would quit if the organization has poor impact. But 48 percent do not seem to care as much about that dimension.

How does this information help companies? Consider gender diversity (or the lack thereof) in financial institutions. Among MBA students, females are much less likely to choose to work for a financial institution. The proportion of female MBA students going into finance is 15 percentage points lower than for their male classmates at Columbia Business School. Given that finance is the highest-paying industry for our graduates, this is not only affecting the institutions but also our female graduates. There are many potential explanations for this discrepancy, such as finance's male-dominant culture or fears of discrimination. But what is the impact of differences in motivation and preferences for different job attributes among job seekers? And can the industry target different segments of potential workers in distinct ways?

My coauthors and I used a traditional technique from marketing and applied it to job preferences of those top talents. A conjoint analysis is normally used to estimate the value of one specific feature. For example, how willing are customers to pay for a phone camera that has fifty megapixels instead of twelve—independent of other features such as screen size or design? It entails asking consumers to choose between different phones while varying the different features (including megapixels and price). We used such a conjoint analysis for jobs that MBA students might apply for and varied factors, such as income, flexibility, status, and how socially responsible the organization was. We found among this very ambitious and skilled talent group that there are clear and distinct segments who care about purpose very differently.

Students in the different segments are interested in different courses while in school, and they eventually choose different industries. In particular, MBA students who value purpose are less likely to select jobs in the finance industry—the industry with the highest wages. Female students are more likely to belong to the segment that cares about purpose. So, if the finance industry wants to increase the proportion of female talent, they need to address this need. However, the industry's emphasis shouldn't be solely on the pursuit of purpose, as the interest in purpose varies among individuals, regardless of gender. Women, just like men, may prioritize purpose to differing degrees. Thus, relying solely on gender for segmentation is inadequate. Behavioral segmentation offers a more nuanced approach, transcending blunt sociodemographic labels like age or gender.

Surveys, such as the ones we have used in our studies, can help create meaningful segments based on employees' motivation, needs, and attitudes. Starbucks did a famous segmentation study in 2010 that focused on the thousands of employees in stores across the globe. Melissa Graves, director of HR's Organizational Insights and Analytics Department, based at the company's Seattle headquarters, said that her team expanded the typical engagement survey using tools from marketing: "We also asked about what marketing calls 'needs states'—lifestyle factors, beliefs and attitudes that differentiate the partners [employees] and drive loyalty and motivation." The findings of Starbucks's study revealed the existence of three distinct segments among its employees: the "skiers," who primarily work to support their other passions; the "artists," who prioritize community and social responsibility in their choice of employer; and the "careerists," who seek long-term career growth opportunities within the company. Segments such as these align closely with the different motivational factors discussed in Part II and illustrate the varying degrees of importance individuals place on flexibility (higher for skiers), purpose (higher for artists), and just right tasks and career development (higher for careerists).

A major Asian telecom company rolled out an incentive plan that was only accepted by 5 percent of its workforce. The company clearly misunderstood what made their employees tick. To address this problem, the company used a survey-based approach to gather data about the motivation of its field force and segment accordingly. The segmentation approach showed that its employees had a variety of different motives and that many were willing to earn less for some of those nonpay attributes such as flexibility. One of the segments was "waiting for retirement." Those were normally very knowledgeable workers (and therefore important to the company) who were financially more secure and were waiting to qualify for their retirement benefits. Others were "hungry and ambitious" who were willing to opt for a pay-for-performance scheme that has a lower base salary but more earning upsides if hitting performance and quality goals.

Based on those different segments, the company was able to target different benefit packages and the respective messages to different groups. The acceptance of the approach and take-up of the different options was overwhelmingly high. For example, the company was able to offer a more flexible work schedule with part-time work for the ones who were waiting for retirement. Those workers only needed to work when needed, which has cost benefit to the company, but still qualified for retirement benefits. Bain & Company, a consultancy, estimated that performance increased by 70 percent and unit costs dropped by 30 percent. The effort allowed the company to also target their training or voluntary separation programs to the right segment—with great success. The logic of this approach is the same as with customers: employees also do not fit into one group that reacts to the same approach. By understanding the differences and offering a customized EX, motivation and engagement go up—and so does firm performance.

In addition to surveys, there is a host of nontraditional data that organizations can easily collect on employee behavior and analyze to personalize EX. As we will discuss below, it is crucial to exercise caution in the utilization of such data to avoid causing unease among employees.

But there does exist a rich source of information, for example, in the form of metadata about email exchanges, Slack communications, or meetings. Research by Microsoft on such data discussed in the previous chapter can detect different segments based on how individuals interact and communicate with others in the organization. The data provides insights into how working together works and the importance of personal connections. It is possible to get more fine-grained insights about individual employees and figure out who needs support because they are isolated or not interacting with a diverse group. Similarly, smart badges can enable companies to analyze who is talking to whom and in this way determine which individuals are central to the flow of information (or should be) and then make tailored changes to the work environment.

Internal marketplaces, like the ones discussed in Chapter 8, are providing opportunities for employees to get matched to employment opportunities within the same organizations. But they can also provide data about employees—their skills, ambitions, and interests. Think about how Netflix knows about your preferences by what you watch, what you search for, and what you just sample by watching a trailer. While most traditional HR data is static and limited to degrees and demographic backgrounds, data from internal marketplaces such as Gloat is dynamically updated and provide more behavioral data. These data sets will provide a more complete picture of what employees are actually interested in. For instance, if an employer is interested in what an employee's just right tasks are, they can create such a personalized experience. This is what IBM has done. According to Diane Gherson, former head of IBM's HR, the company worked together with their workforce to design "a learning platform that is individually personalized for every one of our 380,000 IBMers. [...] it's organized sort of like Netflix."

But remember: it's vital for businesses to keep in mind the different factors that motivate humans to work if they want to create the employee advantage. Only then can they use data in the most powerful way to effectively segment the workforce and personalize EX. This approach will allow leaders to look for different types of data that provide insights into employees' behavior and preferences. Hard data is, however, no substitute for just listening to employees—and doing so frequently.

Understanding employees' needs on a personal level will provide insights into what motivates each employee personally. You have to ask yourself: What are the behavioral segments in my organization? What motivational factors are driving those different segments? What data (hard data or surveys) am I using to isolate what motivates different segments of my workforce?

Now, employers can craft "moments that matter" for the different segments. Something marketers have understood for a long time.

Moments at Work That Matter

Once you are armed with these insights from the data you have gathered and from direct input from your employees, and after you have identified core segments within your organization, the table is set for meaningful improvements to EX. These insights can be used to map the employee journey and define "moments that matter." While there are well-known steps on the employee journey, such as recruiting or onboarding, employee insight work can reveal other "moments that matter," whether they are pain points or opportunities for the organization to delight employees.

Marketing teams in customer-centric organizations have been perfecting the concept of customer journeys and moments that matter for a long time. Customer journeys encompass the entire process of customer interactions with a company, both online and offline. Moments that matter are specific points within this journey that significantly impact the customer's perception of the business. These moments can be positive and strengthen loyalty, or negative and cause dissatisfaction. By identifying and understanding the dynamics of these crucial touch points, businesses can enhance the customer experience through feedback analysis, data interpretation, and behavior observation. Once they know how to enhance these moments, companies can deliver a more satisfying overall experience. The same principles are at work when applied to the employee experience.

Recall how Eli Lilly transformed its marketing team's focus from customer journeys to mapping the journeys of minority groups within the organization, as discussed in Chapter 3. When I talked to Kelly Copes-Anderson, vice president and global head of diversity, equity, and inclusion at Eli Lilly, she mentioned where the journeys originated: "I worked on the commercial side of our business and saw how getting the voices of our customers, our patients, and people that are in the category of the disease area where we have a medicine to really learn what their experiences are—What are the challenges, opportunities, the tensions that they feel? What are their day-to-day realities?—so that it's not only do we give them a medicine, but how do we actually create the right type of experience for them to be successful with their disease that goes beyond the medicine?"

The goal of applying this technique to employees (using interviews, focus groups, and data analysis) was to explore the journeys for minority segments and figure out how to change the moments that mattered in their careers in order to increase their EX and, eventually, their representation in leadership positions. The first journey that focused on women was a huge success and got applied to many more minority segments within the organization—and it has changed how the organization interacts with its employees. Kelly Copes-Anderson mentioned that the journeys showed that "we had to be more intentional. With the gained insight, we were able to determine what areas we should focus on and prioritize in order to achieve our goals. One priority that came out of the first journey with women was that transparency and understanding of career management needed to be increased.... With the understanding of the experience (and the barriers), the company made it much more explicit and normal to ask for assessment for leadership—with significant success."

An important part of all that insight work regarding employees' experiences is to create empathy among the different segments of the workforce. Sharing the experiences and feelings of others creates the opportunity to engage on a deeper level. Copes-Anderson said: "I think part of the personalization is when we educated our entire organization on these employee journeys, so that everybody understood what were those moments of truth ["moments that matter" in Eli Lilly speak], those key opportunity points in the employee experience for women, for Black employees, or for Latinx. It allows us to more intentionally treat individuals as individuals."

Every organization and every segment within those organizations is different in what ultimately motivates and frustrates employees. Recognizing these variations is crucial, but a committed effort is required to understand employees' behavior and what motivates them. Within organizations, there are specialized teams solely dedicated to generating customer insights and enhancing the customer experience. A similar level of attention has to be given to employees and their experiences. In doing so, it is essential to involve the employees themselves.

Involving employees in the process not only creates necessary insights but is also critical to mitigate some of the challenges of moving toward a data-driven personalization of EX.

Involve Employees

If you were to ask a successful marketer whether it is a good idea to talk and listen to consumers once a year, they certainly would respond that this is insufficient if you want to track the changing needs of your customers. Nevertheless, this is how many companies treat their employees—if they even conduct annual employee surveys at all. Customer surveys are enormously valuable. In addition to collecting data about consumers, customer surveys can provide a lot of insights. Constant feedback, customer insight interviews, and focus groups are all core parts of customer-centricity. Executives at Home Depot, for example, are required to spend time each quarter talking to customers. The same tactics can be used to understand what employees or team members want. Just simply listening to workers can create goodwill as employees feel heard and understood. As a Starbucks manager once said after a listening session with CEO Howard Schultz: "I remember how he listened and truly made everyone feel valued." It is the personal touch that makes a difference. As noted in Chapter 9, the Novartis division study showed that promoting one-on-one meetings between managers and team members had a significant overall impact. This was especially true when managers were explicitly encouraged to ask their team members to openly communicate what mattered to them and where they required support. It was this personalized approach to meetings that yielded the most significant positive outcomes.

Involving employees in the process of humanizing and personalizing work is critically important for three reasons. First, effectively personalizing EX requires new and unconventional high-frequency data about employees' behavior. This can involve sensitive material. Think, for example, of metadata about emails or Slack exchanges. Or even more personal, how about the data on employees' wellness and health that some companies have access to? Such information could be very helpful to businesses committed to supporting employees at risk. But, just as there are privacy concerns surrounding the gathering of data about consumer behavior, such as shopping histories or search data, organizations must exercise extreme caution to ensure they do not undermine employees' trust and violate their privacy. Given the temptation of leaders to use data to monitor and surveil employees, being sensitive and careful about using this data is critical.

Transparency and employee involvement are therefore of utmost importance. Organizations must be forthright about the data they are utilizing and the reasons behind it. This will establish a trustworthy signal that the data is being employed to enhance the employee experience, ultimately leading to improved organizational performance. It necessitates a shift in mind-set, recognizing that what benefits the employee experience also benefits the organization as a whole. If leaders are afraid to be completely transparent about the use of data, they are signaling to their employees that the organization does not trust its workforce and that it might be using the data in a way that hurts its employees. Both are clear signs that the organization is not yet employee-centric.

The second rationale for involving employees in the customization of the employee experience (EX) relates to the perception of inequality. By its very nature, personalization will result in different outcomes for employees. Training, benefits, and support will be tailored to individual needs, leading to variations in employee roles and in how workers and employee segments are treated. For example, the opportunity to work remotely differs by type of employee, which can create significant rifts within the workforce. Almost all the executives I talk to confirm that this apparent inequality is perceived negatively—more so than obvious inequalities in organizations such as income. The research on people's acceptance of inequality clearly shows that if humans understand why certain individuals are treated differently (such as why somebody earns more), they accept it. If they do not understand the difference, they will have a visceral negative reaction. When it comes to remote work, for example, the different ways employees are treated may feel very ad hoc—because it often actually is. Transparency, clear communication, and the involvement of employees—and deliberately thinking about why certain workers can and cannot work remotely—will help.

Involving employees and being transparent will lead them to perceive the selection process as fair and accept it. IBM experienced this firsthand when they involved its workforce in the process of overhauling its performance management system—probably one of the more sensitive HR topics within an organization. Instead of the typical top-down, consultant-driven process, IBM began to involve its employees—all of them. The head of HR, Diane Gherson, blogged to her workforce with a suggestion for a new performance management system. "We'd love your input," she wrote. "If you hate it, we'll start over, no problem. But we really want your thoughts." As you can imagine, some of the first reactions were cynical in nature. Employees harbored skepticism, perceiving the situation as a scam because they believed that the executive team had already reached definitive decisions. To address this concern, IBM had to intensify its efforts in clearly communicating and assuring employees that it genuinely valued and sought their input.

Through dedicated efforts to build trust, including transparent communication about the company's foundational principles and its commitment to take employees' inputs seriously, eventually over one hundred thousand employees actively participated in the process. As a result, the entire process proved to be faster than the traditional approach and generated substantial buy-in from the workforce. "That's the power of engaging the whole workforce," Gherson concluded. "People are much less likely to resist the change when they've had a hand in shaping it."

Last but not least, listening to employees will improve an organization's understanding of what motivates its workers to be the most engaged and productive. It is the final and most human aspect of employee-centricity. People are different with all their unique needs, fears, motivations, and preferences. Attentively listening to employees, treating their input with importance, and customizing the employee experience (EX) to meet their needs will create the employee advantage. Whether an organization is large and capable of undertaking extensive employee insights projects, conducting large-scale surveys and focus groups, or leveraging vast amounts of data for insights, or whether it is a small organization with limited resources, the act of listening remains critical. Kelly Copes-Anderson of Eli Lilly said: "We have a whole lot of data, and that richness of the data has allowed us as a large organization to make the kinds of changes that are appropriate for our scale. But why wouldn't you just make the space and time, even if it's a two-hour meeting, to ask really simple questions about what the experience is for your employees? It's really that simple. And being able to hear that voice of the employee allows you to maybe rethink how you're approaching your workplace differently."

Ultimately, the intricate tapestry of human motivation and the unique distinctions among individuals present a significant challenge in managing teams and organizations. However, this very complexity also holds the key to gaining a competitive edge—if managed properly. The most successful organizations grasp the fundamental truth that businesses are comprised of human beings. Thus, they wholeheartedly embrace an employee-centric approach, recognizing two crucial aspects. First, putting employees at the forefront is a mutually beneficial strategy, fostering a win-win situation. Second, this approach necessitates delving deeper into human motivation beyond monetary incentives and customizing the employee experience to cater to the specific needs of each individual.

Epilogue
The Employee-Centric Future

THESE ARE ESPECIALLY challenging times for people in business. Technological and cultural changes have always played a powerful role in shaping our working world, but the last few decades have been particularly disorienting for workers and managers alike. It can be hard to fully appreciate how much and how quickly the workplace has changed due to the constant need for re- and upskilling, innovations in digital communications, robotics, and artificial intelligence. All this change has undeniably been disruptive, and it can be tempting to think that the fundamental dynamics that shape human cooperative endeavors—like engaging in business—have changed. But that's simply not the case.

One fact has remained consistent in successful companies throughout all the decades of technological transformation: the heart at the center of a successful company is its people. Great leaders know that understanding what truly motivates these workers is the key to unlocking their full potential—and the potential of your business. Organizations that understand this basic fact have already taken the first step toward enjoying the employee advantage.

Throughout the book, we've seen how organizations that want to be competitive in a fast-changing business environment can and, indeed must, evolve if they want to effectively harness the potential of their employees. The stories and insights I have shared in these pages come from the work of social scientists and forward-thinking executives from around the world, underscoring the universality of these lessons. Companies that recognize, celebrate, and amplify human potential thrive because they are meeting human needs. The greatest innovations in technology, automation, and strategy will never be enough to make a business thrive if they are not implemented in a human-centric way.

Managers should not be surprised that employees want to be treated as valuable—more than expendable cogs in the machinery of a business. Leaders should not shut their ears when their employees tell them they want better treatment. Workers are not much different than the customers that businesses have been at great pains to please in the past few decades. Just as those customers have grown to expect more from businesses, employees are beginning to do the same. After all, employees are also customers! The same major shifts that affected the changes toward customer-centricity are also pushing businesses to put their people first if they want to thrive.

First, companies must rethink their traditional attitudes about the value of workers and what makes them tick. They need to abandon the outdated notion that when companies put their employees first, shareholders will lose out. This simplistic either-or way of thinking was also once the way many businesses looked at their relationship with consumers. Second, leaders must abandon the old idea that people are solely driven by salaries and bonuses. This is a crude and simplistic model of human motivation. Businesses that want engaged workers need to do the work to truly understand what their employees want.

Of course, there's no one-size-fits-all approach to humanizing work. But we can derive some basic principles from the behavioral science of motivation. Behavioral economics, as we've seen, offers a treasure trove of insights into the motivations, desires, and behaviors of individuals. By integrating these insights into business strategies, leaders can design workplaces that not only meet but exceed employee expectations. This alignment between organizational goals and individual aspirations paves the way for a harmonious, productive, and resilient workforce.

The Intentional Workplace

You can't achieve the employee advantage through half measures. It requires the implementation of a comprehensive plan. If the plan appears deceptively simple, like adding a ping-pong table in the common area or free yoga classes, that is a sign that it will fall short. You cannot "om" your company out of an uninspiring or toxic work culture. Neither can superficial branding strategies alter deeply embedded parts of a company's culture. True change comes from initiatives that are challenging to execute and challenging for competitors to replicate. Such changes may be hard to implement and costly in the short term, but the long-term benefits in brand loyalty, employee satisfaction, and overall profitability can be immense.

Before you can make improvements, you need a candid assessment of where your team or organization currently falls short. Ask yourself: How can a more engaged workforce create more value for the business through increases in productivity, innovation, or better customer service?

Another question you should ask yourself is: What are the core values of our business, and do they align with those of our employees? Answering this question will help you identify the employees that are right for your business. Just as customer-centric businesses identify and market toward the people who are most likely to connect with their products, employee-centric businesses need to identify which types of employees are the right fit and which are not. Traditional skill levels or credentials represent only one facet of this consideration. As the research presented in this book shows, people have many different motivations, and it falls upon you to determine the types of employees that make up the optimal mix within your workforce. Consider factors such as the employees' values, social intelligence, willingness to assist others, and capacity to both provide and receive constructive feedback. Then hire and promote accordingly.

Next comes the most crucial and challenging step: enhancing every facet of operations by adopting an employee-centric perspective. To do this, harness the power of the four key human motivators discussed in the previous chapters: aiming for ambitious goals (shoot for the moon); granting autonomy (a matter of trust); aligning tasks and skills appropriately (just right tasks); and recognizing the effectiveness of collaborative efforts (working together works).

Remember that the approach you take needs to be comprehensive and intentional. The metaphorical andon cord is useless if it is not accompanied by employee-centric practices such as proper training and flat hierarchies where everybody is seen and valued as equal team members. Giving flexibility and autonomy is great, but it needs to be paired with engaged coaching. You need to be intentional about when flexibility is affecting collaboration and how to create the right environment in which working together really works.

Also—and I can't emphasize this enough—listen to your employees. They possess valuable knowledge, and it is essential to trust in their expertise. Eli Lilly gained invaluable insights about its employees' work experiences from its "employee journeys" program because the company was open to feedback from the people it was designed to help. When you listen you get more than just a better-designed work experience. You'll foster transparency and empower your employees to be participants in the company's culture. The outcome, if you do this right, will be a flourishing business, both in the present and in the future.

The Human-Centric Future of Work

Now, before we wrap up, let's talk a little more about the future. Businesses today have access to myriad tools that promise to increase efficiency in the workplace, and we can expect these to grow more powerful and ubiquitous in the coming years. Some of these promise to monitor (some might say spy on) employees in and out of the office. It's easy for managers to be swept away by the allure of cutting-edge technologies, but employee-centric leaders should continually ask themselves: Can these tools be adopted and implemented in a human-centric way? The insights about human motivation can guide leaders in their decisions to leverage technological change to enhance the employee advantage.

As we saw throughout the book, technological advances should support human motivation. There is, for example, a substantial danger in collecting data about employees for the purpose of surveillance. This "digital Taylorism" negatively affects employees' sense of autonomy and leads them, rightly, to feel they are not trusted. Such data is best used to personalize experience and provide supportive feedback. This will help employees become better at their jobs and enable managers to assign them the just right jobs that will allow them to succeed and keep them challenged. A human-centric approach acknowledges the importance of continually evolving just right tasks for employees. Technology can play a pivotal role in identifying these roles and tasks within the organization, facilitating the creation of personalized and empowering development plans. As a leader, you need to be deliberate in creating opportunities for your team members, ensuring they are optimally challenged and engaged, thus mitigating the risk of boredom or attrition.

Technology can also help amplify meaning and purpose for employees. Advancements like GenAI have the potential to liberate individuals from rote tasks, allowing them to concentrate on more meaningful endeavors. The moment I never again have to write a meeting summary or a next-steps email, I will be very happy. That's not only because I will be spared the headache of doing a tedious task, but it also means I will be able to focus on the most important aspects of my job, like meeting with my students and staff and doing my research. If mundane and mindless tasks can be automated, your employees will get a boost in working toward the real purpose of the organization.

It's critical for businesses to understand, however, that technology should be regarded as a tool that augments human capabilities, not as something that will displace them. Many are rightly anxious about the impact of technology on their jobs. The successful integration of technology should revolve around freeing up employees' capacity, enabling them to dedicate more of their efforts to tasks that align with the core purpose of the organization. Be transparent and involve your workforce along the way.

Technology and data can also serve as valuable tools in assisting human-centric leaders in purposefully cultivating positive and influential interactions. Social interactions between workers can be beneficial to work, but not always. We've all been in offices or on teams where relationships can take a negative turn, leading to hostility and toxicity. Or vital connections between employees can simply break down. Data can furnish crucial insights into the dynamics of interactions—revealing who engages with whom and where information flows within the organization. This information can be invaluable in crafting interactions that are truly meaningful and constructive.

Technology has the capacity to enable meaningful connections that transcend geographical and temporal boundaries. For instance, features like the random breakout function on Zoom can foster connections that might not have occurred during traditional in-person meetings. Technological tools can break down physical constraints, such as office layout, to facilitate connections.

However, while virtual teamwork and mentoring offer significant advantages, it's essential to be intentional about fostering in-person social interactions and not allowing electronic distractions to dominate. It is not only acceptable but, in fact, necessary for employees to socialize and have dedicated time and space for personal interaction. As a leader, you play a pivotal role in establishing the stage and setting norms for healthy and supportive social interactions.

Regardless of whether you are a CEO or an emerging leader, running a large organization or a small team, adopting an employee-centric mind-set yields advantages. However, this approach demands a level of dedication to employees comparable to the obsession that customer-centric companies have toward their customers. Achieving this requires not only a profound comprehension of human behavior but also a genuine commitment to humanizing the workplace and treating employees as the new customers. The era of a one-size-fits-all approach has to be left behind. Personalization will emerge as not only the foundation of customer-centricity but also the essential element for building a genuinely employee-centric future. If technology is implemented in a human-centric way, it can help achieve the employee advantage. But this transformation will demand considerable effort and the nurturing of a new generation of leaders. The outcome will be an organization and a workforce poised for the future and driven by heightened engagement and motivation, culminating in a thriving and prosperous business.

Acknowledgments

A FEW YEARS AGO, a book agent approached me and inquired whether I would be interested in crafting a book based on my research on behavioral economics. At that time, I declined the offer, feeling I didn't have a subject that inspired enough passion to embark on the significant endeavor of authoring a book. A few years have passed, though. A pandemic has come and gone, and I've watched as engagement at work has gone down and executives shared with me their struggle to motivate their teams and implement human-centric future-of-work policies. My feelings changed. I felt a burning enthusiasm for applying insights from my research to an important topic: the potential for leaders and organizations to create engaging and motivating workplaces. That passion helped me through the arduous process of writing this book—but I still couldn't have done it alone. There were many people who were crucial in helping me finish the book before and during the process of writing it. I would like to thank them here.

First of all, I want to extend my gratitude to my parents, who have always believed in me and supported my pursuits. Although they did not attend college themselves, only speak German and therefore cannot read any of my academic writings, and were heartbroken when I decided to move an ocean away, they consistently conveyed that whatever I chose to do was the right path.

My journey into an academic career would not have been possible without my adviser, Bruno S. Frey. He instilled in me a passion for social science and economics research. Bruno is an unorthodox economist who posed intriguing and unconventional questions. His pioneering research on the limits of monetary incentives inspired me early on in my career, and his influence is unmistakable throughout this book.

Although I am often studying why employees are not engaged at work, I am happy to say this is not a problem for me at Columbia Business School. No organization is perfect, but I couldn't ask for better colleagues. It is a privilege to work alongside and learn from some of the world's finest scholars. My gratitude goes in particular to my strategy colleagues Bo Cowgill, Bruce Kogut, Dan Wang, Daniel Keum, Jerry Kim, Jorge Guzman, Kathy Harrigan, Nataliya Wright, Soomi Kim, and Vanessa Burbano. They have played a significant role in shaping me into a better strategist. But all my colleagues in the Management Division are incredible scholars from whom I have learned a lot. I have also drawn inspiration from my amazing colleagues outside my immediate division. Special thanks to Jeff Schwartz, with whom I developed our elective on the future of work and the executive education program. His passion for the future of work ignited my own exploration of how firms can improve. And then there are the amazing and dedicated staff and administrators at CBS who actually make the place work. Special thanks to Amanda Eckler, Joyce Blair, Julie Berger, Kathleen Rithisorn, Katie Conway, Kerith Gardner, Lisa Andujar-Ray, Sean Hardwick, and Sherene Alexander.

Throughout Columbia, I interact with hundreds of exceptionally bright, engaging, and ambitious students and participants in our executive education programs. I am fortunate to have a job where I not only teach but also learn. I cherish the fact that I gain as much, if not more, from my students as they hopefully gain from me. Thus, I wholeheartedly thank them for their contributions to my growth.

Special thanks are due to my book agent, Jeff Shreve, who did not give up on me when I said no the first time. He and the team at The Curious Minds Agency believed in my book idea and collaborated closely with me on the book's concept and structure. He did an incredible job. Jeff Alexander worked as my developmental editor, helping me refine my arguments and convey them eloquently. He was also there when I had doubts and downs. Thanks for dealing with me all those months. And then there is Colleen Lawrie at PublicAffairs, who not only believed in this book project but also assisted me in refining the idea. She diligently read multiple versions of my manuscript, improving it each time. She is the epitome of an exceptional editor. My heartfelt thanks extend to her team at PublicAffairs who worked tirelessly to transform my manuscript into something truly remarkable. Their expertise, commitment, and creative input were invaluable in shaping my work into its final form. I could not imagine a better team on my side.

This book owes much to the collective research efforts of colleagues across the globe. My coauthors are a significant part of why I love my job; they contribute to my growth and offer diverse perspectives. Special thanks to Alois Stutzer, Anat Bracha, Armando Meier, Bruno S. Frey, Charles Sprenger, Dan Ariely, Daniel Keum, David Huffman, Devin Pope, Dina Pomeranz, Elizabeth Miskin, Eric Johnson, Erik Wengström, Florian Schneider, Johanna Rickne, Lamar Pierce, Lea Cassar, Leandro Carvalho, Lorenz Goette, Maria Cotofan, Matt Stephenson, Matthias Sutter, Matthias Benz, Nandil Bhatia, Nicolas Padilla, Olivier Toubia, Olle Folke, Patryk Perkowski, Pedro Rey-Biel, Pol Campos-Marcade, Robert Dur, Simon Luechinger, Stephanie Wang, Uri Gneezy, and Vanessa Burbano for their invaluable contributions to our joint work that influenced the content of this book. Engaging discussions with Felix Oberholzer-Gee and Mic Milic Frederickx, enriched this book immensely. While this book draws from my own research, it also integrates many insights from numerous other scholars. Many of them I've had the privilege of knowing personally and interacting with at seminars, conferences, or through personal conversations. Other insights I've gleaned through my daily work, which involves reading scholarly work—what an amazing aspect of my job. Additionally, I've drawn inspiration from executives who continuously strive to make their organizations more employee-centric.

Last but certainly not least, I extend my heartfelt thanks to my family, who supported me during the intense writing process. Our remarkable children, Miguel, Alba, and Henrik, kept me grounded and never complained that I was too obsessed about this book (although I probably was). I love them immensely. And then there is my wife, Susan, to whom this book is dedicated. She is my most fervent champion, always by my side. Susan challenges my ideas, inspires me every day, and is the best partner I could ever imagine. Our relationship proves that working together works. Thank you from the bottom of my heart.

Notes

Introduction

1 **Scholastic and Bloomsbury...were** The story about the Harry Potter book is from: Brad Stone, *The Everything Store: Jeff Bezos and the Age of Amazon* (New York: Random House, 2013).

1 **"I was thinking, holy shit** Stone, *The Everything Store*, 111.

2 **"That either-or-mentality** Stone, *The Everything Store*, 111.

2 **"We will continue to focus** Amazon Staff, "Amazon's Original 1997 Letter to Shareholders," About Amazon US, March 21, 1997, https://www.aboutamazon.com/news/company-news/amazons-orignal-1997-letter-to-shareholders.

2 **"There are many advantages** Amazon staff, "2016 Letter to Shareholders," About Amazon US, April 17, 2017, https://www.aboutamazon.com/news/company-news/2016-letter-to-shareholders.

3 **"We were able to assess** Stone, *The Everything Store*, 111.

3 **In 2015, a now famous** Jodi Kantor and David Steitfeld, "Inside Amazon: Wrestling Big Ideas in a Bruising Workplace," *New York Times*, September 23, 2021, https://www.nytimes.com/2015/08/16/technology/inside-amazon-wrestling-big-ideas-in-a-bruising-workplace.html.

3 **The average rate of "regretted" attrition** Eugene Kim, "Amazon Employees Are Quitting at Twice the Rate of Recent Years, Mostly Due to Low Pay and Increased Competition, Leaked Documents Show," Business Insider, May 24, 2022, https://www.businessinsider.com/amazons-regretted-attrition-rate-more-than-doubled-in-the-past-year-2022-5.

4 **"It is very important that area managers** Jodi Kantor, Karen Weise, and Grace Ashford, "Inside Amazon's Employment Machine," *New York Times*, December 15, 2021, https://www.nytimes.com/interactive/2021/06/15/us/amazon-workers.html.

4 **If you study Bezos's shareholder** Tricia Gregg and Boris Groysberg, "Amazon's Priorities over the Years, Based on Jeff Bezos's Letters to Shareholders," *Harvard Business Review*, 2019.

4 **My colleague at Columbia** Nandil Bhatia and Stephan Meier, "Are Customers 10x More Important to Firms than Employees? Empirical Analysis of

231

Imbalance in Emphasis Between Two Stakeholders," working paper, September 1, 2022, https://papers.ssrn.com/sol3/papers.cfm?abstract_id=4215010.

4 **Our results are similar** Salesforce, "The Experience Advantage: Transforming Customer and Employee Experience for the Future of Work," 2022, https://www.salesforce.com/content/dam/web/en_us/www/images/form/conf/TheExperienceAdvantage_Whitepaper_int_V7.pdf; and Arthur Mazor et al., "Reimagine and Craft the Employee Experience: Design Thinking in Action," *Deloitte Insights*, https://www2.deloitte.com/us/en/pages/human-capital/articles/reimagine-and-craft-the-employee-experience.html.

5 **More than 67 percent of US employees** Jim Harter, "U.S. Employee Engagement Needs a Rebound in 2023," Gallup.com, September 19, 2023, https://www.gallup.com/workplace/468233/employee-engagement-needs-rebound-2023.aspx.

7 **"We have always wanted to be** Jeff Bezos, "2020 Letter to Shareholders," About Amazon US, April 15, 2021, https://www.aboutamazon.com/news/company-news/2020-letter-to-shareholders.

8 **"Leaders work every day** Amazon Jobs, "Leadership Principles," accessed September 29, 2023, https://www.amazon.jobs/content/en/our-workplace/leadership-principles.

Chapter 1: The End of the Status Quo

12 **But the trend of resignations** Heather Long, "It's Not a 'Labor Shortage.' It's a Great Reassessment of Work in America," *Washington Post*, May 10, 2021, https://www.washingtonpost.com/business/2021/05/07/jobs-report-labor-shortage-analysis/.

12 **At Starbucks, for instance** Andrea Hsu, "Starbucks Workers Have Unionized at Record Speed; Many Fear Retaliation Now," NPR, October 2, 2022.

13 **Josie, the barista** Lydia Greene, "Complicated Starbucks Order Drives Barista Crazy," *Wide Open Country*, May 20, 2021, https://www.wideopencountry.com/complicated-starbucks-order/.

13 **"They don't seem to really care** Hsu, "Starbucks Workers Have Unionized."

14 **This command never made it** Winnie Hu, "Solitaire Costs Man His City Job After Bloomberg Sees Computer," *New York Times*, February 10, 2006.

14 **In a sample of forty-seven countries** Robert Dur and Max Van Lent, "Socially Useless Jobs," *Industrial Relations* 58, no. 1 (December 2, 2018): 3–16, https://doi.org/10.1111/irel.12227.

15 **"Jobs are not just** Anne Case and Angus Deaton, *Deaths of Despair and the Future of Capitalism* (Princeton, NJ: Princeton University Press, 2020).

16 **Colin Bryar and Bill Carr** Colin Bryar and Bill Carr, "Why (and How) Amazon Created the Kindle and Changed the Book Industry Forever," *Entrepreneur*, January 27, 2021, https://www.entrepreneur.com/growing-a-business/why-and-how-amazon-created-the-kindle-and-changed-the/363311.

16 **"When we worked backwards** Bryar and Carr, "Why (and How) Amazon."

16 **"If you're competitor focused** Marla Tabaka, "Amazon's 4 Keys to Success, According to Jeff Bezos," *Inc.*, April 15, 2019, https://www.inc.com/marla -tabaka/jeff-bezos-says-these-4-principles-are-key-to-amazons-success -they-can-work-for-you-too.html.

17 **Consider wealth management** Stephan Meier and Jeffrey Schwartz, "Morgan Stanley," Columbia Business School Case.

18 **"The future will see a world** Ciaran Daly, "Implications of AI Go Far Beyond Personalization," *AI Business*, September 28, 2022, https://aibusiness .com/verticals/implications-of-ai-go-far-beyond-personalization.

18 **Jeff Bezos commented that** Daniel Newman, "Customer Experience Is the Future of Marketing," *Forbes*, October 13, 2015, https://www.forbes .com/sites/danielnewman/2015/10/13/customer-experience-is-the-future -of-marketing/?sh=3a81819e193d.

18 **Customers post one billion reviews** Statista, "Number of User Reviews and Ratings on Tripadvisor Worldwide 2014–2022," August 29, 2023, https:// www.statista.com/statistics/684862/tripadvisor-number-of-reviews/.

18 **This research shows** Dante Donati, "The End of Tourist Traps: A Natural Experiment on the Impact of Tripadvisor on Quality Upgrading," CESifo Working Paper 9834, July 15, 2022, https://papers.ssrn.com/sol3/papers.cfm ?abstract_id=4163323.

18 **"The online world has changed** Linda Kinstler, "How TripAdvisor Changed Travel," *Guardian*, August 31, 2021, https://www.theguardian.com/news /2018/aug/17/how-tripadvisor-changed-travel.

19 **They use data from many sources** Blake Morgan, "5 Lessons in Personalization from Stitch Fix," *Forbes*, December 10, 2019, https://www.forbes.com /sites/blakemorgan/2019/12/10/5-lessons-in-personalization-from-stitch -fix/?sh=2bd7b845b4e8.

19 **According to Accenture** "Making It Personal: Why Brands Must Move from Communication to Conversation for Greater Personalization," *Accenture Interactive*, Pulse Check 2018, https://www.accenture.com/t20161011 T222718__w__/us-en/_acnmedia/PDF-34/Accenture-Pulse-Check-Dive -Key-Findings-Personalized-Experiences.pdf.

19 **According to Salesforce research** Salesforce, "State of the Connected Customer Report," n.d., https://www.salesforce.com/resources/research-rep orts/state-of-the-connected-customer/.

21 **One of my studies shows** Maria Cotofan et al., "Macroeconomic Conditions When Young Shape Job Preferences for Life," *Review of Economics and Statistics* 105, no. 2 (2023): 467–473, https://doi.org/10.1162/rest_a_01057.

21 **A good example is** Megan Leonhardt, "Managing Gen Z Is Like Working with People from a 'Different Country,'" *Fortune*, October 10, 2022, https:// fortune.com/2022/10/10/how-to-manage-gen-z-working-culture/.

22 **More than half of responders** Qualtrics, "For Employees, Shared Values Matter More Than Policy Positions," September 14, 2022, https://www.qualtrics.com/news/for-employees-shared-values-matter-more-than-policy-positions/.

23 **Although some employees may require** Aaron K. Chatterji, "The New CEO Activists," *Harvard Business Review*, April 21, 2022, https://hbr.org/2018/01/the-new-ceo-activists; and Vanessa Burbano, "The Demotivating Effects of Communicating a Social-Political Stance: Field Experimental Evidence from an Online Labor Market Platform," *Management Science* 67 (February 1, 2021): 1004–1025.

23 **"Some people don't like** Julia Carrie Wong, "Uber CEO Travis Kalanick Caught on Video Arguing with Driver About Fares," *Guardian*, March 1, 2017, https://www.theguardian.com/technology/2017/feb/28/uber-ceo-travis-kalanick-driver-argument-video-fare-prices.

24 **"We were empowering people** Lizzie Widdicombe, "Improving Workplace Culture, One Review at a Time," *New Yorker*, January 15, 2018, https://www.newyorker.com/magazine/2018/01/22/improving-workplace-culture-one-review-at-a-time.

25 **"There'd been a march** Widdicombe, "Improving Workplace Culture."

25 **Research shows that** Svenja Dube and Chenqi Zhu, "The Disciplinary Effect of Social Media: Evidence from Firms' Responses to Glassdoor Reviews," *Journal of Accounting Research* 59, no. 5 (July 9, 2021): 1783–1825, https://doi.org/10.1111/1475-679X.12393.

25 **"This is just putting on the Internet** Widdicombe, "Improving Workplace Culture."

26 **A study mentioned in** Paul Leonardi and Noshir Contractor, "Better People Analytics: Measure Who They Know, Not Just Who They Are," *Harvard Business Review*, November–December 2018, https://hbr.org/2018/11/better-people-analytics.

27 **While it should be obvious** Team at Slack, "The Great Executive-Employee Disconnect," *Slack*, October 5, 2021, https://slack.com/blog/news/the-great-executive-employee-disconnect.

29 **ING, the global bank** Lucia del Carpio et al., "Embracing Digital: ING's Journey to a New Way of Working," *Harvard Business Review Case Study*, November 30, 2018, https://store.hbr.org/product/embracing-digital-ing-s-journey-to-a-new-way-of-working-part-1-ing-faces-digital-disruption/IN1530.

29 **ING went from having** del Carpio, "Embracing Digital."

29 **ING's former chief operating officer** McKinsey & Company, "ING's Agile Transformation," January 10, 2017, https://www.mckinsey.com/industries/financial-services/our-insights/ings-agile-transformation.

30 **After ING's transformation** McKinsey & Company, "ING's Agile Transformation."

30 **It moved up two ranks** del Carpio, "Embracing Digital."

Chapter 2: Not Either-Or but Win-Win

32   **Post-its are just one** 3M, "The History of 3M: From Humble Beginnings to Fortune 500," accessed October 12, 2023, https://www.3m.com/3M/en_US/company-us/about-3m/history/.

34   **"The changes he** David Gelles, *The Man Who Broke Capitalism: How Jack Welch Gutted the Heartland and Crushed the Soul of Corporate America—and How to Undo His Legacy* (New York: Simon and Schuster, 2022), 3.

34   **The process was welcomed** Don Peppers, "How 3M Lost (and Found) Its Innovation Mojo." *Inc.*, May 9, 2016, accessed October 20, 2023, https://www.inc.com/linkedin/don-peppers/downside-six-sigma-don-peppers.html.

35   **"Six Sigma has this terrifying** Anna Canato, Davide Ravasi, and Nelson Phillips, "Coerced Practice Implementation in Cases of Low Cultural Fit: Cultural Change and Practice Adaptation During the Implementation of Six SIGMA at 3M," *Academy of Management Journal* 56, no. 6 (December 1, 2013): 1724–1753, https://doi.org/10.5465/amj.2011.0093.

35   **During those years the** Peppers, "How 3M Lost (and Found) Its Innovation Mojo."

35   **In fact, in 2010** Barry Jaruzelski, Richard Holman, and Edward H. Baker, "3M's Open Innovation," Strategy+Business, May 30, 2011, https://www.strategy-business.com/article/00078.

35   **In 2023, it was** Jay Woodruff, "Best Workplaces for Innovators 2023: Sustainability," *Fast Company*, July 11, 2023, https://www.fastcompany.com/90919520/holcim-recognized-for-sustainability-innovation; and BCG Global, "17 Years of the Most Innovative Companies," n.d., https://www.bcg.com/publications/most-innovative-companies-historical-rankings.

36   **A headline in the *Wall Street Journal*** Ann Zimmerman, "Costco's Dilemma: Be Kind to Its Workers, or Wall Street?," *Wall Street Journal*, March 26, 2004, https://www.wsj.com/articles/SB108025917854365904.

36   **And an analyst** Wayne F. Cascio, "Decency Means More Than 'Always Low Prices': A Comparison of Costco to Wal-Mart's Sam's Club," *Academy of Management Perspectives* 20, no. 3 (August 1, 2006): 26–37, https://doi.org/10.5465/amp.2006.21903478.

36   **"With all due respect** Kevin Stankiewicz, "Jim Cramer Says to Buy Costco's Stock After Its 'Absurd' Post-Earnings Decline," CNBC, September 25, 2020, https://www.cnbc.com/2020/09/25/jim-cramer-buy-costcos-stock-after-its-absurd-post-earnings-dip.html.

37   **I'll use a simple** Adam Brandenburger and Harborne W. Stuart, "Value-Based Business Strategy," *Journal of Economics & Management Strategy* 5, no. 1 (January 13, 2005): 5–24, https://doi.org/10.1111/j.1430-9134.1996.00005.x.

40   **Jeff Bezos calls this** Stone, *The Everything Store*, 111.

41   **"Everybody was saying** Hubert Joly, "Former Best Buy CEO Hubert Joly: Empowering Workers to Create 'Magic,'" *Harvard Business Review*, interview

by Adi Ignatius, April 25, 2022, https://hbr.org/2021/12/former-best-buy-ceo-hubert-joly-empowering-workers-to-create-magic.

41 **As Joly describes** Hubert Joly, *The Heart of Business: Leadership Principles for the Next Era of Capitalism* (Boston: Harvard Business Publishing, 2021).

42 **"When a business is in trouble** Joly, *The Heart of Business*, 116.

42 **"When a business is in critical** Joly, *The Heart of Business*, 113.

42 **An early set of studies** Alex Edmans, "Does the Stock Market Fully Value Intangibles? Employee Satisfaction and Equity Prices," *Journal of Financial Economics* 101, no. 3 (September 1, 2011): 621–640, https://doi.org/10.1016/j.jfineco.2011.03.021; and Alex Edmans, "The Link Between Job Satisfaction and Firm Value, with Implications for Corporate Social Responsibility," *Academy of Management Perspectives*, 26, no. 4 (2012): 1–19.

43 **A more recent study** Larry Fauver, Michael McDonald, and Alvaro G. Taboada, "Does It Pay to Treat Employees Well? International Evidence on the Value of Employee-Friendly Culture," *Journal of Corporate Finance* 50 (June 1, 2018): 84–108, https://doi.org/10.1016/j.jcorpfin.2018.02.003.

43 **Similar studies** Chenyu Shan and Dragon Yongjun Tang, "The Value of Employee Satisfaction in Disastrous Times: Evidence from COVID-19," *Social Science Research Network*, January 1, 2020, https://doi.org/10.2139/ssrn.3560919; and A. Edmans, L. Li, and C. Zhang, "Employee Satisfaction, Labor Market Flexibility, and Stock Returns Around the World (No. w20300)," National Bureau of Economic Research, 2014; and E. Symitsi, P. Stamolampros, and G. Daskalakis, "Employees' Online Reviews and Equity Prices," *Economics Letters* 162 (2018): 53–55.

44 **"Our main challenges were** David Gelles, "Hubert Joly Turned Around Best Buy. Now He's Trying to Fix Capitalism," *New York Times*, July 15, 2021, https://www.nytimes.com/2021/07/15/business/hubert-joly-corner-office-best-buy.html.

44 **"'Authentic' is about credibility** Joly, *The Heart of Business*, 157.

44 **Before the pandemic** Brett Walsh and Erica Volini, *Rewriting the Rules for the Digital Age* (Dallas, TX: Deloitte University Press, 2017).

45 **"We were making independent** CNBC, "How Domino's Is Winning the Pizza Wars," YouTube video, 14:28, July 25, 2019, https://www.youtube.com/watch?v=FWu2rkffYvg.

46 **It is all about** Danny Klein, "For Sizzling Domino's, the Future Is 100 Percent Digital," *QSR*, July 7, 2023, https://www.qsrmagazine.com/pizza/sizzling-dominos-future-100-percent-digital.

46 **"Engaged employees were** Joly, *The Heart of Business*, 71.

46 **It shows in employee reviews** Glassdoor, "Compare Walmart vs Costco Wholesale," Glassdoor.com, accessed January 14, 2023, https://www.glassdoor.com/Compare/Walmart-vs-Costco-Wholesale-EI_IE715-E2590.htm.

46 **"On Wall Street they're** Cascio, "Decency Means More Than 'Always Low Prices.'"

47 **"We pay much better** Cascio, "Decency Means More Than 'Always Low Prices.'"

Chapter 3: Benefits of Putting Employees First

48 **"Everything was a fight** Ira Glass, "NUMMI (2010)," *This American Life*, March 26, 2010, https://www.thisamericanlife.org/403/nummi-2010.

48 **And the quality differences** Susan Helper and Rebecca Henderson, "Management Practices, Relational Contracts, and the Decline of General Motors," *Journal of Economic Perspectives* 28, no. 1 (February 1, 2014): 49–72, https://doi.org/10.1257/jep.28.1.49.

49 **The answer was** Jeffrey K. Liker, *The Toyota Way: 14 Management Principles from the World's Greatest Manufacturer* (New York: McGraw-Hill, 2004).

51 **In a Toyota plant** Liker, *The Toyota Way*, 229.

51 **So, he closed** Helper and Henderson, "Management Practices."

53 **It is the largest** National Institutes of Health (NIH), "Grants & Funding," n.d., https://www.nih.gov/grants-funding.

53 **Every year, HHMI supports** HHMI, "About HHMI Fundamentals," n.d., https://www.hhmi.org/about/financials.

53 **A research team** Pierre Azoulay, Joshua Graff Zivin, and Gustavo Manso, "Incentives and Creativity: Evidence from the Academic Life Sciences," *RAND Journal of Economics* 42, no. 3 (September 1, 2011): 527–554, https://doi.org/10.1111/j.1756-2171.2011.00140.x.

54 **My former colleague** Casey Ichniowski et al., "What Works at Work: Overview and Assessment," *Industrial Relations* 35, no. 3 (July 1, 1996): 299–333, https://doi.org/10.1111/j.1468-232x.1996.tb00409.x.

54 **Studies confirm the effect** Connie X. Mao and Jamie Weathers, "Employee Treatment and Firm Innovation," *Journal of Business Finance & Accounting* 46, no. 7–8 (June 10, 2019): 977–1002, https://doi.org/10.1111/jbfa.12393.

55 **Mercado, the largest** Hazhir Rahmandad and Zeynep Ton, "If Higher Pay Is Profitable, Why Is It So Rare? Modeling Competing Strategies in Mass Market Services," *Organization Science* 31, no. 5 (September 1, 2020): 1053–1071, https://doi.org/10.1287/orsc.2019.1347.

55 **"The layoffs are part** Nadia Rawlinson, "The Era of Happy Tech Workers Is Over," *New York Times*, January 19, 2023, https://www.nytimes.com/2023/01/19/opinion/tech-layoffs-meta-amazon-silicon-valley.html.

56 **So, a group** Clément Bellet, Jan-Emmanuel De Neve, and George Ward, "Does Employee Happiness Have an Impact on Productivity?," *Management Science* 70, no. 3 (March 2024): 1656–1679.

57 **Other related studies** Christian Krekel, George Ward, and Jan-Emmanuel De Neve, "Employee Wellbeing, Productivity, and Firm Performance,"

Social Science Research Network, January 1, 2019, https://doi.org/10.2139/ssrn.3356581.

57 **The high turnover** Zeynep Ton, Cate Reavis, and Sarah Day Kalloch, "Quest Diagnostics (a): Improving Performance at the Call Centers," MIT Sloan, May 1, 2017, https://mitsloan.mit.edu/teaching-resources-library/quest-diagnostics-a-improving-performance-call-centers.

57 **An amazing turnaround** Ton, Reavis, and Kalloch, "Quest Diagnostics (a)."

58 **"At DHL Express** Arnab Dutta, "Employees Love Long Tenures at DHL Express (India). Here's Why," *Business Today*, March 24, 2022, https://www.businesstoday.in/magazine/cover-story/story/employees-love-long-tenures-at-dhl-express-india-heres-why-326615-2022-03-24.

59 **"Attracting people is** Beau Jackson, "DHL Express CEO: 'There's No Such Thing as a Support Function,'" *HR Magazine*, July 29, 2022, https://www.hrmagazine.co.uk/content/features/dhl-express-ceo-there-s-no-such-thing-as-a-support-function/.

59 **"People got us through** Jackson, "DHL Express CEO."

59 **"My predecessor said** Jackson, "DHL Express CEO."

60 **Meanwhile, turnover at Walmart** Wayne F. Cascio, "The High Cost of Low Wages," *Harvard Business Review*, December 2006, https://hbr.org/2006/12/the-high-cost-of-low-wages.

60 **That would be around** National Retail Federation, "2020 National Retail Security Survey," accessed October 22, 2023, https://cdn.nrf.com/sites/default/files/2020-07/RS-105905_2020_NationalRetailSecuritySurvey.pdf.

60 **Researchers at Harvard Business School** Joseph Fuller and Manjari Raman, "Building from the Bottom Up: What Business Can Do to Strengthen the Bottom Line by Investing in Front-line Workers," Harvard Business School, January 2022, https://www.hbs.edu/managing-the-future-of-work/research/Pages/building-from-the-bottom-up.aspx.

61 **But the report also** Fuller and Raman, "Building from the Bottom Up."

61 **"We're trying to turn** Wayne F. Cascio, "Decency Means More Than 'Always Low Prices Prices': A Comparison of Costco to Wal-Mart's Sam's Club," *Academy of Management Perspectives* 20, no. 3 (August 1, 2006): 26–37, https://doi.org/10.5465/amp.2006.21903478.

61 **According to the Bureau** US Bureau of Labor Statistics, "TED: The Economics Daily," September 29, 2020, https://www.bls.gov/opub/ted/2020/median-tenure-with-current-employer-was-4-point-1-years-in-january-2020.htm.

61 **Even younger workers** Richard Fry, "For Today's Young Workers in the U.S., Job Tenure Is Similar to That of Young Workers in the Past," Pew Research Center, December 2, 2022, https://www.pewresearch.org/short-reads/2022/12/02/for-todays-young-workers-in-the-u-s-job-tenure-is-similar-to-that-of-young-workers-in-the-past/.

61 **Research supports** Krekel, Ward, and De Neve, "Employee Wellbeing, Productivity, and Firm Performance."

62 **DJs and the Wakeland** Giulia Carbonaro, "People Wait 12 Hours in Line for Opening of H-E-B Store in Frisco, Texas," *Newsweek*, September 22, 2022, https://www.newsweek.com/people-wait-twelve-hours-line-opening-heb -store-frisco-texas-1745222.

63 **"If you take care** MIT Sloan, "Creating Good Jobs at a Texas Grocery Chain," October 6, 2016, https://mitsloan.mit.edu/ideas-made-to-matter/creating -good-jobs-a-texas-grocery-chain.

63 **Back in 2017** Dan Solomon, "How H-E-B Took Care of Its Communities During Harvey," *Texas Monthly*, September 6, 2017, https://www.texasmon thly.com/the-daily-post/heb-took-care-communities-harvey/.

64 **"We'd all be better off** Greg Jefferson, "Opinion: Why H-E-B Comes Through in a Crisis When Texas Government Doesn't," *Houston Chronicle*, February 19, 2021, https://www.houstonchronicle.com/business/article/H-E-B-winter -storm-Abbott-Texas-power-grid-15964779.php.

64 **On Glassdoor.com** Glassdoor, "Top CEOs," Glassdoor.com, n.d., https:// www.glassdoor.com/Award/Top-CEOs-LST_KQ0,8.htm.

64 **And the engaged** Daniel Zhao, "Happy Employees, Satisfied Customers: The Link Between Glassdoor Reviews and Customer Satisfaction," Glassdoor Economic Research, December 20, 2021, https://www.glassdoor.com /research/employee-reviews-customer-satisfaction.

64 **"That is what really** Will Grant, "Why a Compassionate Mind-Set Strengthens H-E-B," Profile, September 30, 2021, https://profilemagazine.com/2018 /why-a-compassionate-mind-set-strengthens-h-e-b/.

64 **In 2022, the annual Retail** Business Wire, "Amazon Falls to H-E-B after Two Years as Top U.S. Grocery Retailer, Dunnhumby Retailer Preference Index Concludes," Yahoo! Finance, January 31, 2023, https://finance.yahoo .com/news/amazon-falls-h-e-b-120000799.html.

64 **"H-E-B has consistently** Jeff Wells, "H-E-B Tops Dunnhumby's e-Commerce Preference Index," Grocery Dive, June 28, 2022, https://www.grocerydive .com/news/h-e-b-tops-dunnhumbys-e-commerce-preference-index/626172/.

65 **But he just asked** Carmine Gallo, "Zappos Chief Tony Hsieh Discovered the Formula for Attracting Fiercely Loyal Customers," *Forbes*, November 29, 2020, https://www.forbes.com/sites/carminegallo/2020/11/29/zappos-chief -tony-hsieh-discovered-the-formula-for-attracting-fiercely-loyal-customers /?sh=2d12dcc643c5.

65 **He then told the reporter** Gallo, "Zappos Chief Tony Hsieh Discovered the Formula."

65 **"If I can make** Michael R. Malone, "Zoom CEO and Founder: My Employees' Happiness Is My Number One Job," News@TheU, October 22, 2023, https://

news.miami.edu/stories/2020/10/zoom-ceo-and-founder-my-employees
-happiness-is-my-number-one-job.html.

66 **Employee satisfaction** Krekel, Ward, and De Neve, "Employee Wellbeing, Productivity, and Firm Performance."

66 **The economic research team** Zhao, "Happy Employees, Satisfied Customers."

66 **The results support** Jeremy S. Wolter et al., "Employee Satisfaction Trajectories and Their Effect on Customer Satisfaction and Repatronage Intentions," *Journal of the Academy of Marketing Science* 47, no. 5 (May 18, 2019): 815–836, https://doi.org/10.1007/s11747-019-00655-9.

66 **Research shows** Claes Fornell et al., "Customer Satisfaction and Stock Prices: High Returns, Low Risk," *Journal of Marketing* 70, no. 1 (January 1, 2006): 3–14, https://doi.org/10.1509/jmkg.2006.70.1.3.

66 **Combining those results** Zhao, "Happy Employees, Satisfied Customers."

68 **Seventy-five percent** Deloitte, "Uncovering Talent: A New Model of Inclusion," accessed October 22, 2023, https://www2.deloitte.com/content /dam/Deloitte/us/Documents/about-deloitte/us-about-deloitte-uncovering -talent-a-new-model-of-inclusion.pdf.

68 **The report reveals** Emily Field et al., "Women in the Workplace 2023," McKinsey & Company, October 5, 2023, https://www.mckinsey.com/featured -insights/diversity-and-inclusion/women-in-the-workplace.

68 **Thirty-six percent of women** Field et al., "Women in the Workplace 2023."

68 **"A lot of people** Field et al., "Women in the Workplace 2023."

69 **From 2016 to 2020** Lilly, "Stories," n.d., https://www.lilly.com/news/stories /2020-integrated-summary-report-diversity-inclusion-progress-report.

69 **"It became a catalyst** Samm Quinn, "2022 HR Impact Awards: Eli Lilly and Co. DEI Office," *Indianapolis Business Journal*, October 12, 2022, https:// www.ibj.com/articles/2022-hr-impact-awards-eli-lilly-and-co-dei-office.

70 **"There is also an emotional** Matt Krentz, "More Than Ever, Diversity and Inclusion Matter at Eli Lilly and Company," BCG Global, June 22, 2023, https://www.bcg.com/capabilities/diversity-inclusion/matter-more-than -ever-at-eli-lilly-conversation-with-ceo-dave-ricks.

70 **"This isn't altruism** "U.S. Senate Committee on the Budget," February 25, 2021, https://www.budget.senate.gov/download/craig-jelinek-testimony.

Chapter 4: Employees Don't Play Ping-Pong

71 **But in 2016, the** *Wall Street Journal* Zusha Elinson, "Is the Tech Bubble Popping? Ping Pong Offers an Answer," *Wall Street Journal*, May 3, 2016, https://www.wsj.com/articles/is-the-tech-bubble-popping-ping-pong-offers -an-answer-1462286089#:iihwSoVxf5YOpA.

71 **This "ping-pong index"** Charles Ham, Nicholas Seybert, and Sean Wang, "Narcissism Is a Bad Sign: CEO Signature Size, Investment, and Performance," *Review of Accounting Studies* 23 (2018): 234–264; Marjolein van

Baardwijk and Philip Hans Franses, *The Hemline and the Economy: Is There Any Match?*, No. EI 2010-40. 2010; and Barron's, "A Brief Lesson in PowerPoints and Performance," *Barron's*, November 16, 2008, https://www.barrons.com /articles/a-brief-lesson-in-powerpoints-and-performance-1542418827.

72 **Nine out of ten** Charlotte Lieberman, "What Wellness Programs Don't Do for Workers," *Harvard Business Review*, August 14, 2019, https://hbr .org/2019/08/what-wellness-programs-dont-do-for-workers.

73 **Rigorous research investigating** Damon Jones, David Molitor, and Julian Reif, "What Do Workplace Wellness Programs Do? Evidence from the Illinois Workplace Wellness Study," *Quarterly Journal of Economics* 134, no. 4 (August 16, 2019): 1747–1791, https://doi.org/10.1093/qje/qjz023.

73 **"As an employer** McKinsey & Company, "Addressing Employee Burnout: Are You Solving the Right Problem?," May 27, 2022, https://www.mckinsey .com/mhi/our-insights/addressing-employee-burnout-are-you-solving-the -right-problem.

74 **"It requires consistency** CNET, "Microsoft Promises Culture Change at Activision Blizzard. Here's How," January 21, 2022, https://www.cnet.com /tech/gaming/microsoft-promises-culture-change-at-activision-blizzard -heres-how/.

74 **As a consequence** Cecilia D'Anastasio, "Activision, Once Dinged for 'Frat Boy' Culture, Hires More Women," *Seattle Times*, May 11, 2023, https://www .seattletimes.com/business/activision-once-dinged-for-frat-boy-culture -hires-more-women/.

74 **Researchers say that** Jonathan I. Dingel and Brent Neiman, "How Many Jobs Can Be Done at Home?," National Bureau of Economic Research, Working Paper 26948, April 1, 2020, https://doi.org/10.3386/w26948.

75 **One study compared** Nicholas Bloom et al., "Does Working from Home Work? Evidence from a Chinese Experiment," *The Quarterly Journal of Economics* 130, no. 1 (February 2015): 165–218, https://doi.org/10.1093/qje/qju032.

75 **US companies with higher** Drew Smith, "Weathering the COVID Storm: The Effect of Employee Engagement on Firm Performance During the COVID Pandemic," *Social Science Research Network*, January 1, 2021, https://doi .org/10/2139/ssrn.3841779.

76 **Ichniowski and his coauthors** Casey Ichniowski, Kathryn Shaw, and Giovanna Prennushi, "The Effects of Human Resource Management Practices on Productivity: A Study of Steel Finishing Lines," *American Economic Review* 87, no. 3 (June 1997): 291–313.

77 **"We do all the training** Kimie Page in conversation with the author.

78 **John Pearson, CEO** John Pearson, "DHL Express CEO: 'There's No Such Thing as a Support Function,'" interview by HR, *HR Magazine*, July 29, 2022, https://www.hrmagazine.co.uk/content/features/dhl-express-ceo-there -s-no-such-thing-as-a-support-function/.

78 **"If it just stays in** Bill Kerr and Joe Fuller, "Hubert Joly on Humanizing the Profit Motive," *Managing the Future* (podcast), Harvard Business School, December 1, 2021, https://www.hbs.edu/managing-the-future-of-work/podcast /Pages/podcast-details.aspx?episode=21335069.

78 **A study entitled** Ann P. Bartel et al., "Can a Workplace Have an Attitude Problem? Workplace Effects on Employee Attitudes and Organizational Performance," *Labour Economics* 18, no. 4 (August 1, 2011): 411–423, https://doi .org/10.1026/j.labeco.2011.01.008.

79 **One study analyzed** Edward P. Lazear, Kathryn Shaw, and Christopher Stanton, "The Value of Bosses," *Journal of Labor Economics* 33, no. 4 (October 1, 2015): 823–861, https://doi.org/10.1086/681097.

79 **When interpersonal skills are** M. Hoffman and S. Tadelis, "People Management Skills, Employee Attrition, and Manager Rewards: An Empirical Analysis," *Journal of Political Economy* 129, no. 1 (2021): 243–285.

80 **"Yesterday felt impersonal** David Gelles, "Inside the Revolution at Etsy," *New York Times*, November 25, 2017, https://www.nytimes.com/2017/11/25 /business/etsy-josh-silverman.html.

80 **"We believe these changes** Caroline O'Donovan, "Some Etsy Employees Aren't Happy About the Company's More Corporate Direction," BuzzFeed News, August 4, 2017, https://www.buzzfeednews.com/article/carolineodonovan/as -etsys-new-leadership-celebrates-earnings-some-employees.

81 **"This is what Etsy** Max Chafkin, "Can Rob Kalin Scale Etsy?," *Inc.*, January 5, 2021, https://www.inc.com/magazine/20110401/can-rob-kalin-scale-etsy.html.

81 **"We don't believe** Chad Dickerson, "Etsy's Next Chapter: Reimagining Commerce as a Public Company," Etsy News, Etsy, n.d., https://blog.etsy.com /news/2015/etsys-next-chapter-reimagining-commerce-as-a-public-company/.

81 **Employees were allowed** Amy Larocca, "Etsy Wants to Crochet Its Cake, and Eat It Too," The Cut, April 5, 2016, https://www.thecut.com/2016/04/etsy -capitalism-c-v-r.html.

81 **An article in *New York*** Larocca, "Etsy Wants to Crochet Its Cake, and Eat It Too."

82 **According to *Businessweek*** Max Chafkin and Jing Cao, "The Barbarians Are at Etsy's Hand-Hewn, Responsibly Sourced Gates," Bloomberg, May 18, 2017, https://www.bloomberg.com/news/features/2017-05-18/the-barbarians -are-at-etsy-s-hand-hewn-responsibly-sourced-gates.

82 **Attrition increased** Gelles, "Inside the Revolution at Etsy."

82 **"It was really hard** Ranjay Gulati, Luciana Silvestri, and Monte Burke, "Etsy: Crafting a Turnaround to Save the Business and Its Soul," Harvard Business School Case 821-092, April 2021.

83 **Eighty-one percent of Etsy's** Gulati, Silvestri, and Burke, "Etsy: Crafting a Turnaround to Save the Business and Its Soul."

83   **Around 50 percent** Shaaron A. Alvares, "Why and How Etsy Embraces Differences at the Workplace," InfoQ, May 21, 2019, https://www.infoq.com /news/2019/05/etsy-inclusion-gender/.

83   **Analysis of half** Claudine Madras Gartenberg, Andrea Prat, and George Serafeim, "Corporate Purpose and Financial Performance," *Organization Science* 30, no. 1 (January 1, 2019): 1–18, https://doi.org/10.1287/orsc.2018 .1230.

83   **"The customer isn't always** Peter Fader, *Customer Centricity: Focus on the Right Customers for Strategic Advantage* (Philadelphia: University of Pennsylvania Press, 2020).

84   **"If you've hired** Gallo, "Zappos Chief Tony Hsieh Discovered the Formula."

84   **"It doesn't matter** Max Nisen, "Tony Hsieh's Brilliant Strategy for Hiring Kind People," Business Insider, November 22, 2013, https://www.businessin sider.com/tony-hsieh-zappos-hiring-strategy-2013-11.

84   **It's essential to hire** Björn Bartling, Ernst Fehr, and Klaus M. Schmidt, "Screening, Competition, and Job Design: Economic Origins of Good Jobs," *American Economic Review* 102, no. 2 (2012): 834–864, http://dx.doi.org /10.1257/aer.102.2.834.

85   **Etsy's purpose was clear** Ranjay Gulati, *Deep Purpose: The Heart and Soul of High-Performance Companies* (New York: Harper Business, 2022).

85   **In 2022, Etsy** "Biggest Gains in Employee Engagement in the Management Top 250," *Wall Street Journal*, May 3, 2022, https://www.wsj.com/articles/big gest-gains-in-employee-engagement-in-the-management-top-250-11651590179.

Chapter 5: More Than Money at Work

89   **As its mission statement** PayPal, "Mission, Vision, & Values," n.d., https:// about.pypl.com/who-we-are/mission-vision-values/default.aspx.

89   **"I did [the survey] because** Dan Schulman, "What COVID-19 Means for the Future of Commerce, Capitalism and Cash," TED Talk, 49:08, May 2020, https://www.ted.com/talks/dan_schulman_what_covid_19_means_for _the_future_of_commerce_capitalism_and_cash.

90   **"I think the number one** Schulman, "What COVID-19 Means for the Future of Commerce."

90   **At PayPal, more than** Minda Zetlin, "PayPal Grew Its Profits 28 Percent— by Raising Workers' Wages," *Inc.*, January 17, 2021, https://www.inc.com /minda-zetlin/paypal-wages-ndi-profits-growth-dan-schulman.html.

90   **The plan increased** Zetlin, "PayPal Grew Its Profits 28 Percent."

90   **which cost PayPal** Ainsley Harris, "How PayPal CEO Dan Schulman Is Leading a More Inclusive Way Forward," *Fast Company*, May 22, 2020, https://www.fastcompany.com/90490899/how-paypal-ceo-dan-schulman -is-leading-a-more-inclusive-way-forward.

90 **Despite the high cost** Schulman, "What COVID-19 Means for the Future of Commerce."

90 **A study among manufacturing** Supreet Kaur et al., "Do Financial Concerns Make Workers Less Productive?," *Quarterly Journal of Economics*, January 1, 2021, https://doi.org/10.3386/w28338.

91 **A one dollar per hour increase** Natalia Emanuel and Emma Harrington, "The Payoffs of Higher Pay: Elasticities of Productivity and Labor Supply with Respect to Wages," working paper, 2020.

92 **With the boost** Sarah Cwiek, "The Middle Class Took Off 100 Years Ago... Thanks to Henry Ford?," NPR, January 27, 2014, https://www.npr.org/2014/01/27/267145552/the-middle-class-took-off-100-years-ago-thanks-to-henry-ford.

92 **"It's going to be expensive** Harris, "How PayPal CEO Dan Schulman Is Leading."

92 **During that time** HEICO, "Annual Reports," 2022, https://www.heico.com/investors/annual-reports/.

93 **The HEICO stock** Abram Brown, "The 47,500 Percent Return: Meet the Billionaire Family Behind the Hottest Stock of the Past 30 Years," *Forbes*, January 13, 2020, https://www.forbes.com/sites/abrambrown/2020/01/13/heico-endelson/?sh=6be834334b18.

93 **"It makes me very happy** Michael Larkin, "CEO's Focus on Family Gives Aerospace Company Its Wings," *Investor's Business Daily*, August 27, 2018, https://www.investors.com/news/management/leaders-and-success/family-ties-help-this-ceo-take-small-aerospace-firm-into-orbit/.

93 **Stavros is convinced** "A Stake in Success: Boosting Profits via Employee Ownership," CBS News, February 19, 2023, https://www.cbsnews.com/news/a-stake-in-success-private-equity-and-employee-ownership/.

94 **PayPal's turnover** Zeynep Ton and Sarah Kalloch, "PayPal and the Financial Wellness Initiative," MIT Sloan, November 8, 2022, https://mitsloan.mit.edu/teaching-resources-library/paypal-and-financial-wellness-initiative.

94 **Chipotle, Chobani** PayPal Holdings, Inc., "Chipotle, Chobani, Even, Prudential Financial, Verizon, and Other Leading Companies Join Forces with PayPal and JUST Capital to Improve the Financial Health of America's Workforce," *PR Newswire*, July 13, 2021, https://www.prnewswire.com/news-releases/chipotle-chobani-even-prudential-financial-verizon-and-other-leading-companies-join-forces-with-paypal-and-just-capital-to-improve-the-financial-health-of-americas-workforce-301332075.html.

94 **In a survey from 2021** Tamara Lytle, "When Employee Incentives Go Wrong: How Bonuses Can Backfire," Society for Human Resource Management, April 22, 2023, https://www.shrm.org/hr-today/news/all-things-work/pages/when-employee-incentives-go-wrong.aspx.

95 **Yet, a growing body** Uri Gneezy, *Mixed Signals: How Incentives Really Work* (New Haven, CT: Yale University Press, 2023); and Uri Gneezy, Stephan Meier, and Pedro Rey-Biel, "When and Why Incentives (Don't) Work to Modify Behavior," *Journal of Economic Perspectives* 25, no. 4 (2011): 191–210, https:// doi.org/10.1257/jep.25.4.191.

95 **Studies have shown that** Rafael Di Tella, John Haisken-De New, and Robert MacCulloch, "Happiness Adaptation to Income and to Status in an Individual Panel," *Journal of Economic Behavior & Organization* 76, no. 3 (2010): 834–852, https://doi.org/10.1016/j.jebo.2010.09.016.

95 **Even those who win** Erik Lindqvist, Robert Östling, and David Cesarini, "Long-Run Effects of Lottery Wealth on Psychological Well-Being," *Review of Economic Studies* 87, no. 6 (2020): 2703–2726, https://doi.org/10.1093/restud /rdaa006.

95 **Similarly, while employees** Alois Stutzer and Bruno S. Frey, "Stress That Doesn't Pay: The Commuting Paradox," *Scandinavian Journal of Economics* 110, no. 2 (2008): 339–366, https://doi.org/10.1111/j.1467-9442.2008.00542.x.

95 **A comprehensive meta-analysis** Timothy A. Judge et al., "The Relationship Between Pay and Job Satisfaction: A Meta-analysis of the Literature," *Journal of Vocational Behavior* 77, no. 2 (2010): 157–167, https://doi.org/10.1016/j .jvb.2010.04.002.

96 **In 2004, two researchers** Ernst Fehr and John A. List, "The Hidden Costs and Returns of Incentives—Trust and Trustworthiness Among CEOs," *Journal of the European Economic Association* 2, no. 5 (2004): 743–771, https:// doi.org/10.1162/1542476042782297.

96 **The result was not** Uri Gneezy and Aldo Rustichini, "A Fine Is a Price," *Journal of Legal Studies* 29, no. 1 (January 1, 2000): 1–17, https://doi.org/10 .1086/468061.

97 **Instead of creating** Jakob Alfitian, Dirk Sliwka, and Timo Vogelsang, "When Bonuses Backfire: Evidence from the Workplace," *Management Science*, Articles in Advance (2023), https://doi.org/10.1287/mnsc.2022.00484.

97 **The incentive program** Roland G. Fryer, "Teacher Incentives and Student Achievement: Evidence from New York City Public Schools," *Journal of Labor Economics* 31, no. 2 (2013): 373-407, https://doi.org/10.3386/w16850.

97 **Incentives can sometimes** Gneezy, *Mixed Signals: How Incentives Really Work.*

98 **Dan Ariely, Anat Bracha** Dan Ariely, Anat Bracha, and Stephan Meier, "Doing Good or Doing Well? Image Motivation and Monetary Incentives in Behaving Prosocially," *American Economic Review* 99, no. 1 (February 1, 2009): 544–555, https://doi.org/10.1257/aer.99.1.544.

99 **They paid $3 billion** US Department of Justice, "Wells Fargo Agrees to Pay $3 Billion to Resolve Criminal and Civil Investigations into Sales Practices

Involving the Opening of Millions of Accounts Without Customer Authoriza-
tion," February 21, 2020, https://www.justice.gov/opa/pr/wells-fargo-agrees
-pay-3-billion-resolve-criminal-and-civil-investigations-sales-practices.

99   **Bengt Holmström of MIT** Bengt Holmström, "Pay for Performance and Beyond," *American Economic Review* 107, no. 7 (July 1, 2017): 1753–1777, https://
doi.org/10.1257/aer.107.7.1753.

100   **Some of my colleagues** David Atkin et al., "Organizational Barriers to
Technology Adoption: Evidence from Soccer-Ball Producers in Pakistan,"
Quarterly Journal of Economics 132, no. 3 (March 9, 2017): 1101–1164, https://
doi.org/10.1093/qje/qjx010.

102   **We may think** Mattia Filomena and Matteo Picchio, "Retirement and
Health Outcomes in a Meta-analytical Framework," *Journal of Economic
Surveys* 37, no. 4 (July 28, 2022): 1120–1155, https://doi.org/10.1111/joes.12527.

102   **Some studies even** Andreas Kühn et al., "Fatal Attraction? Extended Unemployment Benefits, Labor Force Exits, and Mortality," *Journal of Public Economics* 191 (November 1, 2020): 104087, https://doi.org/10.1016/j
.jpubeco.2019.104087.

102   **The importance of employment** Reshmaan Hussam et al., "The Psycho-
social Value of Employment: Evidence from a Refugee Camp," *American
Economic Review* 112, no. 11 (November 1, 2022): 3694–3724, https://doi.org
/10.1257/aer.20211616.

103   **For example, in Switzerland** Bruno S. Frey and Alois Stutzer, *Happiness
and Economics: How the Economy and Institutions Affect Human Well-
Being* (Princeton, NJ: Princeton University Press, 2001), https://doi.org/10
.1515/9781400829262.

103   **Even in more conservative** Andreas Knabe and Steffen Rätzel, "Quanti-
fying the Psychological Costs of Unemployment: The Role of Permanent Income," *Applied Economics* 43, no. 21 (August 1, 2011): 2751–2763, https://doi
.org/10.1080/00036840903373295.

103   **In a survey of front-line** Fuller and Raman, "Building from the Bottom Up."

103   **A recent study** Daron Acemoglu, Alex He, and Daniel Le Maire, "Eclipse of
Rent-Sharing: The Effects of Managers' Business Education on Wages and
the Labor Share in the US and Denmark," National Bureau of Economic Research, Working Paper 29874, March 2022.

104   **In fact, there are** Isaac Sorkin, "Ranking Firms Using Revealed Preference," *Quarterly Journal of Economics* 133, no. 3 (2018): 1331–1393, https://doi
.org/10.1093/qje/qjy001.

104   **In a survey with around** Vanessa Burbano, Nicolas Padilla, and Stephan
Meier, "Gender Differences in Preferences for Meaning at Work," *American
Economic Journal: Economic Policy*, 2023.

105   **Moving a US worker** Nicole Maestas et al., "The Value of Working Conditions in the United States and Implications for the Structure of Wages,"

American Economic Review 113, no. 7 (July 2023): 2007–2047, https://doi.org /10.1257/aer.20190846.

106 **These factors** E. L. Deci and R. M. Ryan, *Intrinsic Motivation and Self-Determination in Human Behavior* (New York: Plenum, 1985); and Lea Cassar and Stephan Meier, "Nonmonetary Incentives and the Implications of Work as a Source of Meaning," *Journal of Economic Perspectives* 32, no. 3 (August 1, 2018): 215–238, https://doi.org/10.1257/jep.32.3.215.

Chapter 6: Shoot for the Moon

107 **"We choose to go** John F. Kennedy, "Address at Rice University on the Nation's Space Effort," Historic Speeches, John F. Kennedy Presidential Library and Museum, September 12, 1962, https://www.jfklibrary.org/learn/about -jfk/historic-speeches/address-at-rice-university-on-the-nations-space -effort.

107 **"[NASA] never had** Andrew M. Carton, "'I'm Not Mopping the Floors, I'm Putting a Man on the Moon': How NASA Leaders Enhanced the Meaningfulness of Work by Changing the Meaning of Work," *Administrative Science Quarterly* 63, no. 2 (June 7, 2017): 323–369, https://doi.org/10.1177/000183921 7713748.

108 **"I don't know of** Carton, "'I'm Not Mopping the Floors.'"

109 **In a recent survey, more** Shawn Achor et al., "9 Out of 10 People Are Willing to Earn Less Money to Do More-Meaningful Work," *Harvard Business Review,* November 6, 2018, https://hbr.org/2018/11/9-out-of-10-people-are -willing-to-earn-less-money-to-do-more-meaningful-work.

109 **Undergraduates, for instance** Robert H. Frank, "What Price the Moral High Ground?," *Southern Economic Journal* 63, no. 1 (July 1, 1996): 1, https:// doi.org/10.2307/1061299.

109 **In fact, many** Vanessa Burbano, Nicolas Padilla, and Stephan Meier, "Gender Differences in Preferences for Meaning at Work," *American Economic Journal: Economic Policy,* 2023.

109 **For instance, when** Daniel Hedblom, Brent R. Hickman, and John A. List, "Toward an Understanding of Corporate Social Responsibility: Theory and Field Experimental Evidence," National Bureau of Economic Research, Working Paper 26222, September 2019, https://doi.org/10.3386/w26222.

110 **In fact, according** Unilever, "Unilever's Purpose-Led Brands Outperform," Unilever, September 7, 2023, https://www.unilever.com/news/press-and-media /press-releases/2019/unilevers-purpose-led-brands-outperform/; and Tensie Whelan, "Research: Actually, Consumers Do Buy Sustainable Products," *Harvard Business Review,* September 17, 2021, https://hbr.org/2019/06/research -actually-consumers-do-buy-sustainable-products.

111 **Most of these "purpose" statements** Christopher Michaelson, Douglas A. Lepisto, and Michael G. Pratt, "Why Corporate Purpose Statements

Often Miss Their Mark," Strategy+Business, August 17, 2020, https://www
.strategy-business.com/article/Why-corporate-purpose-statements-often
-miss-their-mark.

111 **Similarly, a McKinsey study of one thousand** McKinsey & Company,
"Purpose: Shifting from Why to How," April 22, 2020, https://www.mckinsey
.com/capabilities/people-and-organizational-performance/our-insights
/purpose-shifting-from-why-to-how.

111 **In a survey** McKinsey & Company, "More Than a Mission Statement: How
the 5Ps Embed Purpose to Deliver Value," November 5, 2020, https://www
.mckinsey.com/capabilities/strategy-and-corporate-finance/our-insights
/more-than-a-mission-statement-how-the-5ps-embed-purpose-to-deliver
-value#/.

111 **"Many executives avoid working** Robert E. Quinn and Anjan V. Thakor, "Creating a Purpose-Driven Organization," *Harvard Business Review* 96, no. 4 (2018):
78–85, https://hbr.org/2018/07/creating-a-purpose-driven-organization.

111 **An analysis of half** Claudine Gartenberg, Andrea Prat, and George Serafeim, "Corporate Purpose and Financial Performance," *Organization Science*
30, no. 1 (2019): 1–18, https://doi.org/10.1287/orsc.2018.1230.

112 **The amount Kraft Heinz** Paul Polman and Andrew Winston, *Net Positive:
How Courageous Companies Thrive by Giving More Than They Take* (Boston:
Harvard Business Publishing, 2021).

113 **"The goal of the USLP** Polman and Winston, *Net Positive*, 22.

114 **Polman concluded** Polman and Winston, *Net Positive*, 23.

114 **"Just as people cannot** Jon Schumacher, "How Whole Foods CEO John
Mackey Is Leading a Revolution in Health and Business," *Entrepreneur,*
January 3, 2019, https://www.entrepreneur.com/leadership/how-whole-foods
-ceo-john-mackey-is-leading-a-revolution-in/325128.

114 **"Profit for a company** Polman and Winston, *Net Positive*, 63.

114 **I have been studying** Stephan Meier, *The Economics of Non-Selfish Behaviour: Decisions to Contribute Money to Public Goods* (Cheltenham, UK:
Edward Elgar, 2006).

115 **My colleagues and I** Vanessa Burbano et al., "The Gender Gap in Meaningful Work," *Management Science*, December 4, 2023, https://doi.org/10.1287
/mnsc.2022.01807.

115 **My colleague and coauthor** Vanessa Burbano, "Social Responsibility Messages and Worker Wage Requirements: Field Experimental Evidence from
Online Labor Marketplaces," *Organization Science* 27, no. 4 (2016): 1010–1028.

115 **Various studies** Lea Cassar and Stephan Meier, "Nonmonetary Incentives
and the Implications of Work as a Source of Meaning," *Journal of Economic
Perspectives* 32, no. 3 (2018): 215–238, https://doi.org/10.1257/jep.32.3.215.

115 **Studies have also shown** Cassar and Meier, "Nonmonetary Incentives."

116 **Given that** James Bell et al., "In Response to Climate Change, Citizens in Advanced Economies Are Willing to Alter How They Live and Work," Pew Research Center, September 14, 2021, https://www.pewresearch.org /global/2021/09/14/in-response-to-climate-change-citizens-in-advanced -economies-are-willing-to-alter-how-they-live-and-work/.

116 **In various businesses** Caroline Flammer, "Does Corporate Social Responsibility Lead to Superior Financial Performance? A Regression Discontinuity Approach," *Management Science* 61, no. 11 (November 1, 2015): 2549–2568, https://doi.org/10.1287/mnsc.2014.2038.

116 **"Purpose-driven companies** Polman and Winston, *Net Positive*, 83.

117 **For example, Volkswagen** Federal Trade Commission, "FTC Charges Volkswagen Deceived Consumers with Its 'Clean Diesel' Campaign," March 29, 2016, https://www.ftc.gov/news-events/news/press-releases/2016/03/ftc-charges -volkswagen-deceived-consumers-its-clean-diesel-campaign.

117 **It is difficult to quantify** Ioannis Ioannou, "How Greenwashing Affects the Bottom Line," *Harvard Business Review*, July 21, 2022, https://hbr .org/2022/07/how-greenwashing-affects-the-bottom-line.

117 **This number rises** Adele Peters, "68 Percent of U.S. Execs Admit Their Companies Are Guilty of Greenwashing," *Fast Company,* April 12, 2022, https:// www.fastcompany.com/90740501/68-of-u-s-execs-admit-their-companies -are-guilty-of-greenwashing.

117 **Most studies focus** Ioannis Ioannou, George I. Kassinis, and Giorgos Papagiannakis, "The Impact of Perceived Greenwashing on Customer Satisfaction and the Contingent Role of Capability Reputation," *Journal of Business Ethics* 185, no. 2 (June 3, 2022): 333–347, https://doi.org/10.1007/s10551-022 -05151-9.

117 **When a company's purpose** Sabrina Scheidler et al., "Scrooge Posing as Mother Teresa: How Hypocritical Social Responsibility Strategies Hurt Employees and Firms," *Journal of Business Ethics* 157, no. 2 (January 24, 2018): 339–358, https://doi.org/10.1007/s10551-018-3788-3.

118 **Moreover, self-reported motivation** Lea Cassar and Stephan Meier, "Intentions for Doing Good Matter for Doing Well: The Negative Effects of Prosocial Incentives," *Economic Journal*, December 18, 2020, https://doi.org/10 .1093/ej/ueaa136.

119 **"If a goal is not** Polman and Winston, *Net Positive,* 138.

119 **"For years, Unilever** Polman and Winston, *Net Positive,* 23.

119 **"The plan was not** Polman and Winston, *Net Positive,* 121.

122 **KPMG rose seventeen spots** Bruce N. Pfau, "How an Accounting Firm Convinced Its Employees They Could Change the World," *Harvard Business Review*, November 30, 2017, https://hbr.org/2015/10/how-an-accounting-firm -convinced-its-employees-they-could-change-the-world.

122 **Studies show this helps** Tara Lomas et al., "Gratitude Interventions: A Review and Future Agenda," in *The Wiley Blackwell Handbook of Positive Psychological Interventions*, ed. Acacia C. Parks and Stephen M. Schueller (Hoboken, NJ: John Wiley, 2014), 1–19.

123 **"I'm so pleased because** Washington Post Live, "Transcript: The Future of Work: Health and Wellness with Leena Nair & Nick Patel," *Washington Post*, October 14, 2021, https://www.washingtonpost.com/washington-post -live/2021/10/14/transcript-future-work-health-wellness-with-leena-nair -nick-patel/.

124 **Similarly, a study of ten thousand** Christiane Bode, Jasjit Singh, and Michelle Rogan, "Corporate Social Initiatives and Employee Retention," *Organization Science* 26, no. 6 (December 1, 2015): 1702–1720, https://doi .org/10.1287/orsc.2015.1006.

125 **When Nordea, a large bank** McKinsey & Company, "Purpose: Shifting from Why to How," April 22, 2020, https://www.mckinsey.com/capabilities /people-and-organizational-performance/our-insights/purpose-shifting -from-why-to-how.

126 **"We had to come up with** Samuel J. Palmisano, "The HBR Interview: Samuel J. Palmisano; Leading Change When Business Is Good," interview by Paul Kemp and Thomas A. Stewart, *Harvard Business Review* 82, no. 12 (2004): 60–70.

126 **"Companies with purpose last** McKinsey & Company, "Talent Management as a Business Discipline: A Conversation with Unilever CHRO Leena Nair," March 9, 2018, https://www.mckinsey.com/capabilities/people -and-organizational-performance/our-insights/talent-management-as-a -business-discipline-a-conversation-with-unilever-chro-leena-nair.

Chapter 7: A Matter of Trust

128 **Consider what can be** Moritz Altenried, "On the Last Mile: Logistical Urbanism and the Transformation of Labour," *Work, Organisation, Labour & Globalisation* 13, no. 1 (April 1, 2019), https://doi.org/10.13169/workorgalaboglob .13.1.0114.

128 **The patents filed** Alessandro Delfanti and Bronwyn Frey, "Humanly Extended Automation or the Future of Work Seen Through Amazon Patents," *Science, Technology, & Human Values* 46, no. 3 (July 29, 2020): 655–682, https://doi.org/10.1177/0162243920943665.

130 **Their study** Matthias Benz and Bruno S. Frey, "The Value of Doing What You Like: Evidence from the Self-Employed in 23 Countries," *Journal of Economic Behavior and Organization* 68, no. 3–4 (December 1, 2008): 445–455, https:// doi.org/10.1016/j.jebo.2006.10.014.

130 **One comprehensive study** Allan Lee, Sara Willis, and Amy Wei Tian, "Empowering Leadership: A Meta-analytic Examination of Incremental

Contribution, Mediation, and Moderation," *Journal of Organizational Behavior* 39, no. 3 (August 18, 2017): 306–325, https://doi.org/10.1002/job.2220.

131   **The use of bossware** Jordan Turner, contributor, "The Right Way to Monitor Your Employee Productivity," Gartner, June 9, 2022, https://www.gartner.com /en/articles/the-right-way-to-monitor-your-employee-productivity.

131   **In 2022, there was** Goh Chiew Tong, "Employee Surveillance Is on the Rise—and That Could Backfire on Employers," CNBC, April 26, 2023, https:// www.cnbc.com/2023/04/24/employee-surveillance-is-on-the-rise-that -could-backfire-on-employers.html.

131   **In a 2019 study** PwC, "Secure Your Future People Experience," Pricewater-houseCoopers, 2019, https://www.pwc.com/gx/en/people-organisation/pdf /secure-your-future-people-experience-pwc.pdf.

133   **The productivity results** Richard M. Locke et al., "Beyond Corporate Codes of Conduct: Work Organization and Labour Standards at Nike's Suppliers," *International Labour Review* 146, no. 1–2 (March 1, 2007): 21–40, https://doi .org/10.1111/j.1564-913x.2007.00003.x.

134   **In return, according to** Gary Hamel, "Yes, You Can Eliminate Bureaucracy," *Harvard Business Review*, October 29, 2018, https://hbr.org/2018/11 /the-end-of-bureaucracy.

135   **"Companies try to learn** McKinsey & Company, "Shattering the Status Quo: A Conversation with Haier's Zhang Ruimin," July 27, 2021, https:// www.mckinsey.com/capabilities/people-and-organizational-performance /our-insights/shattering-the-status-quo-a-conversation-with-haiers-zhang -ruimin.

135   **McKinsey has a term** Aaron De Smet, Caitlin Hewes, and Leigh Weiss, "For Smarter Decisions, Empower Your Employees," McKinsey & Company, September 9, 2020, https://www.mckinsey.com/capabilities/people-and-organizational -performance/our-insights/for-smarter-decisions-empower-your-employees.

136   **"Openness demonstrates** Laszlo Bock, *Work Rules!: Insights from Inside Google That Will Transform How You Live and Lead* (New York: Twelve Books, 2001), 46.

137   **A large spa** Hugh Xiaolong Wu and Shannon X. Liu, "Managerial Attention, Employee Attrition, and Productivity: Evidence from a Field Experiment," *Social Science Research Network*, January 1, 2021, https://doi.org/10.2139/ssrn.3787204.

138   **The home care market** Grand View Research, *Home Healthcare Market Size & Trends: 2023–2030*, n.d., https://www.grandviewresearch.com/indus try-analysis/home-healthcare-industry.

138   **Buurtzorg has been able** Ethan Bernstein et al., "Buurtzorg," Harvard Business School Case 122-101, June 2022. (Revised January 2023.)

138   **"It is important** Bernstein et al., "Buurtzorg."

139   **"Because I had this** Bernstein et al., "Buurtzorg."

139   **Gonnie Kronenberg** Bernstein et al., "Buurtzorg."

140   **A survey by Microsoft** Microsoft, "Hybrid Work Is Just Work. Are We Doing It Wrong?," Work Trend Index Special Report, September 22, 2022, https://www.microsoft.com/en-us/worklab/work-trend-index/hybrid-work-is-just-work.

140   **Research shows** Iris Bohnet, Bruno S. Frey, and Steffen Huck, "More Order with Less Law: On Contract Enforcement, Trust, and Crowding," *American Political Science Review* 95, no. 1 (March 1, 2001): 131–144, https://doi.org/10.1017/s0003055401000211.

140   **Indeed, studies show** Paul J. Zak, "The Neuroscience of Trust," *Harvard Business Review*, January 1, 2017, https://apunteca.usal.edu.ar/id/eprint/1402/.

140   **It is estimated** Deloitte, "The Chemistry of Trust: Part 1: The Future of Trust," https://www2.deloitte.com/content/dam/Deloitte/ca/Documents/deloitte-analytics/ca-chemistry-of-trust-pov-aoda-en.pdf.

140   **An analysis of four thousand** Nicholas Bloom, Raffaella Sadun, and John Van Reenen, "The Organization of Firms Across Countries," *Quarterly Journal of Economics* 127, no. 4 (2012): 1663–1705, https://doi.org/10.3386/w15129.

141   **To examine this causal effect** Stephan Meier, Matthew Stephenson, and Patryk Perkowski, "Culture of Trust and Division of Labor in Nonhierarchical Teams," *Strategic Management Journal* 40, no. 8 (April 11, 2019): 1171–1193, https://doi.org/10.1002/smj.3024.

142   **One of those studies** Marta Angelici and Paola Profeta, "Smart-Working: Work Flexibility Without Constraints," *Management Science*, 2023, https://doi.org/10.2139/ssrn.3556304.

143   **Another study focused** Nicholas Bloom, Ruobing Han, and James Liang, "How Hybrid Working from Home Works Out," National Bureau of Economic Research, Working Paper 30292, July 1, 2022, https://doi.org/10.3386/w30292.

144   **In a survey among three thousand** Mark Murphy, "This Mistaken Belief Is Ruining Most Employee Engagement Surveys," *Forbes*, September 9, 2018, https://www.forbes.com/sites/markmurphy/2018/09/09/this-mistaken-belief-is-ruining-most-employee-engagement-surveys/?sh=29d3e467a1df.

144   **Research supports the notion** McKinsey & Company, "Survey Fatigue? Blame the Leader, Not the Question," May 10, 2021, https://www.mckinsey.com/capabilities/people-and-organizational-performance/our-insights/the-organization-blog/survey-fatigue-blame-the-leader-not-the-question.

144   **"Voice means giving** Bock, *Work Rules!*

144   **But the findings from a large 2017 survey** Thomas A. Kochan et al., "Worker Voice in America: Is There a Gap Between What Workers Expect and What They Experience?," *Industrial and Labor Relations Review* 72, no. 1 (October 11, 2018): 3–38, https://doi.org/10.1177/0019793918806250.

145   **"For many organizations** Bock, *Work Rules!*

145 **Studies consistently show** Kimberly Fox et al., "Organisational- and Group-Level Workplace Interventions and Their Effect on Multiple Domains of Worker Well-Being: A Systematic Review," *Work & Stress* 36, no. 1 (August 26, 2021): 30–59, https://doi.org/10.1080/02678373.2021.1969476.

145 **A Chinese car manufacturing** Jing Cai and Shing-Yi Wang, "Improving Management Through Worker Evaluations: Evidence from Auto Manufacturing," *Quarterly Journal of Economics* 137, no. 4 (April 19, 2022): 2459–2497, https://doi.org/10.1093/qje/qjac019.

147 **As one Nvidia worker** Connie Lin, "Job Seekers, Work at One of These Companies in 2022 if You Want a Better Corporate Culture," *Fast Company*, January 12, 2022, https://www.fastcompany.com/90712131/jobseekers-work -at-one-of-these-100-companies-in-2022-if-you-want-a-good-corporate -culture.

147 **During a talk I helped** Columbia Business School, "NVIDIA CEO Jensen Huang Reveals Keys to AI, Leadership," October 3, 2023, https://www .youtube.com/watch?v=MwiM_nPyx5Y&t=2s.

147 **An examination of evidence** Simon Jäger, Shakked Noy, and Benjamin Schoefer, "What Does Codetermination Do?," *ILR Review* 75, no. 4 (2022): 857–890, https://doi.org/10.1177/00197939211065727.

148 **"Give people slightly more** Bock, *Work Rules!*

Chapter 8: Just Right Tasks

150 **Providing just right** Judith Allen and R. K. W. Van Der Velden, "Educational Mismatches Versus Skill Mismatches: Effects on Wages, Job Satisfaction, and On-the-Job Search," *Oxford Economic Papers-New Series* 53, no. 3 (July 1, 2001): 434–52, https://doi.org/10.1093/oep/53.3.434.

151 **But if the skill** Bryan Lufkin, "The Damaging Effects of 'Boreout' at Work," BBC, July 5, 2021, https://www.bbc.com/worklife/article/20210701-the-dam aging-effects-of-boreout-at-work.

151 **Surveys in the UK and Australia** Peter Boxall, Meng-Long Huo, and Jonathan Winterton, "How Do Workers Benefit from Skill Utilisation and How Can These Benefits Be Enhanced?," *Journal of Industrial Relations* 61, no. 5 (January 16, 2019): 704–725, https://doi.org/10.1177/0022185618819169.

151 **In a survey by McKinsey** Aaron De Smet et al., "The Great Attrition Is Making Hiring Harder. Are You Searching the Right Talent Pools?," McKinsey & Company, July 13, 2022, https://www.mckinsey.com/capabilities/people-and -organizational-performance/our-insights/the-great-attrition-is-making -hiring-harder-are-you-searching-the-right-talent-pools.

152 **In LinkedIn's 2023** LinkedIn Learning, "Building the Agile Future: L&D Puts People and Skills at the Center of Organizational Success," 2023 Workplace Learning Report, https://learning.linkedin.com/content/dam

/me/learning/en-us/pdfs/workplace-learning-report/LinkedIn-Learning
_Workplace-Learning-Report-2023-EN.pdf.

152 **Marc Cenedella** Rachel Gillett, "22 Signs It's Time to Quit Your Job," Business
Insider, July 11, 2017, https://www.businessinsider.com/signs-you-should-quit
-your-job-2017-7#youre-not-growing-9.

152 **In a study quoted** Steve Glaveski, "Where Companies Go Wrong with Learning and Development," *Harvard Business Review*, January 20, 2021, https://hbr
.org/2019/10/where-companies-go-wrong-with-learning-and-development.

154 **He later pointed out** Llm, "Latino Leaders," Latino Leaders, July 14, 2021,
https://www.latinoleadersmagazine.com/heroes-of-the-fight-against
-covid19/2021/7/14/expertise-and-industrial-adaptability-to-address-the
-pandemic-the-general-motors-case.

154 **In an interview with CNN** Peter Valdes-Dapena, "These Are the Workers
Helping GM to Build Ventilators," CNN, May 18, 2020, https://www.cnn.com
/2020/05/18/business/gm-factory-workers-ventilators-coronavirus/index.html.

154 **"It's more assembly** Jamie L. LaReau, "She Thought of Her Mom When
She Volunteered to Make Ventilators for GM," *Detroit Free Press*, April 2,
2020, https://www.freep.com/story/money/cars/general-motors/2020/04/02
/gm-uaw-ventilators-ventec/5113005002/.

155 **So, Mary Barra** Eric D. Lawrence, "Mary Barra: How GM Shifted to High
Gear During Coronavirus Pandemic," *Detroit Free Press*, May 13, 2020,
https://www.freep.com/story/money/cars/general-motors/2020/05/12/gm
-mary-barra-coronavirus-pandemic/3116403001/.

155 **In a study with seventeen hundred** Henry Sauermann and Wesley M.
Cohen, "What Makes Them Tick? Employee Motives and Firm Innovation,"
Management Science 56, no. 12 (December 1, 2010): 2134–2153, https://doi
.org/10.1287/mnsc.1100.1241.

155 **"When you engage** Lawrence, "Mary Barra: How GM Shifted to High Gear."

156 **Patricia Frost** Patricia Frost, "Patricia Frost, CHRO at Seagate," Gloat.com,
video, n.d. https://www.facebook.com/Workey/videos/patricia-frost-chro-at
-seagate/2042408635966875/.

156 **A large and insightful study** Ingrid Haegele, "Talent Hoarding in Organization," *Social Science Research Network*, January 1, 2021, https://doi.org
/10.2139/ssrn.3977728.

157 **Sixty-two percent** Fuller and Raman, "Building from the Bottom Up."

157 **Costco even has an** Wayne F. Cascio, "Decency Means More Than 'Always
Low Prices': A Comparison of Costco to Wal-Mart's Sam's Club," *Academy
of Management Perspectives* 20, no. 3 (August 1, 2006): 26–37, https://doi
.org/10.5465/amp.2006.21903478.

157 **For Mary Barra** Tom Krisher, "GM CEO Says Making Ventilators Changed
the Company Culture," AP News, December 10, 2021, https://apnews.com
/article/business-detroit-mary-barra-78d4fb08fc04c1f88d034aa3b3cd23af.

158 **"One of the most important** Mary Barra, "Mary Barra on the Pandemic Year: Moving at 'Ventilator Speed,'" *Wall Street Journal*, March 19, 2021, https://www.wsj.com/articles/mary-barra-on-the-pandemic-year-moving -at-ventilator-speed-11616169866.

159 **"No organizations can offer** William R. Kerr, Emilie Billaud, and Mette Fuglsang Hjortshoej, "Unilever's Response to the Future of Work," Harvard Business School Case 820-104, April 2020. (Revised October 2020.)

160 **"We wanted to move** Kerr, Billaud, and Hjortshoej, "Unilever's Response to the Future of Work."

161 **According to Unilever's** Kerr, Billaud, and Hjortshoej, "Unilever's Response to the Future of Work."

161 **"Our culture had been** Satya Nadella, *Hit Refresh: The Quest to Rediscover Microsoft's Soul and Imagine a Better Future for Everyone* (New York: HarperBusiness, 2017).

162 **"After Zain, things** Jane Francisco, "Satya and Anu Nadella Open Up About Their Family Life," *Good Housekeeping*, September 27, 2017, https://www .goodhousekeeping.com/life/inspirational-stories/a46221/satya-anu-nadella -microsoft/.

163 **"We can have all the** Nadella, *Hit Refresh*, 93.

163 **His initial, tone-deaf** Kara Swisher, "Microsoft CEO Satya Nadella on Women Pay Gaffe: 'I Answered That Question Completely Wrong,'" Vox, October 9, 2014, https://www.vox.com/2014/10/9/11631778/microsoft-ceo-satya -nadella-on-women-gaffe-i-answered-that-question.

163 **"I said I was looking** Swisher, "Microsoft CEO Satya Nadella on Women Pay Gaffe."

164 **"The fixed mindset** Carol S. Dweck, *Mindset: The New Psychology of Success* (New York: Random House, 2006).

165 **Research in collaboration** Jana Gallus, "Fostering Public Good Contributions with Symbolic Awards: A Large-Scale Natural Field Experiment at Wikipedia," *Management Science* 63, no. 12 (December 1, 2017): 3999–4015, https://doi.org/10.1287/mnsc.2016.2540.

166 **"We're super proud** Valentino Lucio, "H-E-B Driver Achieves 4 Million Consecutive Safety Miles Behind the Wheel," H-E-B Newsroom, May 12, 2022, https://newsroom.heb.com/h-e-b-driver-achieves-4-million-consecutive -safety-miles-behind-the-wheel/.

166 **Research supports** Bruno S. Frey and Jana Gallus, *Honours Versus Money: The Economics of Awards* (Oxford, UK: Oxford University Press, 2017).

167 **A number of studies** Carly D. Robinson et al., "The Demotivating Effect (and Unintended Message) of Awards," *Organizational Behavior and Human Decision Processes* 163 (March 1, 2021): 51–64, https://doi.org/10.1016/j .obhdp.2019.03.006; and Timothy Gubler, Ian Larkin, and Lamar Pierce, "Motivational Spillovers from Awards: Crowding Out in a Multitasking

Environment," *Organization Science* 27 (2016): 286–303, https://doi.org/10
.1287/orsc.2016.1047.

168 **Additionally, offering a monetary** Dan Ariely, Anat Bracha, and Stephan
Meier, "Doing Good or Doing Well? Image Motivation and Monetary Incentives in Behaving Prosocially," *American Economic Review* 99, no. 1 (February 1, 2009): 544–555, https://doi.org/10.1257/aer.99.1.544.

168 **In surveys of around sixteen thousand** Deloitte Greenhouse, "The Practical
Magic of 'Thank You': How Your People Want to Be Recognized, for What, and by
Whom," Deloitte, June 2019, https://www2.deloitte.com/content/dam/Deloitte
/us/Documents/about-deloitte/us-about-deloitte-the-practical-magic-of-thank
-you-june-2019.pdf.

169 **Well, unfortunately** Amit Kumar and Nicholas Epley, "Undervaluing Gratitude: Expressers Misunderstand the Consequences of Showing Appreciation," *Psychological Science* 29, no. 9 (June 27, 2018): 1423–1435, https://doi
.org/10.1177/0956797618772506.

Chapter 9: Working Together Works

171 **With my coauthors** Lorenz Goette, David Huffman, and Stephan Meier, "The
Impact of Group Membership on Cooperation and Norm Enforcement: Evidence
Using Random Assignment to Real Social Groups," *American Economic Review*
96, no. 2 (April 1, 2006): 212–216, https://doi.org/10.1257/000282806777211658.

172 **Research around the globe** Ernst Fehr and Simon Gächter, "Altruistic
Punishment in Humans," *Nature* 415, no. 6868 (January 1, 2002): 137–140,
https://doi.org/10.1038/415137a.

172 **Research confirms** Joël Berger and Debra Hevenstone, "Norm Enforcement
in the City Revisited: An International Field Experiment of Altruistic Punishment, Norm Maintenance, and Broken Windows," *Rationality and Society*
28, no. 3 (March 4, 2016): 299–319, https://doi.org/10.1177/1043463116634035.

174 **Arthur Brooks** Arthur C. Brooks, "Fully Remote Work Will Make You Less
Happy," *Atlantic*, April 7, 2022, https://www.theatlantic.com/family/archive
/2021/04/zoom-remote-work-loneliness-happiness/618473/.

174 **When asked about** Steven J. Davis, "The Big Shift to Remote Work," Boston
Fed, November 2022.

174 **When employees can** Nicholas Bloom, Ruobing Han, and James Liang,
"How Hybrid Working from Home Works Out," National Bureau of Economic
Research, Working Paper 30292, July 1, 2022, https://doi.org/10.3386/w30292.

174 **From his research, Pentland** Gallup, Inc., "Workplace Socializing Is Productive," Gallup.com, December 12, 2022, https://news.gallup.com/business
journal/111766/news-flash-workplace-socializing-productive.aspx.

175 **In another study at a call** Alex Pentland, "The New Science of Building
Great Teams," *Harvard Business Review* 90, no. 4 (January 1, 2012): 60–69,
https://ci.nii.ac.jp/naid/20001077629/.

176 **"I've been reminded of** Caitlin Huston, "Disney Employees Must Return to Office Four Days a Week, Bob Iger Says," *Hollywood Reporter,* January 9, 2023, https://www.hollywoodreporter.com/business/business-news/disney -employees-office-bob-iger-memo-1235293491/.

176 **Jamie Dimon, CEO** Jane Their, "Jamie Dimon Says Remote Work 'Doesn't Work' for Bosses, Young Workers, or 'Spontaneity,'" Yahoo! Finance, January 20, 2023, https://www.yahoo.com/now/jamie-dimon-says-remote-doesn-222 623977.html#:~:text=Dimon%20expounded%20on%20his%20longstanding,or %20management%2C%E2%80%9D%20Dimon%20said.

176 **"In-person time** Steven Rattner, "Is Working from Home Really Working?," *New York Times,* March 22, 2023, https://www.nytimes.com/2023/03/22 /opinion/remote-work-salesforce-meta-working-from-home.html.

176 **The bank's annual report** Antoine Gara and Tabby Kinder, "'It Is Not Cut-Throat like Goldman Sachs': SVB's Culture in Focus," *Financial Times,* March 16, 2023, https://www.ft.com/content/6e23a2fb-484e-418d-b309-bf558b3a6a17.

176 **In a survey in 2019** SHRM, "The Impact of Toxic Work Culture: Comes with a Quarter-Trillion Dollar Cost," SHRM Talk Work Culture, October 10, 2019, https://www.talkworkculture.com/advice-info/toxic-workplace/.

177 **According to recent studies** Nupur Sharma and Rajib Lochan Dhar, "From Curse to Cure of Workplace Ostracism: A Systematic Review and Future Research Agenda," *Human Resource Management Review* 32, no. 3 (September 1, 2022): 100836, https://doi.org/10.1016/j.hrmr.2021.100836.

177 **It has been estimated** Olle Folke and Johanna Rickne, "Sexual Harassment and Gender Inequality in the Labor Market," *Quarterly Journal of Economics* 137, no. 4 (May 12, 2022): 2163–2212, https://doi.org/10.1093/qje/qjac018.

177 **As a Black, woman vice president** Field et al., "Women in the Workplace 2023."

178 **But in the Swiss army study** Lorenz Goette, David Huffman, Stephan Meier, and Matthias Sutter, "Competition Between Organizational Groups: Its Impact on Altruistic and Antisocial Motivations," *Management Science* 58, no. 5 (2012): 948–960, https://doi.org/10.1287/mnsc.1110.1466.

180 **When my colleagues and I** Sophie Cho et al., "Social Networks Have Fewer Weak Ties and Less Homophily in Virtual Organizations," working paper, 2022.

180 **Analyzing the collaboration** Longqi Yang et al., "The Effects of Remote Work on Collaboration Among Information Workers," *Nature Human Behaviour* 6, no. 1 (September 9, 2021): 43–54, https://doi.org/10.1038/s41562 -021-01196-4.

180 **Furthermore, Melanie Brucks** Melanie S. Brucks and Jonathan Levav, "Virtual Communication Curbs Creative Idea Generation," *Nature* 605, no. 7908 (April 27, 2022): 108–112, https://doi.org/10.1038/s41586-022-04643-y.

181 **For example, at mixers** Paul Ingram and Michael W. Morris, "Do People Mix at Mixers? Structure, Homophily, and the 'Life of the Party,'"

Administrative Science Quarterly 52, no. 4 (December 1, 2007): 558–585, https://doi.org/10.2189/asqu.52.4.558.

181   **Analysis of data for** Zoë Cullen and Ricardo Perez-Truglia, "The Old Boys' Club: Schmoozing and the Gender Gap," *American Economic Review* 113, no. 7 (2023): 1703–1740, https://doi.org/10.1257/aer.20210863.

181   **About half the companies** Jason Sandvik et al., "Should Workplace Programs Be Voluntary or Mandatory? Evidence from a Field Experiment on Mentorship," NBER Working Paper Series, August 1, 2021, https://doi.org/10.3386/w29148.

182   **A sales call center conducted** Sandvik et al., "Should Workplace Programs Be Voluntary or Mandatory?"

182   **According to a study** Marcus Alexander and Fotini Christia, "Context Modularity of Human Altruism," *Science* 334, no. 6061 (December 9, 2011): 1392–1394, https://doi.org/10.1126/science.1202599.

183   **The bank looked at** Alex Pentland, "The Data-Driven Society," *Scientific American* 309, no. 4 (September 17, 2013): 78–83, https://doi.org/10.1038/scientificamerican1013-78.

186   **"Employees told us** LEGO, "LEGO Campus Grand Opening," LEGO.com, November 13, 2020, https://www.lego.com/en-us/aboutus/news/2019/october/lego-campus-grand-opening?locale=en-us.

186   **"We've done [the redesign]** Tim Ahrensbach, "Get Reworked Podcast: What Makes an Office Worth Coming To?," interview by Mike Prokopeak and Siobhan Fagan, *Get Reworked* podcast, June 21, 2022, https://www.reworked.co/digital-workplace/get-reworked-podcast-what-makes-an-office-worth-coming-to/.

188   **But there was** Steve, "Howard Schultz Tells the Truth Behind Starbuck Success in China," Simplify, April 13, 2019, https://simplifyway.com/articles/howard-schultz-tells-the-truth-behind-starbucks-success-in-china/.

188   **"So," he explained** Steve, "Howard Schultz Tells the Truth."

189   **"We had an annual meeting** BCG Global, "Howard Schultz on Global Reach and Local Relevance at Starbucks," July 4, 2021, https://www.bcg.com/publications/2012/leadership-management-two-speed-economy-howard-schultz-global-reach-and-local-relevance.

189   **They conducted a six-week** Chris Rider, "Proven Tactics for Improving Teams' Psychological Safety," *MIT Sloan Management Review*, March 27, 2023, https://sloanreview.mit.edu/article/proven-tactics-for-improving-teams-psychological-safety/.

190   **Research in a US sales** Jason J. Sandvik et al., "Workplace Knowledge Flows," *Quarterly Journal of Economics* 135, no. 3 (2020): 1635–1680, https://doi.org/10.1093/qje/qjaa013.

191   **In the United States** SHRM, "SHRM Reports Toxic Workplace Cultures Cost Billions," press release, Society for Human Resource Management,

September 25, 2019, https://www.shrm.org/about-shrm/press-room/press
-releases/pages/shrm-reports-toxic-workplace-cultures-cost-billions.aspx.

191 **"In most organizations** Tera Allas and Bill Schaninger, "The Boss Factor: Making the World a Better Place Through Workplace Relationships," McKinsey & Company, September 22, 2020, https://www.mckinsey.com /capabilities/people-and-organizational-performance/our-insights/the-boss -factor-making-the-world-a-better-place-through-workplace-relationships.

191 **They worked together** Sule Alan, Gözde Çörekçioğlu, and Matthias Sutter, "Improving Workplace Climate in Large Corporations: A Clustered Randomized Intervention," *Quarterly Journal of Economics* 138, no. 1 (September 28, 2022): 151–203, https://doi.org/10.1093/qje/qjac034.

192 **Cognitive routine tasks** Enghin Atalay et al., "The Evolution of Work in the United States," *American Economic Journal: Applied Economics* 12, no. 2 (April 1, 2020): 1–34, https://doi.org/10.1257/app.20190070.

192 **The share of jobs** David Deming, "The Growing Importance of Social Skills in the Labor Market," *Quarterly Journal of Economics* 132, no. 4 (June 6, 2017): 1593–1640, https://doi.org/10.1093/qje/qjx022.

193 **The resulting study** Anita Williams Woolley et al., "Evidence for a Collective Intelligence Factor in the Performance of Human Groups," *Science* 330, no. 6004 (October 29, 2010): 686–688, https://doi.org/10.1126/science.1193147.

195 **Research by a team** Ben Weidmann and David J. Deming, "Team Players: How Social Skills Improve Team Performance," *Econometrica* 89, no. 6 (2021): 2637–2657, https://doi.org/10.3982/ECTA18461.

196 **"It is the company's choice** Jensen Huang, "Jensen Huang: Employee Selection Affects Culture," Stanford eCorner, YouTube video 3:20, May 2, 2011, https://www.youtube.com/watch?v=Pnr_TVjYlj4.

196 **Research with around forty thousand** Alan Benson, Danielle Li, and Kelly Shue, "Promotions and the Peter Principle," *Quarterly Journal of Economics* 134, no. 4 (August 16, 2019): 2085–2134, https://doi.org/10.1093/qje/qjz022.

197 **"We changed it** SHRM, "In First Person: Indra Nooyi," Society for Human Resource Management, March 31, 2022, https://www.shrm.org/executive /resources/people-strategy-journal/spring2022/pages/in-first-person-indra -nooyi.aspx.

Chapter 10: Customize EX

202 **But surveys showed that** Jose Maria Barrero, Nicholas Bloom, and Steven J. Davis, *Why Working from Home Will Stick*, Working Paper 28731, National Bureau of Economic Research, 2021.

202 **"It is very important** Jodi Kantor, Karen Weise, and Grace Ashford, "Inside Amazon's Employment Machine," *New York Times*, December 15, 2021, https://www.nytimes.com/interactive/2021/06/15/us/amazon-workers .html.

202 **Neuroscientists, for example** Dennis P. Carmody and Michael Lewis, "Brain Activation When Hearing One's Own and Others' Names," *Brain Research* 1116, no. 1 (October 1, 2006): 153–158, https://doi.org/10.1016/j.brainres.2006.07.121.

203 **For instance, we know** Maria Cotofan, Robert Dur, and Stephan Meier, "Macroeconomic Conditions When Young Shape Job Preferences for Life," *Review of Economics and Statistics* 105, no. 2 (March 1, 2023): 467–473, https://doi.org/10.1162/rest_a_01057.

203 **According to a survey** Deloitte Insights, "The Postgenerational Workforce," May 15, 2020, https://www2.deloitte.com/us/en/insights/focus/human-capital-trends/2020/leading-a-multi-generational-workforce.html.

204 **According to estimates** Cody Cook et al., "The Gender Earnings Gap in the Gig Economy: Evidence from over a Million Rideshare Drivers," *Review of Economic Studies* 88, no. 5 (2021): 2210–2238, https://doi.org/10.1093/restud/rdaa081.

205 **My research on financial literacy** Kristopher Gerardi, Lorenz Goette, and Stephan Meier, "Numerical Ability Predicts Mortgage Default," *Proceedings of the National Academy of Sciences of the United States of America* 110, no. 28 (June 24, 2013): 11267–11271, https://doi.org/10.1073/pnas.1220568110.

206 **To analyze whether** Stephan Meier and Elizabeth Miskin, "Knowledge or Preferences? Explaining Earnings Heterogeneity Among Ride-Share Drivers," working paper, 2022.

207 **Survey evidence** Net Impact, "7.2: Millennials Rank Impact over Pay, but Companies Are Stuck," in "Chapter 7: Why We Work," in *Talent Report: What Workers Want in 2021*, https://netimpactreport.com/chapter-7?anchor=millennials#millennials.

207 **My coauthors and I** Vanessa Burbano, Nicolas Padilla, and Stephan Meier, "Gender Differences in Preferences for Meaning at Work," *American Economic Journal: Economic Policy*, 2023.

208 **"We also asked about** Bill Roberts, "Celebrate Differences," Society for Human Resource Management, December 1, 2012, https://www.shrm.org/hr-today/news/hr-magazine/pages/1212-employee-segmentation.aspx.

209 **To address this problem** "Using Employee Segmentation to Bring Out the Best in Your Workforce," Bain, January 28, 2020, https://www.bain.com/insights/using-employee-segmentation-to-bring-out-the-best-in-your-workforce/.

210 **According to Diane Gherson** Lisa Burrell, "Co-Creating the Employee Experience," *Harvard Business Review*, July 7, 2021, https://hbr.org/2018/03/co-creating-the-employee-experience.

213 **"I remember how** Justin Bariso, "In His First Week Back as Starbucks CEO, Howard Schultz Made a Brilliant Move. It Just May Save the Company," *Inc.*,

May 1, 2022, https://www.inc.com/justin-bariso/starbucks-ceo-howard-schultz
-how-to-build-trust-problem-solving-emotional-intelligence.html.

214 **Or even more personal** Rachel Emma Silverman, "Bosses Tap Outside Firms
to Predict Which Workers Might Get Sick," *Wall Street Journal*, February 18,
2016, https://www.wsj.com/articles/bosses-harness-big-data-to-predict-which
-workers-might-get-sick-1455664940.

215 **"We'd love your input** Burrell, "Co-Creating the Employee Experience."

216 **"That's the power** Burrell, "Co-Creating the Employee Experience."

Index

STEPHAN MEIER is the James P. Gorman Professor of Business Strategy and the Chair of the Management Division at Columbia Business School (CBS). He is an award-winning teacher at CBS, and every year hundreds of students learn from him about the human side of strategy in Columbia's MBA and executive education programs. Before Columbia, he worked as the first senior economist at the Center for Behavioral Economics and Decision-Making at the Federal Reserve Bank, where he began to deeply appreciate the value and importance of evidence-based policy making.

In his role as the coordinator for CBS's core strategy class—the mandatory class that all of the roughly 1,100 MBA and EMBA students who start every year at CBS have to take—Meier shapes how the students learn about business strategy and has, himself, developed many of the case studies used in the class. In recent years, Meier developed a popular new elective and executive education program, "Future of Work," which features many of the core ideas that inform *The Employee Advantage*. He is also the co-faculty director of the new flagship executive education program "Executive Development Program: Leading into the Future." Through these endeavors, Meier teaches hundreds of executives every year about how humans actually work, and how to design the future of work with those lessons in mind.

He is a world-renowned expert at the intersection of behavioral economics, business strategy, and the future of work. He leads the Lab on "Humans in the Digital Economy" in the Digital Future Initiative at CBS.

His research findings have been published in top academic journals, such as *Science, Nature, American Economic Review*, and *Management Science*; have been featured in popular magazines, such as *Harvard Business Review*; and covered by countless news outlets, such as the *Economist, Wall Street Journal, Financial Times, New York Times, Los Angeles Times*, Bloomberg, and BBC. Meier has also worked as a consultant with Uber Technologies to help them better understand what motivates Uber drivers.

He has a master's degree in history, economics, and political science from the University of Zurich (Switzerland) and then got a doctorate in economics from the same institution. He lives with his family in Manhattan but spends a lot of time each year in Switzerland, his home country. In his free time, he enjoys traveling to as many places as possible, going to all types of art events, making LEGO stop-motion movies, capsizing his sailboat, playing the drums (not good but loud!), and spending time with his family.

PublicAffairs is a publishing house founded in 1997. It is a tribute to the standards, values, and flair of three persons who have served as mentors to countless reporters, writers, editors, and book people of all kinds, including me.

I. F. STONE, proprietor of *I. F. Stone's Weekly*, combined a commitment to the First Amendment with entrepreneurial zeal and reporting skill and became one of the great independent journalists in American history. At the age of eighty, Izzy published *The Trial of Socrates*, which was a national bestseller. He wrote the book after he taught himself ancient Greek.

BENJAMIN C. BRADLEE was for nearly thirty years the charismatic editorial leader of *The Washington Post*. It was Ben who gave the *Post* the range and courage to pursue such historic issues as Watergate. He supported his reporters with a tenacity that made them fearless and it is no accident that so many became authors of influential, best-selling books.

ROBERT L. BERNSTEIN, the chief executive of Random House for more than a quarter century, guided one of the nation's premier publishing houses. Bob was personally responsible for many books of political dissent and argument that challenged tyranny around the globe. He is also the founder and longtime chair of Human Rights Watch, one of the most respected human rights organizations in the world.

• • •

For fifty years, the banner of Public Affairs Press was carried by its owner Morris B. Schnapper, who published Gandhi, Nasser, Toynbee, Truman, and about 1,500 other authors. In 1983, Schnapper was described by *The Washington Post* as "a redoubtable gadfly." His legacy will endure in the books to come.

Peter Osnos, *Founder*